新编 GRE 词汇荟萃

下册

主 编 吴英全
副主编 任 利 姜向中

世界图书出版公司
北京·广州·上海·西安

图书在版编目（CIP）数据

新编 GRE 词汇荟萃/吴英全主编. －北京：世界图书出版公司
北京公司，1999.1
ISBN 7－5062－3827－6

Ⅰ.新… Ⅱ.吴… Ⅲ.英语－词汇－研究生－入学考试－美国
－汇编 Ⅳ.H313.1

中国版本图书馆 CIP 数据核字(98)第 38871 号

内 容 简 介

本书精选 GRE 考试中出现的约 7800 词，其特点是：第一，收词全而精。
不含浅显派生词；不含四级以下词汇，以六级以上词汇为主。其次，融汇词汇
记忆与词汇应试于一体，把怪僻词和其特定用法相结合。第三，记忆方式多样
化。不仅提供丰富的例句，而且给出详细的词根和词缀分解，还包括同义词、
反义词归类记忆，以及相近词形、词义关联记忆等等。

本书主要面向 GRE 考生，同时也不愧是 TOEFL，EPT，GMAT 等方面
考生的良师益友。

为配合学习，本书配有录音带 6 盒，由美籍教授以纯正美式发音朗读。

书　　名：新编 GRE 词汇荟萃（下册）
主　　编：吴英全
副 主 编：任　利　姜向中
责任编辑：王志平
出　　版：世界图书出版公司北京公司
印　　刷：北京中西印刷厂
发　　行：世界图书出版公司北京公司（北京朝内大街 137 号，100010）
销　　售：各地新华书店和外文书店
开　　本：1/32　850×1168　印张：12.5　字数：33 万
版　　次：1999 年 3 月第 1 版　1999 年 10 月第 2 次印刷
印　　数：8001-16000
书　　号：ISBN 7-5062-3827-6/H・256
定　　价：38.00 元（上、下册）

Unit Twenty-One

laurel ['lɔrəl] *n.* 月桂树；桂冠

参考：laureate（戴桂冠的，获奖者），sequoia（红杉）

lava ['lɑːvə] *n.* 熔岩

Lava, pumice and other igneous rocks are found in great abundance around Mount Vesuvius near Naples.

那不勒斯附近的维苏威火山那里发现了大量的熔岩，浮石及其他火成岩。

比较记忆：larva（昆虫幼虫）

lave [leiv] *v.* 洗浴，冲刷. cleanse

The running water will *lave* away all stains.

流水可冲洗掉所有污迹。

lavish ['læviʃ] *a.* 挥霍的；   *v.* 挥霍. spendthrift

I never expected a *lavish* reward for my services；I would have been pleased with a token.

我可从不曾指望我的劳动会得到什么丰厚的回报，我只是想能给我 一枚徽章我就很满足了。

比较记忆：ravish（抢夺）

lax [læks] *a.* 懒散的，松弛的. relax

We dislike restaurants where the service is *lax* and inattentive.

我们不喜欢服务懒散，不认真的餐馆。

laxative ['læksətiv] *n.* 轻泻药；   *a.* 通便的；放松的. cathartic

layette [lei'et] *n.* 新生婴儿的全套用品

A pink *layette* is traditional for a girl baby.

传统上，小女孩用粉红色婴儿用品。

layman ['leimən] *n.* 俗人，门外汉. laity

1

The *layman* were barred from the medical convention.

医学会议把门外汉拒之门外。

lea [li:] *n*. 牧场，草地

Herds of cattle moved slowly over the *lea*.

牛群在牧场上缓缓移动。

leaflet ['li:f-lit] *n*. 传单；嫩叶

leaf + let (little) → 嫩叶

lean [li:n] *a*. 瘦骨嶙峋的. skinny

lease [li:s] *n*. 租约；租期； *v*. 出租

She planned to *lease* her apartment to a friend.

她打算把她的公寓租给一个朋友。

leash [li:ʃ] *n*. (拴猎犬的)皮带； *v*. 束缚. fetter

It is horrible that your mind have been *leashed* by the prejudices of your parents.

你的思想为你父母的偏见所约束,真是太可怕了。

leaven ['levn] *n*. 发酵剂； *v*. 发酵. yeast；影响

Be bread dough is *leaven*ed, it puffs up, expanding in volume.

当做面包用的面团发酵时,它会体积增大膨胀起来。

lecherous ['letʃərəs] *a*. 好色的. sensual

lechery ['letʃəri] *n*. 好色，淫荡，纵欲

In his youth he led a life of *lechery* and debauchery；he did not mend his ways until his infecting venereal.

他年轻时过着一种纵情声色的生活；一直不思改悔,直到传染上了性病。

比较记忆：lecher（色狼）

lectern ['lektə(:)n] *n*. 读经台. stand

The chaplain delivered his sermon from a hastily improvised *lectern*.

随军牧师在一仓促搭建的经坛上布道。

ledge [ledʒ] *a*. (墙突出的狭长部分)壁架；暗礁. reef

The climbers advanced across a rocky *ledge*.

登山者向前进跨过一道岩突。

ledger [ˈledʒə] *n*. 分类账

leech [liːtʃ] *n*. 吸血鬼. sponger

John was a *leech* who clung to his friends as long as they had money.

约翰是个吸血鬼,只要朋友还有钱,他就赖着人家不放。

leer [liə] *v*. 斜眼看;送秋波

The nasty old man *leered* at the young girl.

那个龌龊的老人(不怀好意地)斜眼看着那个姑娘。

leery [ˈliəri] *a*. 多疑的;审慎的. skittish

Don't eat the sushi at this restaurant; I am a bit *leery* about how fresh it is.

别吃这家店的寿司,我疑心它有点儿不大新鲜了。

leeward [ˈliːwəd] *a*. 下风的. tailwind. ↔ windward

leeway [ˈliːwei] *n*. 回旋余地. margin

When you set a deadline, allow a little *leeway*.

确定死期限的时候要留有余地。

legacy [ˈlegəsi] *n*. 遗产,遗留之物. bequest, heritage, patrimony

The *legacy* from my parents is an album of family photographs.

我父母留给我的遗产是一本家庭像册。

来自:legate(把……遗赠给)

legend [ˈledʒənd] *n*. 地图里的说明文字或图例

The *legend* at the bottom of the map made it clear which symbols stood for rest areas along the highway and which stood for public camp sites.

地图下面的说明标明了哪些代表高速公路沿途的停留地,哪些又是公共露营地。

legerdemain [ˌledʒədəˈmein] *n*. 手法,变戏法

比较记忆：legerity（轻巧，灵敏）

legible ['ledʒəbl] *a.* 容易辨认的，易读的. ↔ illegible

legion ['li:dʒən] *a.* 兵团，一大群. multitude

Mahatma Gandhi had a *legion* of devoted followers.

圣雄甘地有一大群忠实的追随者。

legislate ['ledʒisleit] *v.* 立法

Congress *legislated* increased benefits for veterans.

议会立法增加了退伍军人的权益。

legislature ['ledʒisleitʃə] *n.* 立法机关

Sponsors of the bill were relieved because there was no opposition to it within the *legislature* until after the measure had been signed into law.

议案提请人松了一口气,因为议案通过签署成为法律前,立法会内没有反对意见。

legitimate [li'dʒitimit] *a.* 合法的，正当的. licit

Divorce is *legitimate* but subject to various legal requirements before taking final effect.

离婚是正当的,但在最后裁定前受各种法律条文要求的制约。

比较记忆：legitimize（使合法，正式批准）

lenitive ['lenitiv] *a.* 缓和的. soothing

A cloudless, sunny day is *lenitive* to the spirits.

阳光明媚,晴空无云的天气(最适于)缓和情绪。

比较记忆：lenient（宽大的，仁慈的）

lento ['lentəu] *a.* (音乐)徐缓的

参考：allegro（(音乐)轻快的）

leonine ['li(:)ənain] *a.* 狮子的

leon (= lion) + ine → 狮子的

leprosy ['leprəsi] *n.* 麻风

Because *leprosy* is such an unsightly disease, its victims have frequently been shunned.

麻风病是十分不雅的疾病,因而人们都躲着麻风病人。

lesion ['liːʒən] *n.* 伤口,损害

比较记忆：legion（大量）

lessee [le'siː] *n.* （房地产）租户. ↔ lessor

lethal ['liːθəl] *a.* 致命的. fatal

It is unwise to leave *lethal* weapons where children may find them.

把致命武器放在孩子们可以找得到的地方可不是明智之举。

lethargic [le'θɑːdʒik] *a.* 昏睡的；冷淡的

Having missed her exercise class for that day, Ms. Dean felt *lethargic* and listless.

没去上那天的运动锻炼课,迪安女士感觉（浑身）倦息乏力,打不起精神来。

lethargy ['leθədʒi] *n.* 嗜眠症；倦息. drowsy

leukemia [luːˈkiːmiə] *n.* 白血病

参考：hemophilia（血友病）

levee ['levi] *n.* 防洪堤,堤岸

levee : freshet ＝ rampart : invasion

leviathan [li'vaiəθən] *n.* 大海兽；巨大之物

参考：mammoth（猛犸；庞然大物）

levitate ['leviteit] *v.* （使）飘浮在空中

As the magician passed his hands over the recumbent body of his assistant, she appeared to rise and *levitate* about three feet above the table.

魔术师的手从他助手平躺着的身体上掠过,他助手的身体看上去升了起来,悬浮在空中,距桌面有 3 英尺。

levity ['leviti] *n.* 轻率,轻浮. flippancy

At such a serious moment in our history, your *levity* is inappropriate and in bad taste.

在我们历史上这样严肃的一个时刻,你轻浮的举止十分不当,不合时宜。

levy ['levi] *v.* & *n.* 征税；征兵. impose；enlist

Voters responded to the *levy* lof a new tax with stolidity because they have become inured to the fickle nature of government policies.

投票人对新的赋税政策无动于衷，他们早已习惯了政府政策的变幻无常。

lewd [luːd] *a.* 好色的，猥亵的. obscene ↔ chaste

They found his *lewd* stories dull and objectionable.

他们发觉他那些色情故事很乏味无聊，令人反感。

lexical ['leksikəl] *a.* 词汇的，词典的

lex（词汇）+ ical → 词汇的

比较记忆：dyslexia（阅读障碍）

lexicographer [ˌleksi'kɔɡrəfə] *n.* 词典编纂人

lexico（= lexicon）+ grapher → 词典编纂人

lexicon ['leksikən] *n.* 词典

I cannot find this word in any *lexicon* in the library.

我在图书馆所有的字典里都找不到这个词。

liability [ˌlaiə'biliti] *n.* 缺陷；债务；易患. ↔ asset

Her lack of an extensive vocabulary was a *liability* that she was able to overcome.

她可以克服词汇量不大的缺陷。

liaison [li(ː)'eizən] *n.* 联系；暧昧关系. affair

As the *liaison*, he had to avoid offending the leaders of the two armies.

作为中间联系人，他得避免冒犯双方军队领导人中的（任何一方）。

liana [li'ænə] *n.* 藤本植物. vane

参考：legume（豆科植物）

libation [lai'beiʃən] *n.* 奠酒（给神献酒），饮酒

参考：baptism（洗礼）

libel ['laibəl] *v.* （文字）诽谤，中伤

参考：slander（口头诽谤）

libelous [ˈlaibələs] *a.* 诽谤的. defamatory

He sued the newspaper because of its *libelous* canard.

他就报纸的诽谤性谎言对其起诉。

liberality [ˌlibəˈræliti] *n.* 慷慨，心胸开阔. generosity

They recompense her for her *liberality*.

他们报答了她的慷慨。

liberated [ˈlibəreitid] *a.* 无拘束的，放纵的. unfettered

来自：liberate（解放）

libertarian [ˌlibəˈtɛəriən] *n.* 自由论者. latitudinarian

比较记忆：totalitarian（极权主义者）

libertine [ˈlibə(ː)tiːn] *n.* （宗教）自由思想者；浪荡子. roue, rake

Although she was aware of his reputation as a *libertine*, she felt she could reform him and help him break his dissolute way of life.

尽管她知道他那浪荡子的名声，却感到她能改造好他，帮他摆脱放荡的生活方式。

libidinous [liˈbidinəs] *a.* 性欲的；好色的. wanton

They objected to his *libidinous* behavior.

他们不赞成他那种好色的行为。

libido [liˈbiːdəu] *n.* 性欲；里比多

The psychiatrist maintained that suppression of the *libido* often resulted in maladjustment and neuroses.

精神病学家坚持认为，性压抑往往会导致机体失调及神经机能症。

libretto [liˈbretəu] *n.* 歌词，剧本

The composer of an opera's music is remembered more frequently than the author of its *libretto*.

人们往往会记住一出歌剧的曲作者，却记不住词作者。

licence [ˈlaisəns] *n.* 自由，放肆；执照，许可

The restaurant applied for a *licence* to sell wine.

餐馆申请卖酒许可证。

licensure [ˈlaisənʃə] *n.* 许可证的发给

　　licensure ∶ driver ＝ certification ∶ teacher

licentious [laiˈsenʃəs] *a.* 纵欲的；不受制约的. lewd；dissolute

　　He took a *licentious* attitude towards all pre-marital affairs.

　　他对各种婚前行为都持放纵态度。

lichen [ˈlaiken] *n.* 地衣

　　参考∶fungus（真菌）

licit [ˈlisit] *a.* 合法的. ↔ illicit

　　It isn't *licit* for a private citizen to own a gun in our country.

　　在我们国家,私人持枪不合法。

lido [ˈliːdəu] *n.* 海滨浴场

　　参考∶natatorium（室内游泳池）,peignoir（妇女浴袍）

liege [liːdʒ] *a.* 忠贞的. faithful

　　Master his own impulses, as a soloist should be, is not *liege* to the conductor.

　　像一个独奏演员该做的那样,抑制住他（想发挥一下）的冲动是对指挥的不忠实。

lien [liən] *n.* 扣押权,留置权

　　lien ∶ claim ＝ subpoena ∶ command

ligature [ˈligətʃuə] *n.* 绑缚物. bond

　　比较记忆∶ligament（韧带）

light-hearted [ˈlaitˈhɑːtid] *a.* 愉快的. delightful

　　The *light-hearted* youngsters sang as they hiked through the woods.

　　心情轻松愉快的年轻人们唱着歌徒步穿越森林。

　　参考∶highhanded（傲慢的）

ligneous [ˈligniəs] *a.* 木质的,木头的. woody

ligneous ∶ wood ＝ osseous ∶ bone

比较记忆：lignum（木材），lignify（木质化）

liken [ˈlaikən] *v.* 比拟

Lilliputian [ˌliliˈpjuːʃən] *a.* 极小的. infinitesimal

The model was built on a *Lilliputian* scale, however, it is delicate.

这一模型建造规模小却很精巧。

lilt [lilt] *n.* 轻快活泼的歌曲；轻快的动作

To make him happy, she hummed a cheerful *lilt*.

为了让他高兴，她哼了一曲轻快活泼的歌曲。

lily [ˈlili] *n.* 百合花

参考：narcissus（水仙花），cucumber（黄瓜）

limber [ˈlimbə] *a.* 可塑的；灵活的. pliant; supple

Hours of ballet classes kept him *limber*.

几小时几小时地上芭蕾课使他（身体）灵活。

limbo [ˈlimbəu] *a.* 中间状态；忽视或遗忘状态

Among the divisions of Hell are Purgatory and *Limbo*.

地狱可划分为地狱边境及炼狱。

limerick [ˈlimərik] *n.* 五行打油诗

The child wrote a humorous *limerick* in class.

这个孩子在班上写了首幽默的打油诗。

limitrophe [ˈlimitrəuf] *a.* 位于边界的，邻接的. adjacent

An entrance hall was *limitrophe* to all the rooms of the apartment.

通向各个公寓房间有一过厅相连。

limn [lim] *v.* 描述，绘画

He was never satisfied with his attempts to *limn* her beauty on canvas.

他从没对他在画布上描绘她的美所做出的尝试满意过。

limnetic [limˈnetik] *a.* 湖泊的

9

参考：limnology（湖泊学）

limousine ['limə(:)zi:n] *n.* (豪华)轿车，(机场、车站)接送旅客的
　　　　交通车

　　　limousine : automobile = mansion : residence.

limpet ['limpit] *n.* 紧随他人者； （软体动物）

　　　参考：snail（蜗牛），slug（鼻涕虫），mussel（贻贝）

limpid ['limpid] *a.* 清澈的，透明的. lucid

　　　A *limpid* stream ran through his latifundium.

　　　一条清澈的小溪流过大庄园。

lineage ['liniidʒ] *n.* 血统，世系. ancestry

　　　He traced his *lineage* back to Mayflower days.

　　　他的家系可以追溯到五月花号时代。

lineal ['liniəl] *a.* 直系的，嫡系的

　　　比较记忆：linear（线的，成直线的）

lineaments ['liniənənts] *n.* 脸形

　　　She quickly sketched the *lineaments* of his face.

　　　她很快勾勒出他的面部轮廓。

linen ['linin] *n.* 亚麻布

　　　Linen wrinkled easily.

　　　亚麻布很容易出皱褶。

　　　参考：dacron（的确良）

lingual ['liŋgwəl] *a.* 舌的；语言的

　　　比较记忆：linguist（语言学家），bilingual（双语言的）

linguist ['liŋgwist] *n.* 语言学家

　　　Although a skilled *linguist*, gifted in many tongs, he
　　　did not understand that particular dialect.

　　　尽管他是个训练有素的语言学家，且对多种语言都颇有天分，他
　　　却不懂那门特别的方言。

linguistics [liŋ'gwistiks] *n.* 语言学

linoleum [li'nəulijəm] *n.* 油毡

10

lim (linum)（flax）+ oleum (oil) → 油毡

lint [lint] *n.* （护伤口）软布；飞花

lionize ['laiənaiz] *v.* 崇拜，看重. venerate

　　　lion + ize（become）→ 崇拜

liquefy ['likwifai] *v.* 液化，溶解. dissolve

　　　参考：solidify（固化）

liquidate ['likwideit] *v.* 清除；清偿. discharge

　　　The dictator brutally *liquidated* all opponents.

　　　独裁者残酷清除所有对手。

liquidity [li'kwiditi] *n.* 流畅

liquor ['likə] *n.* 酒；汁

　　　Use the *liquor* from the roast for the gravy.

　　　用那块烤肉上的汁做肉汁用。

lisp [lisp] *n.* 口齿不清

lissom ['lisəm] *a.* 敏捷的；柔软的. nimble；lithe

　　　This year's champ in Ladies' Singles is a *lissom* teenager
　　　named Jill.

　　　今年"单身女士选美"冠军是个名叫吉尔的敏捷的十几岁少女。

list [list] *v.* 倾斜 tilt；　　*n.* 名单，表；倾侧；愿望

　　　That flagpole should be absolutely vertical；instead ，it
　　　list to one side.

　　　那根旗杆应该笔直地竖立着，而它却斜向一边。

listed ['listid] *a.* 随心所欲的

listless ['listlis] *a.* 无精打采的. indolent

　　　We had expected him to be full of enthusiasm and were
　　　surprised by his *listless* attitude.

　　　我们还期望他满怀热情，结果他那无精打采的态度让我们大吃一
　　　惊。

litany ['litɔni] *n.* 连祷

　　　On this solemn day, the congregation responded to the

11

prayers of the priest during the *litany* with fervor and intensity.

在这庄严的一天,人群在连祷的过程中,不断对牧师的祈祷作出真诚而热烈地反响。

literal [ˈlitərəl] *a.* 精确的,忠实原义的

比较记忆:illiteracy(文盲)

literatus [ˌlitəˈrɑːtəs] *n.* 文人,学者; *pl.* literati

记住:us 结尾的名词的复数形式为 i

lithe [laið] *a.* 柔软的,易弯曲的. supple

Her figure is *lithe* and willowy.

她的身体柔韧苗条。

litigant [ˈlitigənt] *n.* 诉讼当事人

litigious [liˈtidʒəs] *a.* 好诉讼的

比较记忆:litigation(诉讼)

litotes [ˈlaitəutiːz] *n.* 间接肯定法

To say, "he little realizes", when we mean that he does not realize at all, is an example of the kind of under-statement we call *litotes*.

当我们说"他几乎没有意识到"时,就是要表达他根本没有意识到的意思;这是一个我们称之为间接肯定法的一种不充分陈述方式的例子。

litter [ˈlitə] *n.* 垃圾;一窝(动物); *v.* 乱丢

The reporter's desk was *littered* with news releases.

记者桌上乱丢着新闻发布稿件。

litterbin [ˈlitəˌbin] *n.* 垃圾桶

littoral [ˈlitərəl] *a.* 海岸的; *n.* 海滨,沿海地区

参考:lido(海滨浴场)

liturgy [ˈlitə(ː)dʒi] *n.* 礼拜仪式

The visitors were fascinated by the elaborate *liturgy* of the service.

参观者为这种繁杂的礼拜仪式所吸引。

12

liverish ['livəriʃ] *a.* 易怒的，暴躁的. bilious

He was *liverish* when he found out he had flunked.

当他发现考试不及格时，暴跳如雷。

livery ['livəri] *n.* 仆从；（封建贵族侍从、仆人所穿的）制服. uniform

livid ['livid] *a.* （撞伤）青灰色的；（脸色）苍白的；盛怒的

His face was so *livid* with rage that we were afraid that he might have an attack of apoplexy.

他脸色气得发灰，我们都怕他突发中风。

loafer ['ləufə] *n.* 拖鞋；二流子. lounger

That *loafer* will never get the job done.

那个二流子永远也干不完这个活儿。

loam [ləum] *n.* 沃土

参考：humus（腐殖土），barren（贫瘠的）

loathe [ləuð] *v.* 憎恨，厌恶. detest

The scattering of his family made him *loathe* the wicked villain with gnashing teeth.

他的家庭教养使他咬牙切齿地憎恶那个恶棍。

lobe [ləub] *n.* 耳垂；（肺，肝等的）叶

lobster ['lɔbstə] *n.* 龙虾

He likes fish but not *lobster*.

他喜欢吃鱼，却不喜欢吃龙虾。

locale [ləu'kɑ:l] *n.* 事件的现场，地点

We are unable to fix the *locale* of the battle which took place more than a thousand years ago.

我们无法确定一千年前发生的那场战役的地点。

参考：collocate（排列，组合）

locket ['lɔkit] *n.* 纪念品盒

locket：keepsake ＝ purse：money

locomotion [,ləukə'məuʃən] *n.* 运动（力），移动（力）

13

比较记忆：locomotive（运动的，机车）

locus ['ləukəs] *n*. 地点；集中地

Was the culture of medicine in the beginning dispersed from a single focus or did it arise in several *loci*?

开始时，医学文化是从一个中心扩散开来的，还是在几个地点分别出现的？

locution [ləu'kju:ʃən] *n*. 说话风格；惯用语

比较记忆：circumlocution（累赘的表述）

lode [ləud] *n*. 矿脉；丰富的蕴藏. vein

If this *lode* which we have discovered extends for any distance, we have found a fortune.

要是我们发现的这一矿脉延伸一段的话，我们可就发现了一个宝藏了。

比较记忆：lodestar（北极星，目标）

loft [lɔft] *n*. 阁楼，顶楼. garret

比较记忆：lofty（崇高的；高傲的）

log [lɔg] *v*. （航海）日志；记录

logistics [ləu'dʒistik] *n*. 后勤学

logjam ['lɔgdʒæm] *n*. 浮木阻塞，僵局 deadlock

log ＋ jam → 浮木阻塞

loiter ['lɔitə] *v*. 虚度光阴. loaf

loiter ['lɔitə] *v*. 游荡. loaf, linger

The policeman told him not to *loiter* in the alley.

警察告诉他别在街巷间游荡。

loll [lɔl] *v*. 懒洋洋地靠；松垮地下垂. lounge；droop

They *lolled* around in their chairs watching television.

他们懒懒靠在椅子里看电视。

longanimity [ˌlɔŋgə'nimiti] *n*. 坚忍，忍受（痛苦）

long ＋ anim (soul) ＋ ity → 忍受（痛苦）

参考：magnanimous（大度的）

longevity [lɔn'dʒeviti] *n.* 长寿；资历

long + ev (age) + ity → 长寿

参考：medieval（中世纪的），primeval（原始的）

longitude ['lɔndʒitjuːd] *n.* 经度. ↔ latitude（纬度）

All degrees of *longitude* converge at the North and South Poles.

所有的经线交汇在南北极两点上。

longueur [lɔːŋ'gəː] *n.* 枯燥部分

The *longueur* in this book makes it almost unreadable.

这本书枯燥乏味的部分使人几乎没法读下去。

longwinded [,lɔŋ'windid] *a.* 冗长的. diffuse

The lecture was so *longwinded* that people began to leave the auditorium before it was half over.

演讲太冗长了，还没讲到一半，听众就开始退出讲演厅了。

参考：longface（忧郁）

·**loom** [luːm] *n.* 织机； *v.* 隐约出现

The rocky mountains *loomed* in front of the travelers.

石山在旅行者面前时隐时现。

loon [luːn] *n.* 愚人；懒人. goon；sluggard

It is such a *loon* who keeps setting himself on fire by smoking in bed.

他真是个懒人，在床上吸烟结果点着了火。

比较记忆：loop（金属线圈）

loot [luːt] *n.* 掠夺品； *v.* 掠夺. plunder

The thieves hid their *loot* in a deserted warehouse.

窃贼把脏物藏在一废弃的仓库里。

lop [lɔp] *v.* 剪（枝）；删削；剪除. snip

We had to *lop* of whole pages of the report before presenting it to the committee.

我们把报告呈递给委员会前，不得不整页整页地删改。

lope [ləup] *n.* 大步慢跑； *v.* (使)大步慢跑

As the horses *loped* along，we had an opportunity to admire the ever-changing scenery.

骑在马上轻快前行，我们得以欣赏不断变幻的美景。

lopsided [ˌlɔpˈsaidid] *a.* 不平衡的，倾侧的

参考：odds（不平衡）

loquacious [ləuˈkweiʃəs] *a.* 多话的，饶舌的. talkative

loqu (speak) + acious (多……的) → 多话的

lore [lɔ:] *n.* 知识；口头传说

The scholar steeped in medieval *lore*.

这个学者沉醉于中世纪传说的研究。

比较记忆：lorn（被遗弃的）

lotion [ˈləuʃən] *n.* 洗剂 (used as cosmetic or external medicine)

lottery [ˈlɔtəri] *n.* 抽彩给奖法

lounge [laundʒ] *v.* (懒散地)斜靠； *n.* 休息室

On Sundays a lot of people just like to *lounge*.

在星期天，许多人只想懒懒躲在起居室里（歇着）。

lout [laut] *n.* 粗鄙之人. boor

That *lout* doesn't even known you are supposed to thank your hostess.

那个粗鄙之人甚至不懂应该对女主人表示感谢。

low [ləu] *v.* (牛)叫. moo

From the hilltop, they could see the herd like ants in the distance; they could barely hear the cattle *low*.

从山顶上，他们看到远处的畜群像蚂蚁一样，几乎听不见牛叫声。

baa : sheep = low : cattle

lowbred [ˌləuˈbred] *a.* 粗野的，低贱的. ↔ highbred

lubricant [ˈljuːbrikənt] *n.* 润滑剂

比较记忆：lubricate（润滑）

lubricious [ljuːˈbriʃəs] *a.* 好色的；光滑的. lecherous；smooth

16

He took the *lubricious* glances at every passing woman.

他色迷迷的眼光扫过每位过路妇女。

也写作 lubricous

lucid ['lju:sid] *a.* 清晰的；透明的；易懂的

His explanation was *lucid* and to the point.

他的解释中肯明了。

lucrative ['lju:krətiv] *a.* 赚钱的；有利可图的

He turned his hobby into a *lucrative* profession.

他把业余爱好变成了一项有利可图的职业。

lucre ['lju:kə] *n.* 钱；收益. spoils

Preferring *lucre* to undying fame，he wrote stories of popular appeal.

他更爱钱而不在乎什么永恒的功名，因此（选择）写作通俗小说。

lucubrate ['lju:kju(:)breit] *v.* 埋头苦干. meditate

比较记忆：luculent（清楚的，易懂的）

ludicrous ['lju:dikrəs] *a.* 滑稽可笑的. ridiculous

Although his attempts to appear psychotic were so clumsy as to be almost *ludicrous*，there is evidence that Ezra was able to avoid standing trial for treason merely by faking symptoms of mental illness.

尽管他装成个精神病的努力如此笨拙，以致看上去都有些滑稽可笑，但很明显伊兹拉却能逃脱受到叛国罪的审判，就因为他装出精神病患者的症状。

lug [lʌg] *v.* （用力）拉，强拉. tug

You should not *lug* personalities into a discussion of philosophy.

你不该把性格讨论硬拖进哲学讨论中去。

lugubrious [lju:'gju:briəs] *a.* 郁郁不乐的，悲哀的

We may recognize the pessimist by his *lugubrious* mood on life.

我们可以从他对生活郁郁不乐的情绪上看出（他是）悲观主义

者。

lukewarm [ˈljuːk-wɔːm] *a.* 微温的，不热心的. tepid

Fabrics must be washed in *lukewarm* water.

纤维必须用温水洗。

lull [lʌl] *n.* 间歇；　*v.* 使安静；使松弛. interval；soothe

Not wanting to get wet, they waited under the awning for a *lull* of the rain.

不想淋湿了,他们在雨篷下等雨停。

lullaby [ˈlʌləbai] *n.* 摇篮曲

The young mother hummed a *lullaby* to her sleeping baby.

年轻的母亲哼着摇篮曲哄她的孩子睡觉。

lumber [ˈlʌmbə] *n.* 杂物；　*v.* 笨拙地走. ↔ glide

Still somewhat torpid after its long hibernation, the bear *lumbered* through the woods.

长长的冬眠后,还有点儿不活跃,熊笨拙地走过森林。

lumen [ˈluːmin] *n.* 流明(光通量单位)

luminance [ˈluːminəns] *n.* 亮度

比较记忆：luminous（发光的，清晰的）

luminary [ˈluːminəri] *n.* 杰出人物. dignitary.

A leading light of the American stage, Ethel Barrymore was a theatrical *luminary* whose names lives on.

埃塞尔·巴里莫尔作为美国戏剧舞台上的重要人物,是一个名垂青史的戏剧界杰出人物。

lump [lʌmp] *v.* 笨拙地行走；把……混为一谈

An example of an illegitimate method of argument is to *lump* dissimilar cases together deliberately under the pretense that the same principles apply to each.

不合逻辑的辩论方法的一个例子是把不同的案例混在一起,故意假装同一理论可以应用在每一例子上。

lumpish [ˈlʌmpiʃ] *a.* 笨拙的. bungling

lunacy [ˈljuːnəsi] *n.* 精神错乱；愚蠢的行为. insanity

lunatic [ˈluːnətik] *a.* 神智不清的；极蠢的. deranged；inane

The man's *lunatic* behavior is a menace to society.

这人愚昧的行为是对社会的威胁。

lunge [lʌndʒ] *v.* 猛刺；冲刺

The boxer made a *lunge* at his opponent.

拳击手猛扑向他的对手。

lurch [ləːtʃ] *v.* 突然倾倒；蹒跚. pitch

Suddenly, the train *lurched* forward.

火车猛向前倾。

lure [ljuə] *n.* & *v.* 诱惑，引诱. allurement, entice

The coquette used all her wiles to *lure* me into following her.

那个卖弄风骚的女子使尽手段诱惑我随她去。

lurid [ˈljuərid] *a.* 苍白的；耸人听闻的，可怕的. sensational

The *lurid* stories he told shocked his listeners.

他讲的那耸人听闻的故事使听众震惊。

lurk [ləːk] *v.* 潜伏，埋伏. ambush

Who knows what evils *lurk* in the hearts of winning her? The Shadow knows.

谁知道藏在她心中的是什么，邪恶迷惑了她，鬼才知道。

luscious [ˈlʌʃəs] *a.* 美味的；肉感的. dainty；sensuous

The ripe peach was *luscious*.

熟透的桃子很鲜美。

lush [lʌʃ] *a.* 茂盛的；使感官愉快的； *n.* 酒鬼. voluptuous

The *lush* forest housed many different animals and birds.

茂密的森林是许多动物和鸟儿的家园。

lust [lʌst] *n.* (不正常)渴望；强烈性欲. craving

He was so rapacious in his *lust* for money that he impoverished whole families at a time.

19

他对钱太贪婪了，一下子榨穷了那一家子人。

luster [ˈlʌstə] *n.* 光亮，光泽

The soft *luster* of the silk in the dim light was pleasing.

丝在暗淡的光下发出柔和的光泽，令人愉悦。

lustrous [ˈlʌstrəs] *a.* 有光泽的

Her larger and *lustrous* eyes gave a touch of beauty to an otherwise drab face.

她那双富有光泽的大眼睛给平淡的脸庞添几分美丽。

lusty [ˈlʌsti] *a.* 精力充沛的；好色的. robust；risque

His six brothers were tall and healthy and *lusty*.

他六个兄弟都是又高又壮，精力充沛。

luxuriant [lʌgˈzjuəriənt] *a.* 繁茂的，肥沃的. bounteous

↔ small（稀少的）

比较记忆：luxurious（奢侈的，丰富的），luxury（丰富，奢侈）

luxuriate [lʌgˈzjuərieit] *v.* 纵情享乐；迅猛发展. revel；thrive

As a parvenu, you can *luxuriate* in new acquired wealth.

作为一个暴发户，你尽可享用新获取的财富。

lymph [limf] *n.* 淋巴

参考：platelet（血小板）

lynch [lintʃ] *v.* 私刑处死

In the southern part of the United States, Negroes have often been *lynched* by angry crowds.

在美国南部，黑人常被愤怒的人群私刑处死。

lyric [ˈlirik] *a.* 抒情的； *n.* 抒情诗

参考：limerick（五行打油诗）

macabre，**macaber** [məˈkɑːbə] *a.* 骇人的. grisly

The city morgue is a *macabre* spot for the uninitiated.

市陈尸所是保存身份不明尸体的可怕地方。

20

macadam [mə'kædəm] *n.* 碎石；碎石路面

A *macadam* surface is easy to drive on.

碎石路面上行车得容易。

mace [meis] *n.* 权杖；狼牙棒（一种中世纪武器）

The Grand Marshal of the parade raise his *mace* to signal that it was time for the procession to begin.

游行队伍统帅举起指挥棒示意游行该开始了。

参考：diadem（王冠）

macerate ['mæsəreit] *v.* 浸软；使消瘦

The strawberries had been soaking in the champagne for so long that they had begun to *macerate*; they literally fell apart at the touch of a spoon.

草莓在香槟里浸泡了很长时间开始变软,严格地讲,用勺一碰就碎了。

machete [mə'tʃeiti] *n.* 大砍刀

参考：saber（军刀）, lance（长矛）

Machiavellian [mækiə'veliən] *a.* 狡诈的,不择手段的. crafty

I don not think he will be a good ambassador because he is not accustomed to the *Machiavellian* maneuverings of foreign diplomats.

我认为他不会成为一位好大使,因为他不习惯外交家那些不择手段的行径。

machination [ˌmæki'neiʃən] *n.* 阴谋. scheme

I can see through your wily *machinations*,although you plan it deliberately.

尽管你精心设计,我还是得看得穿你的阴谋诡计。

mackintosh ['mækintəʃ] *n.* 雨衣,防水胶布

来自防水胶布发明者 Macintosh

macrocosm ['mækrəkɔzəm] *n.* 宇宙,宏观世界

macro + cosm (university) → 宇宙

maculate ['mækjulit] *v.* 玷污. stain

比较记忆：macula（皮肤上的斑点）

madden ['mædn] *v.* 发疯；大怒. enrage

mad ＋ en（make）→ 发疯

Unit Twenty-Two

madrigal ['mædrigəl] *n.* 情歌，牧歌

His program of folk songs included several *madrigals* which he sang to the accompaniment of a lute.

他的民歌节目包括几首牧歌，是他在琵琶的伴奏下演唱的。

maelstrom ['meilstrəum] *n.* 大漩涡，灾祸. whirlpool

mael (great) + strom (stream) → 大漩涡

The canoe was tossed about in the *maelstrom*.

独木舟在漩涡中颠簸翻滚。

maestro [mɑː'estrəu] *n.* 音乐大师

maggot ['mægət] *n.* 蛆（蝇的幼虫）；狂想. whim

magisterial [ˌmædʒis'tiəriəl] *a.* 有权威的；威风的. imperious

The learned doctor laid down to his patient in a *magisterial* tone of voice.

博学的医生用一种权威的口吻给他的病人下诊断。

magistracy ['mædʒistrəsi] *n.* 地方行政官的职位

magistrate ['mædʒistreit] *n.* 地方行政官

magistrate：bailiwick = bishop：diocese（辖区）

magnanimous [mæg'næniməs] *a.* 宽宏大量的，慷慨的. forgiving

magn (great) + anim (spirit) + ous → 心胸宽的

参考：equanimity（沉着）

magnate ['mægneit] *n.* 财主，巨头. tycoon

The steel *magnate* decided to devote more time to city politics.

钢铁巨头决定多在市府政界花些时间。

magnetism ['mægnitizəm] *n.* 磁；魅力. fascination

23

来自：magnet（磁铁）

magnify ['mægnifai] *v.* 放大；赞美. extol

She tends to *magnify* all her problems.

她似乎总把问题放大来看。

magniloquent [mæg'niləkwənt] *a.* 夸张的. grandiloquent

magni (great) + loqu (speak) + ent → 说大话的

magnitude ['mægnitju:d] *n.* 重要，星球的光亮度

Because it is difficult to measure all the business costs related to employee discontent, an accurate estimate of the *magnitude* of these costs is not easily calculated.

因为不太容易估测同雇员不满有关而造成的商业损失，也就不大好计算出这些损失造成的数量上的精确估计。

magpie ['mægpai] *n.* 鹊；饶舌者. chatterbox

参考：parrot（鹦鹉），vulture（秃鹫）

mahatma [mə'hɑ:tmə] *n.* 伟人，圣贤. sage

mahout [mə'haut] *n.* 驭象者 (keeper and of driver of elephant)

maim [meim] *v.* 使残废. mutilate

The hospital could not take care of all who had been mangled or *maimed* in the railroad accident.

医院接纳不了所有在铁路事故中伤残的病人。

maitre ['meitrə] *n.* 主人；领导人. butler；headwaiter

maize [meiz] *n.* 玉米

参考：rape（油菜），millet（小米），sorghum（高粱）

makeshift ['meikʃift] *n.* 权宜之计，代用品. expediency，substitute

He was guided by *makeshift* rather than by ethical consideration.

他只是遵循了权宜之计，而不是出于道德伦理的考虑（才那么去做）。

maladroit ['mælə'drɔit] *a.* 笨拙的. ↔ adroit

mal (bad) + adroit → 不灵巧的

malady ['mælədi] *n.* 疾病；弊病

She had a strange *malady*, and they couldn't discover a cure.

她得了种怪病，谁也不知该怎么治。

malaise [mæ'leiz] *n.* 萎靡不振，沮丧

mal (bad) + aise (comfort) → 萎靡不振

She felt a sudden vague *malaise* when she heard sounds at the door.

她一听到门响，突然感到一阵莫名其妙的沮丧。

malapropism ['mæləprɔpizəm] *n.* 字的误用

源自 Malaprop，爱尔兰喜剧人物马勒普罗普太太，以荒唐地误用词语而出名

malapropism : verbal = gaffe : social

malaria [mə'lɛəriə] *n.* 疟疾；瘴气. miasma

参考：leukemia（白血病），hemophilia（血友病）

malcontent ['mælkən‚tent] *n.* 反叛者； *a.* 不满的

She knew he was a *malcontent* young man when she married him.

她嫁给他时就知道了他是个反叛的年轻人。

malediction [mæli'dikʃən] *n.* 诅咒. ↔ benediction

male (bad) + dict (speak) + ion → 诅咒

malevolent [mə'levələnt] *a.* 恶意的，恶毒的. ↔ benevolent

male (bad) + vol (volition) + ent → 恶意的

malfeasance [mæl'fi:zəns] *n.* 渎职. ↔ feasance

malfunction ['mæl'fʌŋkʃən] *n.* 故障，障碍. handicap

mal (bad) + function → 故障

malicious [mə'liʃəs] *a.* 恶意的，怨恨的. spleenish

比较记忆：malice（恶意，怨恨）

malign [mə'lain] *a.* 邪恶的； *v.* 诽谤. ↔ benign

mal (bad) + lign (beget) → 诽谤

malignant [mə'lignənt] *a.* 恶性的；恶毒的. virulent

This is a *malignant* disease; we may have to use drastic measures to stop its spread.

这是种恶疾，我们应采取有效措施防止其扩散开来。

malinger [mə'liŋgə] *v.* 装病（以逃避工作或职责）. goldbrick

malinger : duty = recluse : humanity

mall [mɔːl] *n.* 林荫道

The *Mall* in Central Park has always been a favorite spot for Sunday strollers.

中央公园的林荫大道一直是星期天来漫步的人们喜爱的去处。

malleable ['mæliəbl] *a.* 可塑的，易改变的. ↔ brittle

The artist was able to use gold because it was so *malleable.*

艺术家可以用金子，因为它十分（柔软）易塑。

比较记忆：malleate（锻，锤薄）

mallet ['mælit] *n.* 木槌，大头锤

He used a wooden *mallet* to tap the shelf into place.

他用大木锤把架子钉好到其位置上。

malnutrition ['mælnju(ː)'triʃən] *n.* 营养不良. dystrophy

mal (bad) + nutrition → 营养不良.

malodorous [mæ'ləudərəs] *a.* 有臭味的；极其令人反感的

mal (bad) + odor + ous → 臭味的

maltreat [mæl'triːt] *v.* 虐待. abuse

mal (bad) + treat → 虐待

mamma ['mæmə] *n.* 乳腺

比较记忆：mammal（哺乳动物）

mammoth ['mæməθ] *a.* 巨大的； *n.* 猛犸（已绝迹）；庞然大物

The *mammoth* corporations of the twentieth century are a mixed blessing.

20 世纪的大公司是一令人忧喜参半的混合体。

manacle ['mænəkl] *n.* 手铐. handcuff

The *manacles* bit into his wrists.

手铐卡进他手腕。

mandate ['mændeit] *v.* 命令，指令

International law *mandates* that a country accredit diplomatic representatives of countries with whom it maintains friendly relations.

国际法指明一个国家应向与其保持友好关系的国家派驻外交使节。

mandatory ['mændətəri] *a.* 命令的，强迫的. obligatory

These instructions are *mandatory*, any violation will be severely punished.

这些指令是强制性的，对任何违反行为都将严惩不贷。

maneuverable [mə'nu:vərəbl] *a.* 可移动的，操纵灵敏的

maneuver [mə'nu:və] *v.* (军队)调动；用策略，耍花招

He *maneuvered* his way into the confidence of the enemy.

他曲折迂回地赢得了敌人的信任。

mangle ['mæŋgl] *v.* 撕成碎片，压碎

The book was *mangled* by the broken machine.

书被碎纸机撕得粉碎。

比较记忆：mingle（混合），wrangle（争论）

mangy ['meindʒi] *a.* 破烂的. shabby

We finally threw out the *mangy* rug that the dog had destroyed.

我们最终把被狗弄坏的那块破地毯给扔了。

mania ['meinjə] *n.* 癫狂，狂热

Hitler's *mania* is often cited as the cause of World War II.

人们常把二战的起因归为希特勒的狂热。

maniacal [mə'naiəkəl] *a.* 发狂的，狂热的

His *maniacal* laughter frightened us.

他的狂笑吓坏了我们。

manicure ['mænikjuə] *v.* 修指甲

参考：nail（指甲），toenail（脚指甲），fingernail（手指甲）

manifest ['mænifest] *a.* 明白的； *n.* 载货清单； *v.* 表明，显示

Her true feelings *manifested* themselves in her sarcastic asides; only then was her bitterness revealed.

她真实的情感在她满怀嘲讽的旁白中表露无遗,只有那一时刻才暴露出她内心的苦涩。

manifesto [ˌmæni'festəu] *n.* 宣言，声明

The Communist *Manifesto* by Marx proclaimed the principles of modern communism.

马克思的《共产党宣言》表明了现代共产主义的宗旨。

manifold ['mænifəuld] *a.* 繁多的，多种的. varied

mani (many) + fold → 多层次的

manikin ['mænikin] *n.* 侏儒；人体模型；时装模特. pygmy

manipulate [mə'nipjuleit] *v.* 窜改. color；操纵

The magician *manipulated* the cards and ace vanished.

魔术师把牌给变了, A 不见了。

How can you *manipulate* these puppets?

你怎么操纵这些木偶的?

manipulative [mə'nipjulətiv] *a.* 操纵别人的；控制的

来自：manipulate（熟练地操作，摆布）

mannequin ['mænikin] *n.* 时装模特儿，假人（用以展示服装）

mannered ['mænəd] *a.* 不自然的. affected

Attempting to copy the style of his wealthy neighbors, Gatsby adopted a *mannered*, artificial way of speech.

28

为了仿效他那些有钱的邻居的作派,盖茨比采用了一种做作的不
自然的说话方式。

mannerism ['mænərizəm] *n.* 特殊癖性

His most annoying *mannerism* was his habit of drinking
soup loudly.

他最恼人的怪癖就是他大声喝汤的习惯。

manqué [mãŋkei] *a.* 受挫的，不成功的

A *manque* bard never produced a single book of verse.

一个不成功的游唱诗人,一本诗集也写不出来。

mansion ['mænʃən] *n.* 公馆，大厦

The old *mansion* is the town's showplace.

这幢旧大厦是这座镇子的游览胜地。

manslaughter ['mæn‚slɔːtə] *n.* 过失杀人

比较记忆：onslaught（猛攻），slaughter（屠杀）

mantilla [mæn'tilə] *n.* 薄纱短斗蓬，头纱

mantle ['mæntl] *n.* 披风；斗蓬；   *v.* 覆盖

He enveloped her in the voluminous folds of his *mantle*.

他把她裹进他披风宽大的褶层中。

manumit [‚mænju'mit] *v.* 解放（奴隶）. emancipate

Enlightened slave owners were willing to *manumit* their
slaves and thus put an end to the evil of slavery in the
country.

觉醒的奴隶主们自愿解放了奴隶,从而结束了存在于这个国家的
奴隶制的罪恶。

manure [mə'njuə] *n.* （天然）肥料

manure：excrete ＝ compost：decay

maple ['meipl] *n.* 枫树

maple：sap ＝ pine：resin（松脂）

mar [mɑː] *v.* 破坏，损伤. spoil

She had to refinish the *marred* surface of the table.

她得重修损伤的桌面。

maraud [mə'rɔ:d] *v.* 抢劫，掠夺. plunder, pillage

marauder [mə'rɔ:də] *n.* 抢劫者

　　The *marauders* came to the ranch at night and stole the cattle.

　　劫匪半夜来牧场偷走了牛。

mare ['mεə] *n.* 母马. ↔ stallion

margarine [ˌmɑ:dʒə'ri:n] *n.* 人造黄油

　　margarine : butter = saccharin : sugar

marginal ['mɑ:dʒinəl] *a.* 边缘空白处的，不重要的

　　margin : page = shoulder : roadway

mariculture ['mærikʌltʃə] *n.* 海上养殖

　　mari (sea) + culture → 海上养殖

mariner ['mærinə] *n.* 水手，海员. seafarer

marionette [ˌmæriə'net] *n.* 木偶. puppet

　　The singular *marionette* danced on its strings.

　　单人木偶在线绳上跳舞。

marital ['mæritl] *a.* 婚姻的. matrimonial

　　After the publication of his book on *marital* affairs, he was often consulted by married people on the verge of divorce.

　　他有关婚姻生活那本书出版之后，许多处于离婚边缘的人来向他讨教。

maritime ['mæritaim] *a.* 海上的；航海的. nautical

　　The *maritime* country depends on the sea for their wealth.

　　海上国家向大海要财富。

marksmanship ['mɑ:ksmənʃip] *n.* 射击术

　　参考：marksman（射手），fencing（击剑术）

maroon [mə'ru:n] *v.* 使人处于孤独无助之境

In the film *Lifeboat*, an ill assorted group of passengers from a sunken ocean liner are *marooned* at sea in a dinghy.

在电影《生命航船》中，一队各怀心腑事的海上沉船的幸存者乘一艘小橡皮艇在茫茫大海上孤助无依地漂流。

marquetry ['mɑːkitri] *n.* 镶嵌细工

比较记忆：coquetry（卖弄风情）

marrow ['mærəu] *n.* 骨髓；精华. quintessence

It was so cold that he felt frozen to the *marrow*.

太冷了，他觉得简直是寒冷刺骨。

marsh [mɑːʃ] *n.* 沼泽地，湿地. swamp

marsh : sodden = desert : barren

marshal ['mɑːʃəl] *n.* 警察局长； *v.* 排列；整理

At a debate tournament, extemporaneous speakers have only a minute or two to *marshal* their thoughts before addressing their audience.

在一辩论冠军赛上，雄辩的演讲家们只有一两分钟的时间整理他们的思路，而后就得向听众讲话。

marsupial [mɑːˈsjuːpjəl] *n.* 有袋动物

The most common *marsupial* in North America is the o-possum.

北美最常见的有袋动物是负鼠。

martial ['mɑːʃəl] *a.* 战争的；军事的

The sound of *martial* music was always inspiring to the young cadet.

军歌声总会令年轻的军校生为之振奋。

martinet [ˌmɑːtiˈnet] *n.* 要求严格服从纪律的人. ↔ rake

来自 17 世纪法国路易十四世时的军事教官 Martinet

martyr ['mɑːtə] *n.* 烈士，殉道者

The early Christian Church had many *martyrs*.

早期基督教堂有许多殉道者。

masculine ['mɑːskjulin] *a.* 男性的

masculinity [ˌmæskjuˈliniti] *n.* 男子气概

Stringberg's plays are marked by his misogyny; he felt modern woman needed to dominate man and invalidate his *masculinity*.

斯特林贝里的作品总带有仇视女性的色彩,他认为现代妇女总要统治男性且打破男性的权威。

mash [mæʃ] *v.* 捣成糊状;调情. flirt

mash : pestle = piece : awl

mask [mɑːsk] *n.* 假面具; *v.* 隐藏(感情)

masochist [mæsəˈkist] *n.* 自虐狂. ↔ sadist

The *masochist* begs, "hit me", the sadist smiles and says "I won't".

自虐狂请求道:"打我吧";施虐狂微笑着说:"我不打你"。

mason ['meisn] *n.* 石工,石匠

参考:lapidary(宝石匠)

masonry ['meisnri] *n.* 石工(业);石屋

masquerade [ˌmæskəˈreid] *n.* 化装舞会; *v.* 伪装. camouflage

In the *masquerade*, she tried to camouflage as a crone.

在化装舞会上,她想装扮成个老太婆。

massacre ['mæsəkə] *n.* & *v.* 大屠杀,残杀. pogrom

Teutonic hordes advanced across Europe, sacking and *massacring*.

日尔曼游牧民族穿越欧洲,一路上烧杀劫掠。

比较记忆:massage(按摩)

massive ['mæsiv] *a.* 巨大的,粗重的. bulky

We must make *massive* efforts to improve things.

我们得做出很大努力改善情形。

masticate ['mæstikeit] *v.* 咀嚼;把……磨成浆

We must *masticate* our food carefully and slowly in order to avoid digestive disorders.

我们必须细嚼慢咽下食物,以避免造成消化不良。

mastitis [mæs'taitis] *n.* 乳腺炎

参考：arthritis（关节炎），inflammation（发炎）

mastodon ['mæstədən] *n.* 乳齿象（已绝迹）

参考：dinosaur（恐龙），pterodactyl（翼手龙）

matador ['mætədɔ:] *n.* 斗牛士. picador

A *matador* is a man who kills the bull in the sport of
bullfighting.

斗牛士是在斗牛运动中杀死公牛的人。

materialize [mə'tiəriəlaiz] *v.* 使具有物质形式，实现

material ＋ ize (form) → 使具有物质形式

比较记忆：materialism（唯物主义）

maternal [mə'tə:nl] *a.* 母亲的

Many animals display *maternal* instincts only while
their offspring are young and helpless.

许多动物只在幼崽婴幼期孤助无援时表现出母性。

maternity [mə'tə:niti] *n.* 怀孕. conception

matriarch ['meitriɑ:k] *n.* 女家长，女族长

The *matriarch* ruled her gypsy tribe with a firm hand.

女族长用强有力的手段统治着她的吉普赛部落。

matriarchy ['meitriɑ:ki] *n.* 母权制，妇女统治

matri (mother) ＋ archy (state) → 母权制

matricide ['meitrisaid] *n.* & *v.* 杀母（罪）

matri (mother) ＋ cide (kill) → 杀母

比较记忆：parricide（杀父）

matriculate [mə'trikjuleit] *v.* 录取入学

matriculate：student ＝ inaugurate：official

matrimony ['mætriməni] *n.* 婚姻

The hostess attempted to contrive a romantic atmosphere that would bring the two young people together in *matrimony*.

女主人想要营造出一种浪漫气氛,撮合两个年轻人走到一起,结成良缘。

参考: matron (妻子,主妇)

matrix ['meitriks] *n.* 模子;矩阵

matrix : numbers = crystal : atoms

matting ['mætiŋ] *n.* 草席. mat

Matting of dried grasses on the floor is usually seen in the huts of the South Pacific islands.

在南太平洋岛屿的小茅屋中,通常可以看到地上铺着干草织就的草席。

比较记忆: mattress (床垫)

mattock ['mætək] *n.* 鹤嘴锄

The old man used a *mattock* to loosen the topsoil and dig up the roots.

老人用鹤嘴锄刨开表层土壤,挖出根须。

matutinal [ˌmætju(:)'tainl] *a.* 早晨的

参考: nocturnal (夜间的), crepuscular (黄昏的)

maudlin ['mɔ:dlin] *a.* 感情脆弱的. ↔ intelligent

来自人名 Maudalene,常被描绘成哭泣的典型形象

maul [mɔ:l] *v.* 撕裂皮肉;殴打. bruise

The rock star was *mauled* by his overexcited fans.

过分激动的歌迷撕扯着那个摇滚歌星。

maunder ['mɔ:ndə] *v.* 胡言乱语;无精打采地走. babble

比较记忆: launder (洗衣)

People who *maunder* talk much but say little.

胡言乱语的人尽管说的不少,却言之无物。

mausoleum [ˌmɔ:sə'liəm] *n.* 陵墓

His body was placed in the family *mausoleum*.

他的遗体安放在家族墓地里。

maverick ['mævərik] *n*. 独行者

maverick∶conformity = renegade∶vassalage

maw [mɔː] *n*. 动物的胃或喉

The tiger held the lamb in its *maw*.

老虎咬住羊羔咽喉。

mawkish ['mɔːkiʃ] *a*. 令人作呕的. mushy

Your *mawkish* sighs fill me with disgust.

你那故作多情的叹息真令我恶心。

maxim ['mæksim] *n*. 格言，普遍真理

参考：proverb（谚语），adage（谚语），apothegm（格言），epigram（警句），motto（座右铭）

比较记忆：maximum（最大）

mayhem ['meihem] *n*. 严重伤害罪；伤害

The riot was marked not only by *mayhem*, with its attendant loss of life and limb, but also by arson and pillage.

骚乱不仅造成参与者生命和肢体上的伤害，还有纵火抢劫。

maze [meiz] *n*. 迷宫. labyrinth

The *maze* was an artificer created by Daedalus to imprison the violent Minotaur.

迷宫是工匠代达罗斯为困住狂野的半人半牛的（克里特食人）怪物而设计出来的。

meager ['miːgə] *a*. 贫乏的，削瘦的. scanty

His salary was far too *meager* for him to afford to buy a new car.

他的工资对他而言少得可怜，远不够买辆新车的。

mealymouthed ['miːlimauðd] *a*. 委婉的. devious

Rather than tell Jill directly what he disliked, Jack made a few *mealymouthed* comments and tried to change the subject.

不是直言相告吉尔他不喜欢什么,杰克转弯抹角地评价了几句,
又尽力转换了话题。

meander [mi'ændə] *v.* 蜿蜒而流;漫步. ramble

来自 Meander 河,以其蜿蜒曲折而著名

It is difficult to sail up this stream because of the way it *meanders* through the countryside.

顺这条小溪而上很困难,因为它蜿蜒穿过乡间。

measles ['mi:zlz] *n.* 麻疹

参考:fester (化脓),ophthalmia (眼炎)

measured ['meʒəd] *a.* 精确的,慎重的. prudent

mecca ['mekə] *n.* 众人渴望去的地方

来自宗教圣地麦加 Mecca

mechanical [mi'kænikl] *a.* 机械的;无意识的. ↔ meditated

meddlesome ['medlsəm] *a.* 爱管闲事的

He felt his marriage was suffering because of his *meddlesome* mother-in-law.

有这么个爱管闲事儿的岳母,让他觉得他的婚姻简直是遭罪。

median ['mi:djən] *a.* 中间的; *n.* (三角形)中线

medi (middle) + an → 中间的

mediate ['mi:dieit] *v.* 调停. arbitrate

medi (between) + ate (make) → 调停

mediator : deadlock = judge : case

比较记忆:meditate (沉思)

medieval [ˌmedi'i:vəl] *a.* 中世纪的,中古的

medi (middle) + ev (age) + al → 中古的

比较记忆:primeval (远古的)

mediocre ['mi:diəukə] *a.* 平庸的,平凡的. commonplace

mediocrity [ˌmi:di'ɔkriti] *n.* 平庸;平凡;平庸的人

Broadway audiences have become inured to *mediocrity* and so desperate to be pleased as to make their ready ovations meaningless as an indicator of the quality of the production before them.

百老汇的观众已习惯了平庸,不再指望会看到什么令人满意的演出,以致于他们那时不时的鼓掌喝彩也不过是敷衍了事而已,不再能体现出他们对呈现在他们面前的作品质量的好坏(的看法态度了)。

medium ['mi:djəm] *n.* 媒介,(细菌等)生存环境

medi (middle) + ium (mass) → 中间物,媒介

medium : organism = soil : plant

medley ['medli] *n.* 混杂;集成曲. pastiche

The band played a ***medley*** of Gershwin tunes.

乐队上演了一曲格什温主题联奏。

meed [mi:d] *n.* 报酬,工资. recompense

The God will pay you the equivalent ***meed*** for your endeavor

上帝会对你的努力作出相应报答的。

比较记忆:meek(温顺的;驯服的)

meek [mi:k] *a.* 温顺的,谦和的. amiable

The boy was ***meek*** as a lamb when he was reproved.

男孩受到责备时,温顺得像只小羊羔。

megalith ['megəliθ] *n.* (古建筑物用的)巨石

megalomania ['megələu'meinjə] *n.* 自大狂

mdgalo (great) + mania → 自大狂

mélange [mei'lɑ:nʒ] *v.* 混合物. mingle

This anthology provides a ***melange*** of the author's output in the fields of satire criticism and political analysis.

这本集子集成了作者的讽刺批评和政治分析领域的作品。

meld [meld] *v.* 合并. blend

melee ['melei] *n.* 混战

The captain tried to ascertain the cause of the ***melee***

that had broken out among the crew members.

船长试图确认船员间爆发的混乱的起因。

mellifluous [me'lifluəs] *a.* (音乐)柔美流畅的. ↔ raucous

melli (honey) ＋ flu (flow) ＋ ous → 似流蜜的

参考：mellow（甘美的；柔和的）

melodious [mi'ləudjəs] *a.* 悦耳的. euphonic

He was attracted by her sweet, *melodious* voice.

他被她甜美悦耳的嗓音迷住了。

melodrama ['melə͵drɑ:mə] *n.* 情节剧，音乐戏剧

melody ＋ drama → 音乐戏剧

melody ['melədi] *n.* 旋律，歌曲

参考：lullaby（摇篮曲），symphony（交响乐）

membrane ['membrein] *n.* 薄膜，细胞膜

cell：membrane ＝ seed：hull

memento [mi'mentəu] *n.* 纪念品. keepsake，token

Take this book as a *memento* of your visit.

把这本书拿去作你的参观纪念吧。

memoir ['memwɑ:] *n.* 传记； *pl.* 回忆录

The duchess's *memoirs* caused a sensation.

公爵夫人的回忆录引起一阵轰动。

memorials [mi'mɔ:riəls] *n.* 编年史

menagerie [mi'nædʒəri] *n.* 兽群；动物园

mendacious [men'deiʃəs] *a.* 假的，撒谎的. spurious

Our only hope is to prove that the witness was *menda-cious* and guilty of perjury.

我们唯一的希望是证明目击证人撒了谎，犯了伪证罪。

mendicant ['mendikənt] *a.* 行乞的； *n.* 乞丐

From the moment we left the ship, we were surrounded by *mendicants* and peddlers.

我们一下船，就被乞丐和小贩给围住了。

menial ['miːnjəl] *a.* 卑微的，乏味的； *n.* 奴仆. mean

Although Ms. Brown found some of her duties to be *menial*, her supervision of forty workers was a considerable responsibility.

尽管布朗夫人认为她的有些职责乏味，管理四十名工人还是个不小的责任。

mentor ['mentɔː] *n.* 导师. counselor, tutor

During this very trying period, she could not have had a better *mentor*, for the teacher was sympathetic and understanding.

在这一试用期，她的老师真是再好不过的了，因为老师既富于同情心，又十分善解人意。

mercantile ['məːkəntail] *a.* 商品的；商业的

I am more interested in the opportunities available in the *mercantile* field than I am in those in the legal profession.

我对商业领域内的机遇比对法律界的更感兴趣些。

mercenary ['məːsinəri] *a.* 唯利是图的； *n.* 雇佣兵. hessians

I am certain that your action was prompted by *mercenary* motives.

我肯定你的行动出于唯利是图的目的。

mercurial [məːˈkjuəriəl] *a.* 善变的；活泼的. fickle

来自：mercury（水银；水星）

mere [miə] *n.* 池塘

比较记忆：sere（枯萎）

meretricious [ˌmeriˈtriʃəs] *a.* 华而不实的，俗艳的. specious

Her jewels were inexpensive but not *meretricious*.

她（佩带）的珠宝便宜但不俗气。

mergence ['məːdʒəns] *n.* 合并，结合；消失；淹没. immersion

merger [məːdʒə] *n.* 合并

39

When the firm's president married the director of financial planning, the office joke was that it wasn't a marriage, it was a *merger*.

当公司总裁同财政计划部门经理结婚时,公司里的人开玩笑说这不叫作结婚,而是合并。

比较记忆:immerge(沉浸于)

meridian [məˈridiən] *n.* 顶点;子午线;鼎盛时期. vertex

meritorious [ˌmeriˈtɔːriəs] *a.* 值得赞赏的

    merit + orious(多······的)→ 值得赞美的

mermaid [ˈməːmeid] *n.* 美人鱼(神话怪物)

    mermaid : fish = centaur : horse

mesa [ˈmeisə] *n.* 阶地;平顶山. tableland

    mesa : valley = saucer : cup

mesmerize [ˈmezməraiz] *v.* 催眠;着迷. hypnotize;spellbind

    The incessant drone seemed to *mesmerize* him and place him in a trance.

    这种不断的嗡嗡声看上去给他催了眠,使他处于一种神思恍惚的状态。

metabolism [meˈtæbəlizəm] *n.* 新陈代谢

    meta (change) + bol (throw) + ism → 新陈代谢

metallurgical [ˌmetəˈləːdʒikəl] *a.* 冶金(学)的

    During the course of his *metallurgical* research, the scientist developed a steel alloy of tremendous strength.

    在冶金学研究进程中,科学家研制出一种有极好的力度钢合金。

metallurgy [meˈtælədʒi] *n.* 冶金学

metamorphosis [ˌmetəˈmɔːfəsis] *n.* 变形,变态

    meta (change) + morph (form) + osis → 变形

metaphor [ˈmetəfə] *n.* 隐喻,暗喻. ↔ simile

    meta (behind) + phor (bear) → 隐喻

metaphysician [ˌmetəfiˈziʃən] *n.* 玄学家

metaphysics [ˌmetə'fiziks] *n.* 形而上学，玄学

    meta (transcend) + physics → 超越物理现实 → 玄学

mete [miːt] *v.* 衡量；分派. allot

    He tried to be impartial in his efforts to *mete* out justice.

    他努力做到不偏不倚，一碗水端平。

meteor ['miːtjə] *n.* 流星；陨星

    Most *meteors* burn up when they enter the Earth's atmosphere.

    许多陨石进入地球大气层时都烧毁了。

meteoric [ˌmiːti'ɔrik] *a.* 流星的；流星般的. ↔ gradual

    We all wondered at his *meteoric* rise to fame.

    我们都惊叹于他像流星般地昙花一现。

meter ['miːtə] *n.* 韵律；仪；表

meticulous [mi'tikjuləs] *a.* 过分细心的

    He was *meticulous* in checking his accounts and never made mistakes.

    他极细心地核查他的账目，从不出错。

mettle ['metl] *n.* 勇气，斗志

    When challenged by the other houses in the race, the thoroughbred proved its *mettle* by its determination to hold the lead.

    在比赛中受到其他马的挑战时，纯种马充分表现出其斗志，坚持领先地位。

mews [mjuːz] *n.* 马厩

    Let us visit the *mews* to inspect the newly purchased horse.

    让我们去马厩视察一下新买的马。

miasma [mi'æzmə] *n.* 瘴气；坏影响

    The smog hung over Victorian London like a dark

cloud, noisome, reeding of decay, it was a visible *mias-ma*.

烟雾像乌云一样地笼罩在维多利亚时代伦敦的上空,有股腐烂的草的难闻的气味,是一种看得见的瘴气。

mica ['maikə] *n.* 云母

参考:uranium（铀），zinc（锌），marble（大理石）

microbe ['maikrəub] *n.* 微生物

microcosm ['maikrəukɔzm] *n.* (人或社会)缩影

In the *microcosm* of our rural village, we find illustrations of all the evils that beset the universe.

在我们乡村这一小小的社会缩影里,可以找到形形色色充斥于宇宙间邪恶现象的明证。

microscopic [,maikrəs'kɔpik] *a.* 极小的. minute

来自:microscope（显微镜）

midget ['midʒit] *n.* 侏儒，极小者. dwarf

midwife ['midwaif] *n.* 助产士

mien [mi:n] *n.* 风采，态度. bearing

The president was a man of calm and refined *mien*.

总统是个风度翩翩、镇定自若的人。

miff [mif] *n.* 小争吵. skirmish

miff : quarrel = peccadillo : offense

migrant ['maigrənt] *n.* 移民，候鸟

比较记忆:immigrant（移入），emigrant（移出）

mildew ['maildju:] *n.* 霉. mold

参考:dew（露珠），toadstool（霉菌）

milestone ['mailstəun] *n.* 里程碑

Some biologists argue that each specifically human trait must have arisen gradually and erratically, and that it is therefore difficult to isolate definite *milestones* in the evolution of the species.

一些生物学家争辩说每一特殊人种的特征都是逐渐地、不规则性反复出现的,因此很难在种类进行上划分出阶段确定性里程碑。

milieu ['miːljəː] *n.* (个人)社会环境,背景

His *milieu* is watercolors, although he has produced excellent oil paintings and lithographs.

他以水彩画出身,尽管也画过极好的油画和版画。

militant ['militənt] *a.* 好战的,好暴力的. bellicose

Although at this time he was advocating a policy of neutrality, one could usually find him adopting a more *militant* attitude.

尽管他这种时候倡导中立,人们往往发现他更喜欢采取一种暴力态度。

比较记忆:military (军事的)

militate ['militeit] *v.* 对……产生影响

The evidence given by eyewitness *militated* against him.

目击证人提供的证据对他不利。

militia [miˈliʃə] *n.* 民兵

Every state has a *militia*.

每个州都有个民兵团。

milk [milk] *v.* 挤奶;榨取

The gangsters who *milked* protection money from small businesses were unable to retaliate

那些压榨小生意人保护费的团伙帮派报复不得。

milksop ['milksɔp] *n.* 懦夫. mollycoddle

milksop : virility = coquette : virginity

Unit Twenty-Three

millennium [mi'leniəm] *n.* 太平盛世；一千年

I do not expect the ***millennium*** to come during my lifetime.

我没想到一生中会遇上什么太平盛世。

miller ['milə] *n.* 磨坊主

miller : grain = tanner : hide

millinery ['milinəri] *n.* 女帽（总称）

来自：milliner（女帽设计者）

bonnet : millinery = suitcase : luggage

mime [maim] *v.* 比划（讲故事）； *n.* 哑剧（演员）

参考：pantomime（哑剧），mimesis（模仿）

mimic ['mimik] *n.* 模仿者； *v.* 模仿. ape

mimicry ['mimikri] *n.* 模仿；（动物）拟态. mimesis

Her gift for ***mimicry*** was so great that her friend said that she should be in the theater.

她有极好的模仿天分，她的朋友们都说她该去演戏。

minaret [ˌminə'ret] *n.* （清真寺旁的）尖塔，叫拜楼. (slender lofty tower)

From the balcony of the ***minaret*** , we obtained an excellent view of the town and the neighboring countryside.

从叫拜楼的阳台上,我们可以把城镇和相邻乡间的美景尽收眼底。

minatory ['minətəri] *a.* 威胁的，恫吓的. menacing

All abusive and ***minatory*** letters received by the mayor and other public officials were examined by the police.

警察仔细研究了市长及其他政府官员接到的辱骂恐吓信。

mince [mins] *v.* 切碎；小步走

mince ：stride ＝ sip ：quaff

mincing ['minsiŋ] *a.* 娇饰的，故作斯文的

She walked across the stage with *mincing* steps.

她拿腔作势地走过桥。

mingy ['mindʒi] *a.* 吝啬的．miserly

She was so *mingy* that she never tipped the grocery boy.

她太吝啬了，从没给过副食品商店的男童一次小费。

miniature ['minitʃə] *n.* 小画像，缩影

While some see in practical jokes a wish for mastery in *miniature* over a world that seems very unruly, others believe that the jokes' purpose is to disrupt, by reducing all transactions to chaos.

一些人把恶作剧看成是对一混乱无序的世界要加以控制的缩影这种愿望的表达，另一些人却认为这些恶作剧不过是通过把所有事物都弄乱而达到分裂的目的。

minimize ['minimaiz] *n.* 最小化，轻视．↔ maximize

Unlike a judge, who must act alone, a jury discusses a case and then reaches its decision as a group, thus *minimizing* the effect of individual bias.

同法官必须独自做出决断不同的是，陪审团讨论一案例而后得出集体意见，这样把个人偏见降到最小。

参考：minimal（最小的），maximal（最大的）

minion ['miniən] *n.* 奴才；宠儿；偶像．idol

He was always accompanied by several of his *minions* because he enjoyed their subservience and flattery.

他身边总有几个奴才跟着，因为他喜欢听他们的阿谀奉承。

ministrant ['ministrənt] *a.* 服侍的； *n* 服侍者

来自：minister（伺候）

45

minnow [ˈminəu] *n.* 米诺鱼；小淡水鱼

参考：octopus（章鱼），carp（鲤鱼）

minstrel [ˈminstrəl] *n.* 音乐家；诗人. bard

The *minstrel* strolled through the garden.

诗人漫步走过花园。

mint [mint] *n.* 造币厂；　*v.* 铸造

The United States recently *minted* ＄2 bills for general public use.

美国最近制造了一种公众流通使用的两元币。

minuet [ˌminjuˈet] *n.* 小步舞

Although the *minuet* appeared simple, its intricate steps had to be studied very carefully before they could be gracefully executed in public.

尽管小步舞看上去简单，想当众优雅地跳上一曲之前，还真得好好研习一下它那复杂的舞步。

minuscule [ˈminəskju:l] *a.* 微小的. microscopic

Why should I involve myself with a project with so *minuscule* a chance for success.

我干嘛要牵扯进一个成功机会如此之小的项目里去呢？

minute [ˈminit] *a.* 微小的；详细的. diminutive；explicit

A molecule is a *minute* particle of a substance.

分子是一种微小的物质粒子。

minutes [ˈminits] *n.* 会议记录

minutes：agenda ＝ itinerary：log

minutia [naiˈnju:ʃiə] *n.* 细枝末节，细节；　*pl.* minutiae

She would have liked to ignore the *minutiae* of daily living.

她倒宁愿不睬日常生活中的一些细枝末节。

minx [miŋks] *n.* 顽皮姑娘. pert girl

The *minx* learned that she could have almost anything if

46

she went into tantrum.

这个顽皮的姑娘知道她要是发了脾气,几乎想要怎样就能怎样。

比较记忆:sphinx(谜一般的人)

mirage ['mirɑ:ʒ] *n.* 幻影,海市蜃楼

The lost prospector was fooled by a *mirage* in the desert.

迷路的探矿人被沙漠中的海市蜃楼愚弄了。

参考:miraculous(神奇的)

mire ['maiə] *n.* 泥沼;困境; *v.* 使陷入困境. swamp. ↔ extricate

Their rear wheels became *mired* in mud.

他们的后轮陷在泥里。

mirth [mə:θ] *n.* 欢乐,欢笑. jollity, glee

The festive Christmas dinner was a merry one, and old and young alike joined in the general *mirth*.

充满节日气氛的圣诞晚宴真是一个欢乐时刻,无论是老年人还是年轻人都(受到感染)加入这一欢乐的大阵营。

misadventure ['misəd'ventʃə] *n.* 不幸. mischance

mis (bad) + adventure → 不幸

misanthrope ['mizənθrəup] *n.* 愤世嫉俗者. ↔ philanthropist

mis (hatred) + antrope (man) → 恨世者

miscegenation [ˌmisidʒi'neiʃən] *n.* 异族通婚

Some states passed laws against *miscegenation*.

一些州通过了反对异族通婚的法律。

miscellaneous [ˌmisi'leinjəs] *a.* 多方面的;混杂的. promiscuous

miscellany [mi'seləni] *n.* 杂集

This is an interesting *miscellany* of nineteenth-century prose and poetry.

这是一本有关 19 世纪诗歌散文的有趣的杂集。

mischievous ['mistʃivəs] *a.* 淘气的;有害的. naughty

mis（bad）＋ chief（head）＋ ous → 淘气的

miscible ['misibl] *a.* 易于混合的

misconstrue ['miskən'stru:] *v.* 误解，曲解. distort

mis（wrong）＋ construe → 误解

miscreant ['miskriənt] *n.* 恶棍；异教徒. villain；infidel

His kindness to the *miscreant* amazed all of us who had expected to hear severe punishment pronounced.

我们都还以为会听到严惩的宣判，而他对这个恶棍的善良令我们所有的人都吃惊。

misdemeanor [ˌmisdi'mi:nə] *n.* 小罪过

The culprit pleaded guilty to a *misdemeanor* rather than face trial for a felony.

犯罪者请求判罪行为小罪过，而不愿面对重罪的宣判。

misery ['mizəri] *n.* 贫困；悲惨. dismay

比较记忆：miserly（吝啬的）

misgiving ['misgiviŋ] *n.* 疑虑，担忧. qualm

Hamlet described his *misgivings* to Horatio but decided to fence with Laertes despite his foreboding of evil.

汉姆雷特把他的疑虑同霍雷肖说了，但决定瞒着累尔提斯，尽管他预言了邪恶。

mishap ['mishæp] *n.* 不幸，坏运气

mis（bad）＋ hap（luck）→ 坏运气

misnomer ['mis'nəumə] *n.* 误称

His tyrannical conduct proved to all that his nickname，King Eric the Just，was a *misnomer*.

他那铁拳统治向所有的人证明了他号称公正的埃里克之王纯属误称。

misogamy [mi'sɔgəmi] *n.* 厌婚症，婚姻嫌忌

miso（hatred）＋ gamy（marry）→ 厌恶结婚

misogyny [mai'sɔdʒini] *n.* 厌女

48

miso (hatred) + gyny (woman) → 厌女

misogynist : feminism = bureaucrat : anarchy

missal ['misəl] *n.* 祈祷书

The child received a *missal* for his birthday.

这个孩子得到本祈祷书作生日礼物。

比较记忆：missile（发射物体，导弹）

misshapen [ˌmis'ʃeipən] *a.* 畸形的；丑陋的. deformed

mission ['miʃən] *v.* 布道 homily

missionary ['miʃənəri] *n.* 传教士； *a.* 传教的

Some TV *missionaries* are more interested in their own
interests than in the interests of the people or of the
Lord.

一些电视传教士对他们自身的利益比对公众的或上帝的利益更
为关注。

missive ['misiv] *n.* 信件，公文

The ambassador received a *missive* from the Secretary of
State.

大使收到国务卿的一封公文。

mistimed ['mis'laimt] *a.* 不合时宜的. timed

mis（wrong）+ timed → 不合时机的

mistral ['mistrəl] *n.* 冷而干燥的强风

mists [mists] *n.* 雾

mite [mait] *n.* 少许；小虫

比较记忆：mote（微粒）

mitigate ['mitigeit] *v.* 减轻，缓和. appease

Nothing he did could *mitigate* her wrath, she was un-
forgiving.

什么也不能减轻她的罪过，她是不可饶恕的。

mitten ['mitn] *n.* 连指手套

mitten : hand = shawl : neck

49

mixer ['miksə] *n.* 混合器；交际家

mnemonics [ˌniːmə'niks] *n.* 记忆法，记忆规则

参考：amnesia（健忘症）

moat [məut] *n.* 壕沟，护城河. fosse

比较记忆：moan（呻吟）

mock [mɔk] *v.* 嘲笑，嘲弄式地模仿. mimic

mock：imitate ＝ taunt：challenge

moderator ['mɔdərit] *n.* 调解人，仲裁人. referee

来自：moderate（适度的；使和缓）

modicum ['mɔdikəm] *n.* 少量. pinch

Although his story is based on a *modicum* of truth,
most of the events he describes are fictitious.

尽管他的故事多少有些事实基础,他描绘的大多数事件纯属杜
撰。

modish ['məudiʃ] *a.* 时髦的. stylish

She always discarded all garments which were no longer
modish.

她总把过时的衣服扔掉。

modulate ['mɔdjuleit] *v.* 调整（音的强弱），变调

比较记忆：moderate（适度的；调解）

mogul [məu'gʌl] *n.* 显要人物，权势之人. magnate

The oil *moguls* made great profits when the gasoline up-
surges.

石油大亨们在汽油大潮中大发横财。

moiety ['mɔiəti] *n.* 一半，半份

The judge ordered that the dead man's 2 children should
each receive a *moiety* of his possessions.

法官裁断死者的两个子女各得一半财产。

moil [mɔil] *v.* 辛苦工作. drudge

molar ['məulə] *n.* 臼齿（used for grinding food）

50

The dentist removed a loose *molar* from the boy's mouth.

医生从小男孩嘴里拔下颗松动的白齿。

mold [məuld] *n.* 模子； *v.* 塑造

I made the mousse in my new copper *mold*.

我用新铜模具做的奶油冻。

moldy ['məuldi] *a.* 发霉的；陈腐的. fusty

molest [məu'lest] *v.* 骚扰，干扰. bother

That big kid is always *molesting* the children.

这个大孩子总去骚扰小孩子们。

mollify ['mɔlifai] *v.* 安慰，安抚. soothe

We tried to *mollify* the hysterical child by promising her many gifts.

我们努力安抚那个歇斯底里的小姑娘，许诺会送她许多礼物。

参考：emollient（润肤剂）

mollusk ['mɔləsk] *n.* 软体动物

参考：limpet（蝛），snail（蜗牛），slug（蛞蝓），octopus（章鱼），mussel（贻贝），cuttlefish（乌贼），oyster（蚝）

mollycoddle ['mɔlikɔdl] *v.* 娇惯. pamper, coddle

Don't *mollycoddle* the girl, or you'll spoil her.

别娇宠这小丫头，要不会惯坏她的。

molt [məult] *v.* 脱毛，换羽毛

molt : feature = shed : hair

momentous [məu'mentəs] *a.* 极重要的，严重的

He made the *momentous* decision to leave his high-pay job.

他做出个重要决定，要放弃这一报酬优厚的工作。

比较记忆：momentary（短暂的，瞬间的）

momentum [məu'mentəm] *n.* 推进力，势头

The car lost *momentum* as it tried to ascend the steep

hill.

车要下那个陡坡时(发动机)熄火了。

monarch ['mɔnək] *n.* 君主，帝王

　　mon (single) ＋ arch (ruler) → 君主

monastery ['mɔnəstəri] *n.* 男修道院，寺院

　　参考：nunnery（女修道院）

monastic [mənæstik] *n.* 修道士；　*a.* 禁欲生活的

　　Wanting to live a religious life, he took his *monastic*
　　vows.

　　想过一种宗教生活，他宣誓接受禁欲主义。

monasticism [mə'næstisizəm] *n.* 修道生活，禁欲生活

monetary ['mʌnitəri] *a.* 金钱的. pecuniary

　　Jane held the family purse strings; she made all *mone-*
　　tary decisions affecting the household.

　　简掌管着家里的财政大权，有关影响家庭开支的所有用钱决定都
　　由她作出。

mongrel ['mʌŋgrəl] *n.* 杂种动物，混血儿

　　The dog was cute, but he was only a *mongrel*.

　　这只狗逗人喜爱，但它是只混血狗。

monitory ['mɔnitəri] *a.* 劝告的，告诫的. admonitory

　　来自：monitor（监视）

monk [mʌŋk] *n.* 僧侣

　　monk : habit（法衣）＝ soldier : uniform（制服）

monochromat ['mʌnəkrəumæt] *n.* 全色盲者

　　mono (single) ＋ chrom (color) ＋ at → 全色盲

monocle ['mɔnɔkl] *n.* 单片眼镜

　　mono (single) ＋ cle (eye) → 单片眼镜

monody ['mɔnədi] *n.* 挽歌

　　The mourning throng was preparing for a *monody*.

　　送殡人群准备唱挽歌。

monogamy [mɔ'nɔgəmi] *n.* 一夫一妻制

    mono (single) ＋ game (marry) ＋ y → 一夫一妻制

    参考：neogamist（新婚者），bigamous（重婚的）

monograph ['mɔnəgrɑːf] *n.* 专题论文

    mono (single) ＋ graph (write) → 专题论文.

monolithic [ˌmɔnəu'liθik] *a.* 独块巨石的；坚如磐石的；整体的

    mono (single) ＋ lith (rock) ＋ ic → 单块大石头

    比较记忆：lithiasis（结石病）

monologue ['mɔnəlɔg] *n.* 独白，个人长篇演说

    mono (single) ＋ logue (speak) → 独白

monotonous [mə'nɔtənəs] *a.* 单调的，无聊的. tedious

    mono (single) ＋ ton (＝ tune) ＋ ous → 单调的

    It was incredible that a leader singer of her reputation should have such a ***monotonous*** voice.

    真令人难以置信，像她那样有声望的走红歌手，嗓子会那么平淡。

monsoon [mɔn'suːn] *n.* 季雨，季风

    参考：cyclone（旋风），typhoon（台风）

monstrous ['mɔnstrəs] *a.* 巨大的；可怕的. colossal；hideous

    Two ***monstrous*** sharks crossed the bow of the boat.

    两条巨鲨划过般头。

monumental [ˌmɔnju'mentl] *a.* 巨大的；不朽的. immortal

    比较记忆：monument（纪念碑）

mooch [muːtʃ] *v.* 闲荡，溜达. loiter

    The couple decided to ***mooched*** another week in the lively sea-side village.

    这对夫妇决定再在这生机勃勃的海边小村闲逛一个星期。

moody ['muːdi] *a.* 沮丧的，忧郁的. melancholy

    We could not discover the cause of her recurrent ***moodiness***.

    我们找不出她时不时变得沮丧的原因。

moon [mu:n] *v.* 闲逛；如痴如醉地想. loaf；daydream

Teenage girls *moon* over the latest pop idols.

十几岁的少女都在梦想那些流行乐坛的最新偶像。

比较记忆：moonish（反复无常的），moony（幻想的）

moor [muə] *n.* 荒野；　*v.* 停泊. berth

Hounds pursued the escaped convict across the *moor*.

猎犬追踪猎物穿越整个荒野。

moot [nu:t] *a.* 争论的；不实用的；　*v.* 争论. ↔ austere

Whether life exists on other planets is a *moot* question.

外星球是否存在生命是一个没有什么用的问题。

mope [məup] *v.* 抑郁不乐，生闷气. sulk

She *moped* in her room after her father told her that she could not buy that coat.

她爸爸告诉她不能买那件衣服后，她躲进屋闷闷不乐。

比较记忆：mop（拖把）

moppet ['mɔpit] *a.* 小孩，女孩. toddler

When the *moppet* displayed signs of illness, the anxious parents called in a pediatrician.

当小女孩出现生病迹象时，焦虑的父母请来位儿科医生。

morale [mɔ'rɑ:l] *n.* 士气，精神力量

Even though his writings were rejected by the papers, his *morale* remained high.

尽管报纸拒绝了他的作品，他仍保持士气高昂。

比较记忆：moral（道德的）

moralist ['mɔrəlist] *n.* 道德家

moralistic [ˌmɔrə'listik] *a.* 道德的；说教的

morass [mə'ræs] *n.* 沼泽地；困境；　*v.* （使）陷入困境. bog

He *morassed* down in another useless man-to-man talk with his father.

他又一次陷入同他父亲那毫无用途（白费劲儿的）所谓坦诚对话中去。

moratorium [ˌmɔrəˈtɔːriəm] *n.* 延期偿付，暂禁

The breathing spell provided by the ***moratorium*** on arms shipments should give all the combatants a chance to reevaluate their positions.

武器禁运所带来的这一段喘息间隙让交战双方都得到一个重新评价他们自己所处位置的机会。

morbid [ˈmɔːbid] *a.* 病态的，不正常的. abnormal

These ***morbid*** speculations are dangerous, we must lighten our spirits by emphasizing more pleasant matters.

这种病态冥思是很危险的,我们必须更关注令人愉快的事,从而提起精神来。

mordant [ˈmɔːdənt] *a.* 讥讽的；锐利的. sarcastic; stinging

Actors feared the critic's ***mordant*** pen.

演员们都怕评论家手中那锋利的笔。

mores [ˈmɔːriːz] *n.* 风俗习惯

The ***mores*** of Mexico are those of Spain with some modifications.

墨西哥风俗习惯是加以变化的西班牙方式的。

morganatic [ˌmɔːgəˈnætik] *a.* 贵贱通婚的

Refusing the suggestion of a ***morganatic*** marriage, the king abdicated from the throne when he could not marry the woman he loved.

一桩贵贱之间的通婚被拒绝了,国王无法同他心爱的女子结婚,因而他退位了。

moribund [ˈmɔ(ː)ribʌnd] *a.* 即将结束的；垂死的

The doctors called the family to the bedside of the ***moribund*** patient.

医生把垂危的病人的家属叫到病床边。

moron [ˈmɔːrɔn] *n.* 低能儿. imbecile

What a ***moron*** I was to let that bargain slip away!

55

眼睁睁丢掉了那么桩好买卖,我多笨啊!

morose [mə'rəus] *a.* 脾气坏的；忧郁的. sullen

When we first meet Wu, we find him *morose* and depressed.

我们第一次见到吴时,就发现他忧郁沮丧。

morphemics [mɔː'fiːmiks] *n.* 词素学

比较记忆：morphology（形态学）

morsel ['mɔːsl] *n.* 一小块(食物),小吃

You must taste just a *morsel* of this cake.

你一定得尝一小块蛋糕。

mortar ['mɔːtə] *n.* 臼,研钵；迫击炮

参考：flak（高射炮）, shell（炮弹）

mortar ['mɔːtə] *n.* (砌砖用的)灰浆

The mason patched the crack with *mortar*.

泥瓦匠用灰浆抹上了那道缝。

mortician [mɔː'tiʃən] *n.* 殡仪业者

The *mortician* prepared the corpse for burial.

殡仪工作人员把尸体清理好准备下葬。

mortify ['mɔːtifai] *v.* 羞辱；禁欲. humiliate

She was so *mortified* by her blunder that she ran to her room in tears.

她深为自己的过失而羞悔,流着泪跑回自己房间。

mortify ∶ embarrass = mollycoddle ∶ indulge（先人后己）

mortise ['mɔːtis] *n.* 榫眼；   *v.* 用榫接合

mortuary ['mɔːtjuəri] *n.* 太平间

mosaic [mə'zeiik] *n.* 镶嵌细工；马赛克

mosaic ∶ glass = parquet ∶ wood

mosque [mɔsk] *n.* 清真寺

There are many beautiful *mosques* in Saudi Arabia.

在沙特阿拉伯有许多美丽的清真寺。

mote [məut] *n.* 微粒；灰尘. speck

The tiniest *mote* in the eye is very painful.

微小的细尘进到眼睛里也会很疼的。

motet [məut] *n.* 赞美诗，圣歌. chant

motif [məu'ti:f] *n.* 主题，主旨. theme

The cloud is a favorite *motif* in Chinese rugs.

中国地毯图案中常喜欢用白云作主题。

motility [məu'tiliti] *n.* 能动

Certain organisms exhibit remarkable *motility*, motile spores, for example, may travel for miles before coming to rest.

一些生物体表现出惊人的能动性,比如运动孢子在停留驻某地前可能走过了好儿英里。

比较记忆：mobility（流动性）

motley ['mɔtli] *a.* 混杂的，杂色的. medley

The captain had gathered a *motley* crew to sail the vessel.

船长招集了各色人等组成他的船员驾驶那艘船。

mottled ['mɔtld] *a.* 有杂色的. dappled

When he blushed, his face took on a *mottled* hue.

他脸红时,脸上红一块,白一块的。

motto ['mɔtəu] *n.* 座右铭，箴言

motto : shield = epitaph : tombstone

moulder ['məuldə] *v.* 渐趋腐朽

His remains *mouldered* in the mausoleum.

他的遗骸在墓冢中渐渐腐烂。

mountebank ['mauntibæŋk] *n.* 江湖郎中. charlatan

The patent medicine man was a *mountebank*.

那个专卖秘方药的人是个江湖郎中。

move [mu:v] *v.* 提议；感动. proffer

movement ['mu:vmənt] *n.* (交响乐)乐章

You can play the first *movement* of *the Piano Concerto the Yellow River*.

你能演奏《黄河钢琴协奏曲》的第一乐章。

mow [məu] *v.* 刈(草等)

参考：hoe（锄头）

muck [mʌk] *n.* 粪肥；污物

We must get rid of the *muck* of the exploiting classes before we construct the new world.

在我们建设一个新世界之前，得先清除剥削阶级的脏东西。

muckrake ['mʌkreik] *v.* 揭发丑闻

muddle [mʌdl] *v.* 混乱；弄乱. bungle

Her thought was *muddled* and chaotic.

他的思想混乱无绪。

比较记忆：muddy（泥泞的；混乱的）

muffle ['mʌfl] *v.* 降低(声音)；裹住

He went into the snow *muffle* in two woolen coats.

他裹上两件羊毛衣冲进风雪中。

muffler ['mʌflə] *n.* 消声器；围巾

mufti ['mʌfti] *n.* 便装 (civilian clothes). ↔ uniform

mug [mʌg] *n.* 酒杯；　*v.* (为抢劫)猛袭

比较记忆：tug（用力拉），jug（罐子）

muggy ['mʌgi] *a.* 潮闷的

The weather stayed *muggy* for days after the hot spell was over.

一段炎热的天气之后是一连几天潮闷的天气。

mugwump ['mʌgwʌmp] *n.* 政治独立分子

When he refused to support his party's nominees，he was called a *mugwump* and deprived of his seniority privileges in Congress.

58

当他拒绝支持他的党派的提名人后，人们称他为政治独立分子，
也剥夺了他在议会内的资深（人士）特权。

mulatto [mju(ː)'lætəu] *n.* （黑白）混血儿

mulch [mʌltʃ] *n.* 护根

      mulch : erosion ＝ baste : dry

mulct [mʌlkt] *v.* 诈骗；罚款. defraud

      The lawyer was accused of trying to *mulct* the girl of
her legacy.

      人们指责律师企图诈骗女孩应得的遗产。

mull [mʌl] *v.* 沉思；磨碎. meditate；pulverize

      I haven't decided what to do；I'm *mulling* over it.

      我还没决定要做什么呢，我还在想。

multifarious [ˌmʌlti'fɛəriəs] *a.* 多种的，各式各样的

      multi（many）+ fari（do）+ ous → 多种多样的

      参考：multilayered（多层的）

mumble ['mʌmbl] *v.* 喃喃. murmur，mutter

      I *mumbled* to conceal my lack of information.

      我喃喃低语，以掩饰我对此的无知。

mummery ['mʌməri] *n.* 化装表演；滑稽表演

      The masks of the performers in the *mummery* were
exquisite.

      化装表演上演员们的面具精致优美。

mundane ['mʌndein] *a.* 现世的，世俗的. earthly

      He was concerned only with *mundane* multitude.

      他只同世俗大众相关联。

munificent [mju(ː)'nifisnt] *a.* 慷慨的，大方的. ↔ stingy

      The *munificent* gift was presented to the bride by her
rich uncle.

      新娘子眼前是她那有钱的叔叔慷慨大方地送她的礼物。

muniments ['mjuːnimɔntə] *n.* 契据，档案. deed

munitions [mju(ː)'niʃəns] *n.* 军火，弹药. materiel

Dry socks are an important item of *munitions*.

干爽的袜子是重要军需物资。

mural ['mjuərəl] *a.* 墙壁的； *n.* 壁画

murkiness ['məːkinis] *n.* 黑暗；朦胧

The *murkiness* and fog of the waterfront that evening depressed me.

那晚海滨的朦胧和雾气给我留下深刻的印象。

murky ['məːki] *a.* 黑暗的，朦胧的. gloomy

murrain ['mʌrin] *n.* 瘟疫. pestilence

"A *murrain* on you" was a common malediction in that period.

"让你得瘟疫"是那一时期最常见的诅咒。

muse [mjuːz] *v.* 沉思，冥想. ponder

The old man *mused* over the harsh finality of life.

老人在沉思着有关生命的严格终极性这一令人不快的话题。

mushroom ['mʌʃrum] *n.* 蘑菇； *v.* 迅速增长

参考：carrot（胡萝卜），eggplant（茄子）

mushy ['mʌʃi] *a.* 多愁善感的；软绵绵的

His *mushy* self-pity was not taken seriously by his friends, who knew him to be different when sober.

朋友们都知道他清醒的时候像换了个人似的（什么事儿也没有），所以也不把他多愁善感的自怜当真。

musket ['mʌskit] *n.* 火枪，滑膛枪

Musket is an early type of gun used before the invention of rifle.

滑膛枪是发明来复枪前用的一种早期枪型。

muss [mʌs] *v.* 弄污. defile

A man is not allowed to wear shoes in a mosque, lest he *muss it*.

在清真寺里不能穿鞋，否则是一种玷污。

muster ['mʌstə] *v.* 召集，聚集. congregate

60

Washington *mustered* his forces in the Trenton.

华盛顿把部队召集到特伦顿。

比较记忆：master（主人，大师）

musty ['mʌsti] *a.* 发霉的，陈腐老朽的. stale

The attic was dark and *musty*.

阁楼里黑乎乎的，有股发霉的味道。

mutation [mju(:)'teiʃən] *n.* 突变，变异

比较记忆：immutable（不可变的）

mute [mjuːt] *a.* 哑的，沉默的； *n.* 弱音器

In funeral parlor, the mourners' voices had a *muted* quality.

在葬礼大厅里，吊唁者的声音都有些黯哑。

比较记忆：mutable（易变的）

mutilate ['mjuːtileit] *v.* 使残废；切断. maim

The torturer threatened to *mutilate* his victim.

拷问者威胁要杀了他的受害者。

mutineer [ˌmjuːti'niə] *n.* 反叛者，背叛者. renegade

来自：mutiny（叛变）

mutinous ['mjuːtinəs] *a.* 叛变的，反抗的. rebellious

The captain had to use force to quiet his *mutinous* crew.

船长不得不暴力平息船员们的叛变。

mutter ['mʌtə] *v.* 嘟哝，抱怨. grumble

There is no use *muttering* over your own mistakes.

抱怨你自己的错误是毫无用处的。

mutton ['mʌtn] *n.* 羊肉

mutton : sheep = pork : swine

参考：beef（牛肉），venison（鹿肉）

muzzle ['mʌzl] *n.* 口套；炮口

Those who know the truth have been *muzzled* by those in power.

那些了解真相的人都被当权人物封住了口。

muzzy ['mʌzi] *a.* 模糊不清的；昏迷的；含糊的

mycology [mai'kɔlədʒi] *n.* 真菌学

参考：fungus（真菌）

myna ['mainə] *n.* 八哥

参考：magpie（鹊），parrot（鹦鹉）

myopia [mai'əupiə] *n.* 近视，缺乏远见

In thinking only of your present needs and ignoring the future, you are being rather *myopia*.

只顾当前需要，不看长远利益，你太缺少远见了。

myriad ['miriəd] *n.* 许多，无数

Myriad of mosquitoes from the swamps invaded our village every twilight.

每天黄昏，沼泽地那里飞来大批蚊子入侵我们村子。

myrmidon ['məːmidən] *n.* 忠实的追随者

mystify ['mistifai] *v.* 使神秘化；迷惑. perplex

myth [miθ] *n.* 神话故事

mythology [mi'θɔlədʒi] *n.* 神话，神话学

Generally, Babylonian *mythology* lacks the transcendental quality of the myth of Osiris; it is more earthbound and more materialistic.

一般来说，巴比伦神话没有那些地狱判官的先验特点的荒诞，更加世俗唯物。

nab [næb] *v.* 逮捕；攫取. apprehend；snatch

Police *nabbed* him as he ran out of the raided nightclub.

当他跑出砸坏的夜总会的时候，警察抓住了他。

nadir ['neidiə] *n.* 最低点；天底. ↔ zenith

When I first began to study words in families, I was unaware that protagonist was the opposite of antagonist, that *nadir* was the opposite of zenith.

在我开始研究家族语言时，没有意识到支持者是对手的对立面，天底是天顶的对立面。

nag [næg] *n.* 驽马； *v.* 唠叨，烦扰. pester, bother

A wise leader knows how to get results without constant *nagging*.

一个明智的领导人知道怎样不用唠叨不停就可以得到结果。

比较记忆：sag（下垂），lag（落后）

naiad ['naiæd] *n.* （湖中）仙女

希腊神话中保护泉河的女神

The painting showed a *naiad* dancing gracefully on the water surface.

画中画着个优雅地在水面上舞蹈的仙女。

nailery ['neiləri] *n.* 制钉厂

比较记忆：nail（钉；指甲）

naivete [nɑ:'i:vti] *n.* 天真，纯朴，幼稚. puerile

We realized that John was still young and impressionable, but were nevertheless surprised at his *naivete*.

我们知道约翰还年轻易受影响，但还是为他的纯朴幼稚吃惊。

来自：naive（天真的）

nap [næp] *v.* 小睡，打盹. snooze, doze

That six-minute *nap* really refreshed me.

小睡六分钟真令我精神振奋。

narcissism [nɑ:'sisizəm] *n.* 自恋，自爱

narcissism：love ＝ guilty：blame

narcissuses [nɑ:'sisəs] *n.* 水仙花. daffodil

Narcissus 是希腊神话中的美男子，因爱恋自己水中的影子憔悴而死，死后化为水仙花

narcotic [nɑ:'kɔtik] *n.* 麻醉剂；催眠药； *a.* 催眠的；麻醉的

The doctor prescribed a *narcotic* to ease the pain.

医生开了麻醉药给他止痛。

nasal ['neizl] *a.* 鼻的

比较记忆：naval（海军的，军舰的）

nascent ['næsnt] *a.* 初生的，萌芽的. incipient

If we could identify these revolutionary movements in their ***nascent*** state, we would be able to eliminate serious trouble in later years.

要是在革命的萌芽阶段就加以辨明,就可以在其后的那些年里避免许多麻烦了。

natal ['neitl] *a.* 出生的. inchoate

He refused to celebrate his ***natal*** day because it remined him of few years he could look forward to.

他拒绝庆贺生日,因为那会使他想到末日不多了。

natation [nei'teiʃən] *n.* 游泳

The Red Cross emphasizes the need for courses in ***natation***.

红十字会强调游泳课程的需要。

natatorium [ˌneitə'tɔːriəm] *n.* 室内游泳池

比较记忆：sanitarium（疗养院）

nativity [nə'tivəti] *n.* 出生，诞生

比较记忆：cognate（同族的）

natty ['næti] *a.* 整洁的，漂亮的. dapper, smart

Priding himself on being a ***natty*** dresser, the gangster Bugsy collected a wardrobe of imported suits and ties.

一向以漂亮的衣着而自豪,匪徒巴格西收藏了一衣橱的进口西装和领带。

nausea ['nɔːsiə] *n.* 作呕，恶心. queasiness

nauseate ['nɔːsieit] *v.* 使作呕，使厌恶

The noisome smell ***nauseated*** him and made him dizzy.

这种难闻的味道令他恶心晕眩。

nautical ['nɔːtikl] *a.* 船员的，航海的. maritime

The Maritime Museum contains many middles of clipper ships, logbooks, anchors and many other items of a *nautical* nature.

航海博物馆里有许多快速帆船的中间物,航海日志,锚和许多其他的航海用品。

Unit Twenty-Four

nave [neiv] *n.* （教堂的）中殿，信众席

    The **nave** extends from the main entrance to the transepts.

    信众席从主入口处一直延伸到耳堂。

neap [ni:p] *a.* 最低潮的

    We shall have to navigate very cautiously over the reefs as we have a **neap** tide this time of the month.

    我们正赶上这个月的最低潮，所以航行过珊瑚礁时要格外小心。

nebula ['neibjulə] *n.* 星云；喷雾剂

nebulous ['nebjuləs] *a.* 星云的

    His theories were so **nebulous** that few could see what he was trying to establish.

    他的理论十分云山雾罩，没有几个人弄得明白他想要说些什么。

necessitous [ni'sesitəs] *a.* 贫困的，急需的. destitute

    A **necessitous** family was evicted for not paying rent.

    这个贫困的家庭由于交不上租金被赶了出去。

necromancy ['nekrəumænsi] *n.* 巫术，通灵术. sorcery，witchery

    necro (corpse) + mancy (technology) → 通灵术

necrophagous [ne'krɔfəgəs] *a.* 食尸的

    necro (corpse) + phag (feed) + ous → 食尸的

necropolis [ne'krɔpəlis] *n.* 公墓

    necro (corpse) + polis (city) → 公墓

    比较记忆：metropolis（大都市）

nefarious [ni'fɛəriəs] *a.* 凶恶的，邪恶的. miscreant，vicious

    ne (not) + far (fair) + ious → 不公正的，邪恶的

negate [ni'geit] *v.* 取消，否认. veto, gainsay

比较记忆：renegade（叛徒）

negative ['negətiv] *n.* （照相的）底片

negligence ['neglidʒəns] *n.* 疏忽，粗心. delinquency

比较记忆：negligible（可忽略的，微不足道的）

negotiable [ni'gəuʃiəbl] *a.* 可商量的；（支票）可流通的

neigh [nei] *v. & n.* 马嘶，马嘶声

参考：purr（猫叫），bark（犬吠）

nemesis ['nemisis] *n.* 报应，天罚

来自希腊神话中的报应女神 Nemesis

Neolithic ['ni(:)ə'liθik] *a.* 新石器时代的. ↔ Paleolithic

neo（new）+ lith（stone）+ ic → 新石器时代的.

neologism [ni(:)'ɔlədʒizəm] *n.* 新词，新义

neo（new）+ log（word）+ ism → 新词

neonate ['ni:əneit] *n.* 新生婴儿

neo（new）+ nate（born）→ 新生婴儿

neophyte ['ni(:)əufait] *n.* 初学者，新手. tyro

neo（new）+ phyte（plant）→ 新手

nephritis [ne'fraitis] *n.* 肾炎

nephr（= nephritic）+ itis（inflammation）→ 肾炎

比较记忆：nephrolith（肾结石）

nepotism ['nepətizəm] *n.* 裙带关系

比较记忆；nepotistic（任人唯亲的）

nepotism : relative = cronyism : friend

neronian [ni'rəumiən] *a.* 荒淫无度的；残暴的. atrocious

来自荒淫无度的罗马暴君 Nero

nerveless ['nə:vlis] *a.* 无力的，无生气的. shiftless

nescience ['nesiəns] *n.* 无知. ignorance

Knowledge cannot thrive where there is *nescience*.

无知的土壤上不会有知识的繁荣。

nestle ['nesl] *v.* 舒适地安顿，依偎. snuggle

    He *nestled* himself into the hay for a short nap.

    他舒服地偎在草垛上小憩。

nestling ['nestliŋ] *n.* 未离巢的小鸟

    nest ＋ ling (young) → 幼鸟

nether ['neðə] *a.* 下部的，下面的

nethermost ['neðəməust] *a.* 最低的，最下方的. neap

nettle ['netl] *n.* 荨麻；   *v.* 使烦恼，激恼. provoke

    Do not let him *nettle* you with his sarcastic remarks.

    别为他的冷嘲热讽烦恼。

    nettle : plant ＝ jaundice : disease

neurasthenia [ˌnjuərəs'θi:njə] *n.* 神经衰弱

neurology [njuə'rɔlədʒi] *n.* 神经病学

    neur (nerve) ＋ ology (science) → 神经病学

neurosis [njuə'rəusis] *n.* 神经病

    neur (nerve) ＋ osis (disease) → 神经病

neurotic [njuə'rɔtik] *n.* 神经病患者

    She became so *neurotic* that her friends began to worry about her well-being.

    她变得如此神经质，她的朋友们都开始为她的健康担忧了。

neutralize ['nju:trəlaiz] *v.* 使无效，中和. invalidate

    比较记忆：neutron（中子），neuter（中性的，无性的）

nexus ['neksəs] *n.* 联系，连结

    I fail to see the *nexus* which binds these two widely separated events.

    我看不出这大相径庭的两件事间有什么联系。

nib [nib] *n.* 钢笔尖；鸟嘴. beak

    The *nibs* of fountain pens often became clotted and corroded.

    自来水笔尖常会凝结和磨损。

nibble ['nibl] *v.* 慢慢啃

      nibble：gobble ＝ sip：swill

niche [nitʃ] *n.* 壁龛；合适的位置. recess，nook

      The statue was placed in a ***niche*** on the stairway.

      雕像放在走廊里的壁龛中。

nick [nik] *n.* 小伤口；小刻痕；关键时刻. crux

      It is the ***nick*** of the problem in the interpretation of the
      evidence.

      这是怎样理解证据的关键问题。

nicotine ['nikəti:n] *n.* 尼古丁

      nicotine：tobacco ＝ caffeine：coffee

nictitate ['niktiteit] *v.* 眨眼. wink

nifty ['nifti] *a.* 时髦的. stylish

      Her mien was graceful and ***nifty***, as were her words.

      她的仪表像她的语言一样优雅时髦。

niggard ['nigəd] *n.* 吝啬鬼. miser

niggardly ['nigədli] *a.* 小气的；   *adv.* 吝啬地

      The ***niggardly*** pittance the widow receives from the
      government cannot keep her from poverty.

      她得到的那点微薄的政府救济金根本无法救她摆脱贫困。

niggle ['nigl] *v.* 找岔子；挑剔，吹毛求疵. carp

niggling ['nigliŋ] *a.* 琐碎的，费神的. paltry

      It is boring to quibble about a ***niggling*** difference in ter-
      minology.

      这么避重就轻地讨论些术语间的琐碎差异真是无聊。

nightmare ['naitmɛə] *n.* 恶梦；可怕的事物. incubus

      比较记忆：mare（母马）

nihilism ['naiilizəm] *n.* 虚无主义

      比较记忆：annihilate（消灭）

nil [nil] *n.* 无，零. zilch，cipher

nimble ['nimbl] *a*. 敏捷的，灵活的. nippy

He was *nimble* enough to jump the fence.

他很敏捷，一下就能跳过篱笆墙。

nimbus ['nimbəs] *n*. 光轮. halo

The candidate was encompassed with a *nimbus* of fame.

候选人头上罩着圈名望的光环。

nimiety [ni'maiəti] *n*. 过剩. redundancy

nip [nip] *v*. 摧残；夹住. pinch

When the plant begins to ramify, it is advisable to *nip* off most of the new branches.

一株植物开始发枝时，最好剪掉大多数新枝。

比较记忆：nim（偷窃）

nippers ['nipəs] *n*. 钳子，镊子

nippy ['nipi] *a*. 辛辣的；寒冷的. pungent；frigid

This cheese has a good, *nippy* taste.

这种乳酪有种好吃的辛辣味。

nirvana [niə'vɑːnə] *n*. 心灵的平静，解脱

Despite his desire to achieve *nirvana*, the young Buddhict found that even the buzzing of a fly could distract him from his meditation.

尽管年轻的佛教徒有想得到心灵的平静的愿望，但他却发觉一只苍蝇的嗡嗡声也会分散他沉思的注意力。

nit-pick ['nitpik] *v*. 挑剔，吹毛求疵. cavil

An undutiful official preferred to *nit-pick* rather than took steps to correct a situation.

一个不尽职的官员只是吹毛求疵，而不去采取改正这种形势的措施。

nitrogen ['naitridʒən] *n*. 氮（元素）

比较记忆：ozone（臭氧），silicon（硅）

nocturnal [nɔk'təːnl] *a*. 夜间的. ↔ diurnal（白天的）

Mr. Jones obtained a watchdog to prevent the *nocturnal*

raids on his chicken coops.

琼斯先生弄了条看门狗，防止别人夜间来他的鸡笼偷鸡。

nocturne ['nɔktəːn] *n.* 夜曲，夜景画

参考：noctambulance（梦游），noctilucence（夜间发光）

noisome ['nɔisəm] *a.* 恶臭的；有害的. putrid；baneful

I never could stand the *noisome* atmosphere surrounding the slaughter hours.

我从来都受不了屠宰时周围那种难闻的气味。

nomad ['nəumæd] *n.* 流浪者，游牧部落的人. vagrant

The Bedouins of Saudi Arabia are among the world's most famous *nomads*.

沙特阿拉伯的贝都因人是世界上最为著名的游牧民族之一。

nomadic [nəu'mædik] *a.* 游牧的，流浪的. vagabond

Several *nomadic* tribes of Indians would hunt in this area each year.

印度有几个游牧民族每年都在这个地区狩猎。

nomenclature [nəu'menklətʃə] *n.* 术语，命名法. terminology

nomen（name）+ clature（structure）→ 术语

nominal ['nɔminl] *a.* 名义上的，有名无实的. titular

nominate ['nɔmineit] *v.* 提名，指派. designate

nomin（name）+ ate → 提名

nonchalance ['nɔnʃələns] *n.* 无动于衷，冷淡. insouciance

non（no）+ chal（concern）+ ance → 不关心

noncommittal ['nɔnkə'mitl] *a.* 态度暧昧的

比较记忆：committal（交托，承诺）

nonconformity ['nɔnkən'fɔːmifi] *n.* 不遵从（传统）

nondescript ['nɔndiskript] *a.* （因无特征）难以归类的；难以形容的

non（no）+ descript → 没有特征可描述的

nonentity [nɔn'entiti] *n.* 无名小卒；不存在. ↔ entity

Don't dismiss John as a *nonentity* in his quiet way，he is
very important to the form.

别以为约翰喜欢安静的方式就把他小看成无名小卒，他这种方式
是很重要的。

nonobservance [nɔnəb'zə:vəns] *n.* 违反（规则等）. ↔ observance

nonpareil ['nɔnpərəl] *n.* & *a.* 无比的（人）

nonplus ['nɔn'plʌs] *v.* 使窘困；使狼狈. perplex

Jeck's uncharacteristic rudeness *non plused* Jill，leaving
her uncertain how to react.

杰克异乎寻常的粗鲁把吉尔搞得很狼狈,都不知该怎么应对好。

non sense ['nɔnsəns] *n.* 胡扯；无价值的东西

His comments in class are always *nonsense*.

他在班上说的话都是些胡扯。

non sequitur ['nɔn'sekwitə] *n.* （不合前提的）推理

Your term paper is full *non sequitur*；I cannot see how
you reached the conclusions you state.

你的学期论文不切题,我看不出你怎么能得出你所说的那个结
论。

nonskid ['nɔn'skid] *a.* （轮胎）防滑的

nook [nuk] *n.* 隐蔽处，内隅. recess

A shade *nook* is ideal for relaxation.

一处荫凉的隐蔽所是放松放松的理想去处。

normative ['nɔ:mətiv] *a.* 规范的，标准的

来自：norm（规范）

nose-dive ['nəuzdaiv] *v.* （飞机）俯冲；暴跌

nosegay ['nəuzgei] *n.* 花束. bouquet

These spring flowers will make an attractive *nosegay*.

这些春天里绽放的花朵可以扎成一束美丽的花束。

nostalgia [nɔs'tældʒiə] *n.* 怀旧之情，思乡病

nost（home）＋ alg（ache）＋ ia（disease）→ 思乡病

参考：nostmania（怀乡狂）

nostrum ['nɔstrəm] *n.* 江湖秘方药

nostrum ∶ remedy = alchemy ∶ science

nosy ['nəuzi] *a.* 好管闲事的. meddlesome

notarize ['nəutəraiz] *v.* 公证

You must certify the sale of your house by having the paper ***notarized***.

你必须有书面公证才能证明你卖房的合法性。

notary ['nəutəri] *n.* 公证人

notch [nɔtʃ] *v.* V 形刻痕；峡谷；等，级

This restaurant is a ***notch*** above the others.

这家饭店比其他饭店高出一筹。

noted ['nəutid] *a.* 显要的，著名的. notable

noteworthy ['nəut₁wəði] *a.* 显著的，值得注意的. remarkable

notoriety [₁nəutə'raiəti] *n.* 臭名昭著

notorious [nəu'tɔːriəs] *a.* 臭名昭著的

Number theory is rich in problem of an especially vexing sort; they are tantalizingly simple to state but ***notorious*** difficult to solve.

数字理论是特别容易引起争议的那种问题,它们说起来简单地让人满怀希望,解决起来却极其地困难。

nouveau riche ['nuːvəu 'riːʃ] *n.* 暴发户. parvenu

novelettish [₁nɔvə'letiʃ] *a.* 多愁善感的. sentimental

I don't like such ***novelettish*** pictures，I call them fear-jerkers.

我可不喜欢这种多愁善感的影片,我把它们叫做恐惧反射物。

novelty ['nɔvlti] *n.* 新奇(的事物)

nov (new) + elty (noun) → 新奇

novice ['nɔvis] *n.* 生手，新手. neophyte

nov (new) + ice → 新手

novice ∶ nun = tyro ∶ virtuoso

73

novocaine ['nɔvəkein] *n.* 奴佛卡因（一种麻醉药）

　　novocain : anesthetic ＝ jaundice : disease

noxious ['nɔkʃəs] *a.* 有害的，有毒的. toxic

　　We must trace the source of these ***noxious*** gases before they asphyxiate us.

　　我们必须在这些有毒气体使我们窒息之前找到其来源。

nozzle ['nɔzl] *n.* 喷嘴

　　He adjusted the ***nozzle*** so that the water came out in a fine spray.

　　他调了调喷嘴，让水均匀洒出来。

　　比较记忆：fizzle（失败）

nuance [nju:'ɑ:ns] *n.* 细微的差异

　　The unskilled eye of the layman has difficulty in discerning the ***nuances*** of color in the paintings.

　　外行那未经训练过的眼光很难辨别出画上色彩的细微差异。

　　比较记忆：nuisance（麻烦事）

nub [mʌb] *n.* 要旨；小块. pith

　　The students couldn't go far wrong if they get the ***nub*** of the idea in their first lesson.

　　学生们要是在第一课就掌握了这一思想的要旨，就不会出什么大错。

nubile ['nju:bail] *a.* （女孩）到婚嫁年龄的

　　Mrs. Wu, In Pride and Prejudice by Jane, was worried about finding suitable husbands for her five ***nubile*** daughters.

　　《傲慢与偏见》中的伍夫人成天担扰（能不能）给五个待嫁的女儿找到合适的丈夫。

nude [nju:d] *a.* 赤裸的；　*n.* 裸体者. bare, naked

　　She couldn't wear bikinis because they made her feel ***nude***.

　　她不能穿比基尼，那使她感觉像什么也没有穿一样。

nudge [nʌdʒ] *v.* (用肘)轻触，轻推(以引起注意). elbow

nugatory [ˈnjuːɡətəri] *a.* 无价值的，琐碎的. futile

This deed is *nugatory* for no court will enforce it.

这件事太琐碎了,没有一个法庭会承接的。

nullify [ˈnʌlifai] *v.* 使无效，取消. invalidate

null (zero) ＋ ify → 使无效

比较记忆：nullity（无效）

numb [nʌm] *a.* 麻木的； *v.* 使失去感觉

By the time the mountain climbers had reached the snowy top, their hands and feet were *numb* with cold.

登山者爬到积雪的山顶时,手脚都冻木了。

numerology [ˌnjuːməˈrɔlədʒi] *n.* 数字命理学

numer (＝ number) ＋ ology (science) → 根据数字算命的学科

numerology : mathematics ＝ astrology : astronomy

numinous [ˈnjuːminəs] *a.* 神秘的；神圣的. ethereal

That element in artistic expression remains *numinous*.

艺术表现的因素一直是神秘的。

numismatic [ˌnjuːmizˈmætik] *a.* 钱币学的

numismatist [njuːˈmizmətist] *n.* 钱币学家，钱币收藏家

The *numismatist* had a splendid collection of antique coins.

这位钱币收藏家收藏了令人叹为观止的古钱币。

numskull [ˈnʌmskʌl] *n.* 笨蛋. dunce

参考：sage（圣贤）

nunnery [ˈnʌnəri] *n.* 女修道院，尼姑庵. convent

nun ＋ nery (place) → 尼姑庵

参考：nun（修女）, heaven（天堂）, mission（传道）

nuptial [ˈnʌpʃl] *a.* 婚姻的，婚礼的； *pl.* 婚礼. marital, monjugal, connubial

They were divorced because they were unable to deal with their ***nuptial*** matters.

他们处理不好婚姻问题，于是离了婚。

参考：puberty（青春期）

nurture ['nəːtʃə] *v.* 培养，养育

That dealer is patient enough to ***nurture*** a young modern painter's career rather than plunder it is not impossible, but the public's insatiable appetite for modern art makes such dealers less and less likely.

商人可能有足够的耐心培养一个年轻的现代画家的事业，而不仅仅是拿走他的画作，这并非不可能，但公众对现代艺术贪婪的胃口使得这样的商人愈来愈少。

nut [nʌt] *n.* 螺母；坚果

nutrient ['njuːtriənt] *a.* 营养的. nutritious

During the convalescent period, the patient must be provided with ***nutrient***.

在康复期，病人仍需输营养液。

nuzzle ['nʌzl] *v.* 用鼻触；依偎. nestle

She ***nuzzled*** her head on his shoulder.

她把头靠在他肩上。

nymph [nimf] *n.* 仙女；美女

nymphomania [ˌnimfə'meiniə] *n.* 女子淫狂

组合词：nymph ＋ mania → 女子淫狂

oaf [əuf] *a.* 呆子的，白痴的

They called the unfortunate waiter a clumsy ***oaf***.

他们把那不幸的侍者叫做笨手笨脚的白痴。

oasis [əu'eisis] *n.* 绿洲. ↔ desert

Except for a few scattered ***oasis***, the desert is quite barren.

沙漠很荒凉，只零零星星有几块绿洲。

obbligatos [ˌɔbli'gɑːtəu] *n.* 伴奏

参考：trio（三重奏），solo（独奏），duet（二重奏）

obdurate [ˈɔbdjurit] *a.* 固执的，顽固的. ↔ obedient

ob（against）+ dur（hard）+ ate → 坚韧地对抗 → 固执的

obeisance [əuˈbeisəns] *n.* 鞠躬，敬礼

来自：obey（服从）

obelisk [ˈɔbilisk] *n.* 方尖塔

Cleopatra's Needle is an *obelisk* in Central Park, New York City.

在纽约市的中央公园有一名为克娄巴特拉之方尖石碑的方尖塔。

obese [əuˈbiːs] *a.* 极肥胖的

It is advisable that *obese* people try to lose weight.

肥胖的人最好减减肥。

obfuscate [ˈɔbfʌskeit] *v.* 使困惑，使迷惑. muddle

ob（toward）+ fusc（dark）+ ate → 走向黑暗，弄糊涂

obituary [əˈbitʃuəri] *n.* 讣告. necrology

I first learned of her death when I read the *obituary* column in the newspaper.

我是先从报的讣告栏看到她的死讯的。

oblate [ˈɔbleit] *n.* 献身宗教工作的人； *a.* 扁球形的. nun；oval

oblation [əuˈbleiʃən] *n.* 宗教祭品

The wealthy man offered *oblations* so that the Church might be able to provide for the needy.

那个有钱的人捐了些祭品以使教堂可以给那些陷入困境的人（一点帮助）。

obligatory [ɔˈbligətəri] *a.* 强制性的，义务的. mandatory

A reply is desirable but not *obligatory*.

给个答复是最理想不过了，但并不强制。

obliging [əˈblaidʒiŋ] *a.* 恳切的，热心助人的. accommodating

The clerk was most *obliging*.

这个职员最热心肠了。

oblique [ə'bli:k] *adv.* 成 45°角地； *a.* 间接的；斜的. slanting

The sergeant ordered the man to march "*oblique* right".

中尉命令那个人"向右转"走。

obliterate [ə'blitəreit] *v.* 涂掉，毁掉. delete

ob (against) + liter (litter) + ate → 擦掉(文字等)

oblivion [ə'bliviən] *n.* 遗忘

Her works had fallen into a state of *oblivion*；no one bothered to read them.

他的作品已渐被遗忘,没人会费神去看的。

oblivious [ə'bliviəs] *a.* 不在意的，疏忽的. negligent

Concentrating on his work，the draftsman was *oblivious* to the noise.

绘图员全神贯注于他的工作,不在意周围的噪音。

obloquy ['ɔbləkwi] *n.* 诽谤，斥责. calumny

ob (against) + loqu (speak) + y → 斥责

obnoxious [əb'nɔkʃəs] *a.* 令人不快的，可憎的. repulsive

ob (expose) + nox (toxin) + ious → 有毒的，令人不快的

oboe ['əubəu] *n.* 双簧管

参考：woodwind（木管乐器），bassoon（低音管）

obscene [əb'si:n] *a.* 淫秽的. lewd, licentious

The *obscene* monarch helped bring about his country's downfall.

这个荒淫的君主加速了他的国家的灭亡。

obsequies ['ɔbsikwiz] *n.* 葬礼. servile

When she died，hundreds paid their last respects at her *obsequies*.

当她逝世时,几百人来到她的葬礼上表达他们对她最后的崇敬。

obsequious [əb'si:kwiəs] *a.* 逢迎的. cringing

ob (toward) + sequ (follow) + ious → 谄媚的

observance [əb'zə:vəns] *n.* 遵守，奉行(法律，习俗)

observation [ˌɔbzə:veiʃən] *n.* 观察后的评论

observatory [əb'zə:vətəri] *n.* 天文台

参考：nebula (星云)，comet (彗星)，constellation (星系)

obsession [əb'seʃən] *n.* 入迷，缠住

This *obsession* with the supernatural has made him unpopular with his neighbors.

他迷恋超自然力量，这令他很不受邻居们的欢迎。

obsidian [ɔb'sidiən] *n.* 黑曜岩 (dark volcanic rock)

The deposits of *obsidian* on the mountain slopes were an indication that the volcano had erupted in ancient times.

山坡上的黑曜岩表明古时候这里曾有火山爆发。

obsolescent [ˌɔbsə'lesnt] *a.* 即将过时的

obsole (obsolete) + scent → 即将过时的

obsolete ['ɔbsəli:t] *a.* 废弃的，过时的. outmoded

With this realization, the people suddenly found themselves left with *obsolete* moral values and little ethical perspective.

一旦意识到这种状况，人们突然发觉他们只有那过了时的道德观，几乎没有什么伦理观点了。

obstetrician [ˌɔbste'triʃən] *n.* 产科医生

Unlike the midwives, who care for women giving birth at home, *obstetricians* generally work in a hospital setting.

同那些在家里帮人接生的接生婆不同的是，产科大夫一般在医院中工作。

obstetrics [ɔb'stetriks] *n.* 产科学，助产术

参考：gynecologist（妇科医生），pediatrician（儿科医生）

obstreperous [əb'strepərəs] *a.* 吵闹的；难管束的

ob (against) + strer (noise) + ous → 喧闹的

obstruct [əb'strʌkt] *v.* 阻塞；挡住(视线). impede

ob (against) + struct (build) → 反建筑 → 阻塞

比较记忆：obstacle (障碍物)

obtest [ɔb'test] *v.* 恳求. beseech

The child *obtested* her mother to let her stay up longer.

这个孩子恳求她母亲让她晚点儿睡。

obtrude [əb'truːd] *v.* 突出；强加. extrude

ob (outway) + trude (thrust) → 向外突出

obtrusive [əb'truːsiv] *a.* 突出的；炫耀的

I found her a very *obtrusive* person, constantly seeking the center of the stage.

我发现她是个喜欢炫耀的人物,总设法站在舞台的中央。

obtund [ɔb'tʌnd] *v.* 缓和. dull

He tried to *obtund* the blows from his father.

他企图缓和他父亲打过来的那重重的巴掌。

obtundent [ɔb'tʌndənt] *a.* 止痛的；   *n.* 止痛药

obtuse [əb'tjuːs] *a.* 愚笨的；钝的. opaque；blunt

Because he was so *obtuse*, he could not follow the teacher's reasoning and asked foolish questions.

他太愚钝了,都听不懂老师的解释,总问些愚蠢的问题。

obverse ['ɔbvəːs] *n.* 正面. ↔ reverse

obviate ['ɔbvieit] *v.* 排除；避免. forestall；avert

I hope this contribution will *obviate* any need for further collections of funds.

我希望这点捐赠可以免除将来再来集资的需要。

occidental [,ɔksi'dentl] *a.* 西方的. ↔ oriental

80

occlude [ɔ'kluːd] *v.* 堵塞. choke

A blood clot *occluded* an artery to the heart.

一个血块堵塞了通向心脏的血管。

occult [ɔ'kʌlt] *a.* 秘密的；深奥的；玄的. ↔ fathomable, bare

The *occult* rites of the organization were revealed only to members.

这一组织的秘密地点只对组织成员公开。

ochlocracy [ɔk'lɔkrəsi] *n.* 暴民政治

In a state of *ochlocracy*, we are likely to have havoc.

在暴民政治状况下, 我们有可能有场浩劫。

octogenarian [ˌɔktəudʒi'nɛəriən] *n.* 80 到 89 岁的老人

octo (eight) + genarian (ten) → 80 多岁的老人

octopus [ˈɔktəpəs] *n.* 章鱼

参考：slug (鼻涕虫), mussel (贻贝), flounder (比目鱼)

ocular [ˈɔkjulə] *a.* 眼睛的；目击的

参考：rhinal (鼻的), binocular (双眼的)

oculist [ˈɔkjulist] *n.* 眼科医生

In many states, an *oculist* is the only one who may apply medicinal drops to the eyes for the purpose of examining them.

在许多州, 只有眼科医生可以出于检查眼睛的目的往眼睛里滴药水。

oddments [ˈɔdmənts] *n.* 残余物；零头

odds [ɔdz] *n.* 不平衡

比较记忆：oddity (奇怪的事物)

ode [əud] *n.* 颂诗, 颂歌

"*Ode* on a Grecian Urn" by Keats is a poem studied by most students of English literature.

大多数学习英国文学的学生都要学济慈的《希腊古瓮》。

81

odious [ˈəudjəs] *a.* 可憎的，讨厌的. abominable

比较记忆：odorous（芳香的），tedious（乏味的）

odium [ˈəudiəm] *n.* 憎恶，反感. repugnance

I cannot express the *odium* I feel at your heinous actions.

我无法表达出对你这种凶暴行为的反感之情。

odometer [ɔˈdɔmitə] *n.* 里程表

比较记忆：autometer（速度计）

odoriferous [ˌəudəˈrifərəs] *a.* 有香味的；芳香的

odor + fer (carry) + ous → 带有香味的

odyssey [ˈɔdisi] *n.* 长途旅行. trek

The refugee's journey from Cambodia was a terrifying *odyssey*.

从柬埔寨来的难民们的旅程真是可怕的长途跋涉。

offal [ˈɔfl] *n.* 废物. refuse

The hunters took the meat and left the *offal* for the buzzards.

猎人割下肉，把杂碎片留给了鵟鹰。

offertory [ˈɔfətɔːri] *n.* 做礼拜时的捐款

The donations collected during the *offertory* will be assigned to our mission work abroad.

做礼拜时筹集到的捐赠将分派给我们国外的救济工作用。

offhand [ˈɔːfˈhænd] *a.* 即兴的. ad-lib

Expecting to be treated with due propriety by her hosts, Great-Aunt was offended by their *offhand* manner.

老姑妈本指望会受到主人的礼遇，却为他们那种即席发挥的作派大感受到冒犯。

officious [əˈfiʃəs] *a.* 好忠告的；非正式的. ↔ official

Browning informs us that the Dike resented the bough

of cherries some *officious* fool brought to please the Duches.

勃朗宁告诉我们说那个同性恋女子不喜欢不知是哪个好心的傻瓜拿来取悦公爵夫人的樱桃枝。

ogle [ˈəugl] *v.* 暗送秋波，做媚眼. leer

Sitting for hours at the sidewalk cafe, the old gentleman would *ogle* the young girls and recall his youthful romances.

这位老先生在路边咖啡馆坐了好几个钟头,向年轻姑娘们暗送秋波,回忆他年轻时的浪漫史。

ogreish [ˈəug(ə)riʃ] *a.* 魔鬼似的，丑怪的

ogre 表示吃人的魔鬼

ointment [ˈɔintmənt] *n.* 油膏，软膏. unguent

oleaginous [ˌəutiˈædʒinəs] *a.* 含油的，油腻的

olfactory [ɔlˈfæktəri] *a.* 嗅觉的

olfactory : odor = gustatory : favor

oligarchy [ˈɔligɑːki] *n.* 寡头政治

olig (few) + archy (state) → 寡头统治

参考：oligophagous（寡食的）

omen [ˈəumen] *n.* 征兆，预兆. foretoken

Let's hope this glorious weather is a good *omen* for our vacation.

让我们祝愿这灿烂的天气成为我们假期的好兆头。

ominous [ˈɔminəs] *a.* 不祥的. inauspicious

The clouds are *ominous*, they portend a severe storm.

这乌云可不祥,预示着一场严酷的暴风雨。

omnipotent [ɔmˈnipətənt] *a.* 全能的，万能的

omni (universally) + potent → 全能的

参考：omnifacected（全面的）

omniscient [ɔmˈnisiənt] *a.* 无所不知的，博识的

omni (universally) + scient (science) → 博识的

omnivorous [ɔm'nivərəs] *a*. 杂食的；博览群书的.

    ↔ oligophagous

    omni (all) + vor (devour) + ous → 全吃的

onerous ['ɔnərəs] *a*. 繁重的；负有义务的

    He asked for an assistant because his work load was too *onerous*.

    他的工作负担太重,所以他要求（给他配）一个助手。

onlooker ['ɔn,lukə] *n*. 旁观者

    The *onlookers* were soon drawn into the bloody fray.

    旁观者很快被这场血腥打斗吸引住了。

onomatopoeia [,ɔnəmætə'piə] *n*. 象声词

    rustle∶onomatopoeia = yen∶loan-word

onset ['ɔnset] *n*. 攻击；爆发. assail；outbreak

    on + set → set on → 攻击

onslaught [ɔnslɔːt] *n*. 猛攻，猛袭. assault

    We took an unexpected *onslaught* on the jungle stronghold of the enemy.

    我们对敌人的丛林要塞发动了一场突然袭击。

    比较记忆∶slaughter（屠宰）

ontology [ɔn'tɔlədʒi] *n*. 实体论，本体论

onus ['əunəs] *n*. 义务；责任

    The emperor was spared the *onus* of signing the surrender papers；instead，he relegated the assignment to his generals.

    皇帝推卸掉在投降书上签字的责任,而是委托给他的将军们去签署。

onymous ['ɔniməs] *a*. 署名的. ↔ anonymous

ooze [uːz] *v*. 慢慢流出；逐渐消失

    Ketchup *oozed* out of the crack in the bottle.

蕃茄沙司从瓶子上的裂缝中慢慢淌出来。

opacity [əuˈpæsiti] *n.* 不透明，暧昧

The semantic *opacity* of ancient documents is not u-
nique; even in our own time, many documents are difficult to decipher.

并不是只有古代文件中才有语言的暧昧，即便在当今，许多文件
仍难以读懂。

opalescent [ˌəupəˈlesnt] *a.* 像蛋白石的；发乳白光的. iridescent

The Ancient Mariner admired the *opalescent* sheen on
water.

古代航海家崇拜海上乳白色的光彩。

Unit Twenty-Five

opaque [əu'peik] *a*. 不透明的；难懂的；愚笨的. ↔ transparent

The *opaque* window kept the sunlight out of the room.
不透明的玻璃窗把阳光挡在房间之外。

operetta [ˌɔpə'retə] *n*. 小歌剧

oper（＝ opera）＋ etta（little）→ 小歌剧

ophthalmology [ˌɔfθæl'mɔlədʒi] *n*. 眼科学

比较记忆：ophthalmia（眼炎）

opiate ['əupit] *n*. 镇静剂；鸦片制剂. narcotic

By such *opiates*, she made the people forget their difficulties and accept their repellent circumstances.
用这种鸦片剂，她使人们忘记了他们的困境，接受了让人不开心的环境。

opinionate [ə'pinjəneit] *v*. 固执己见

opinion ＋ ate（furnish）→ furnish own opinion → 固执己见

opportune [ɔ'pɔtjuːn] *a*. 合适的，适当的. apropos

比较记忆：opportunity（机会），opportunist（投机分子）

opprobrious [ə'prəubriəs] *a*. 辱骂的；可耻的. abusive；infamous

op（forward）＋ probr（reproach）＋ ious → 侮辱的

opprobrium [ə'prəubriəm] *n*. 臭名；侮辱. infamy

He refused to defend himself against the slander and *opprobrium* hurled against him by the newspapers; he preferred to rely on his record.

他拒绝就报纸一古脑儿抛向他的侮辱诽谤为自己辩护,他更愿意让事实说话。

oppugn [ə'pjuːn] *v.* 攻击;驳斥. refute

　　op (against) + pugn (fight) → 驳斥

optician [ɔp'tiʃən] *n.* 眼镜商;光学仪器制造商

　　参考:optical (视觉的;光学的), optometer (视力计)

optimism ['ɔptimizəm] *n.* 乐观主义. ↔ pessimism

　　比较记忆:optimize (使完善), optimum (最佳)

optometrist [ɔp'tɔmitrist] *n.* 配镜师

　　Although an ***optometrist*** is qualified to treat many eye disorders, she may not use medicines or surgery in her examinations.

　　尽管合格的配镜师可以诊治许多眼疾,却不能在检查中用药或动手术。

opulence ['ɔpjuləns] *n.* 富裕;丰富

　　Visitors from less wealthy lands are amazed and impressed by the ***opulence*** of this country.

　　那些来自不那么富裕的国度的来访者惊叹于这个国家的富庶。

opulent ['ɔpjulənt] *a.* 富裕的,充足的. affluent

opus ['əupəs] *n.* 作品,杰作

　　Although many critics hailed his, Fifth Symphony, he did not regard it as his major ***opus***.

　　尽管许多评论家对第五交响曲击掌喝彩,他却不认为这是他的代表作。

oracle ['ɔrəkl] *n.* 圣人,哲人. sage

　　oracle : prophecy = beau : flirtation

oracular [ɔ'rækjulə] *a.* 神谕的;隐晦的

　　We were unable to understand the ***oracular*** message of the hermit.

　　我们无法理解隐士那模糊的信息。

oration [ɔ:'reiʃn] *n.* 演说,演讲

The students had to memorize Mark Antony's funeral *oration* from "Julius Caesar."

学生们得记住马克·安东尼在葬礼上从"尤利乌斯·恺撒"开始的一段讲话。

oratorio [ˌɔrə'tɔːriəu] *n.* 清唱剧

The Glee Club decided to present an *oratorio* during their recital.

格利俱乐部决定在他们的演奏会上演一出清唱剧。

oratory ['ɔːrə'tɔːri] *n.* 演讲术；小礼拜堂

Poor *oratory* usually spoils the effect of speech.

状况不佳的小礼拜堂常会破坏演讲的效果。

orb [ɔːb] *n.* 天体；球体

orbicular [ɔː'bikjulə] *a.* 圆的. spherical

参考：conical（圆锥形的），oblate（椭圆的）

orchid ['ɔːkid] *n.* 兰花； *v.* 称赞

参考：orchard（果园），vineyard（葡萄园）

ordain [ɔː'dein] *v.* 任命；命令；注定. mandate；doom

The king *ordained* that no foreigner should be allowed to enter the city.

国王下令任何外国人不得进入城市。

ordeal ['ɔːdiːl] *n.* 严峻考验

Terry Anderson spoke movingly of his long *ordeal* as a hostage in London.

泰里·安德森动人地叙述着他在伦敦作人质的一段漫长而可怕的经历。

ordinance ['ɔːdinəns] *n.* 法令，条例. decree

Passing a red light is a violation of a city *ordinance*.

闯红灯违反市政交通法规。

ordinate ['ɔːdinit] *n.* 纵坐标

参考：abscissa（横坐标）

ordnance ['ɔːdnəns] *n.* 大炮；军械. cannon

The destroyer's *ordnance* consists of several small cannon, two torpedo boats, and a number of anti-aircraft guns.

毁灭者的军械装备包括几门加农炮,两艘鱼雷快艇和一些高射机枪。

参考：flak（高射炮）, mortar（迫击炮）

orgiastic [ˌɔːdʒiˈæstik] *a.* 狂欢的

orgy [ˈɔːdʒi] *n.* 狂欢. carousal

In ancient Rome, many banquets were *orgies*.

在古罗马,许多宴会成了狂欢。

orient [ˈɔːriənt] *a.* 上升的; *v.* 定向；熟悉环境

orifice [ˈɔrifis] *n.* 小开口，小孔

The Howe Cavern were discovered when someone observed that a cold wind was issuing from an *orifice* in the hillside.

有人观察到山侧面的一小洞中有冷风吹出从而发现了豪大山洞。

orison [ˈɔrizn] *n.* 祈祷. prayer

Hamlet greets Ophelia with the request "Nymph, in the *orisons*, be all my sins remembered".

汉姆雷特见到奥菲莉娅时请求道："美人,我祈祷宽恕我所有罪恶吧!"

ornate [ɔːˈneit] *a.* 华美的. decked

The baroque furniture can be recognized by its *ornate* carvings.

从华美的雕饰上我们可以认出巴罗克式的家具。

ornery [ˈɔːnəri] *a.* 坏脾气的. cantankerous

No one can get along with my *ornery* cousin.

谁和我那坏脾气的表兄也处不来。

ornithologist [ˌɔːniˈθɔlədʒist] *n.* 鸟类学家

Audubon's illustration of birds prove that he was a great artist because they have interest not only in the *ornithologists* but also the general public.

对鸟类的描绘证明他是个伟大的艺术家，因为这些图画不仅引起鸟类学家的兴趣，也使普通人大感有趣。

ornithology [ˌɔːniˈθɔlədʒi] *n.* 鸟类学

ornithology : finch = archaeology : skull

orotund [ˈɔ(ː)rəutʌnd] *a.* (声音)洪亮的；说大话的. ↔ hoarse

The politician found that his *orotund* voice was an asset when he spoke to his constituents.

政治家发现他在代表大会上讲话时，他洪亮的嗓音是他的宝贵技能。

orthodontics [ˌɔːθəˈdɔntiks] *n.* 正牙学

ortho (correct) + dont (= dent) + ics (science) → 正牙学

orthodox [ˈɔːθədɔks] *a.* 正统的. ↔ heterodox

ortho (right) + dox (opinion) → 正统观点

orthodoxy [ˈɔːθədɔksi] *n.* 正统性

orthogonal [ɔːˈθɔgənl] *a.* 正交的. vertical

orthography [ɔːˈθɔgrəfi] *n.* 正字法，缀字法

ortho (correct) + graphy (write) → 正字

orthopedics [ˌɔːθəuˈpiːdiks] *n.* 矫形外科，整形外科

ortho (correct) + ped (child) + ics → 原指对畸形儿童的整形

oscillate [ˈɔsileit] *v.* 摆动；犹豫. waver

It is interesting to note how public opinion *oscillates* between the extremes of optimism and pessimism.

观察到这样的现象很有趣，公众意见往往在极端的乐观主义和极端的悲观情绪间摇摆不定。

oscilloscope [ˈɔsiləskəup] *n.* 示波器

oscillo (= oscillate) + scope → 示波器

osmosis [ɔzˈməusis] *n.* 渗透；混合

90

He never studies but seems to learn by *osmosis*.

他从不是研究而是潜移默化地习得。

osseous [ˈɔsiəs] *a.* 骨的，含骨的. bony

参考：ossuary（骨灰瓮）

ossify [ˈɔsifai] *v.* 僵化；骨化

When he called his opponent a bonehead, he implied that his adversary's brain had *ossified* and that he was not capable of clear thinking.

他把对手叫作笨蛋,意思是说他对手的脑子僵化了,不能清醒地思考。

ostensible [ɔsˈtensəbl] *a.* 显而易见的；伪装的. ↔ unexpected

Her sadness was concealed by *ostensible* ebullience.

她用装出来的热情奔放掩盖她的悲伤。

比较记忆：ostentatious（炫耀的）

ostentation [ˌɔstenˈteiʃn] *n.* 夸示，炫耀. pretentiousness

ostentatious [ˌɔstenˈteiʃəs] *a.* 夸示的，炫耀的

The real hero is modest, never *ostentatious*.

真正的英雄是谦虚的,从不会炫耀。

ostraccan [ɔsˈtreiʃiən] *n.* 牡蛎. oyster

参考：shrimp（虾），lobster（龙虾）

ostracize [ˈɔstrəsaiz] *v.* 放逐，排斥. exclude

As soon as the newspapers carried the story of his connection with the criminals, his friends began to *ostracize* him.

报纸一登出有关他同那个罪犯的关系的故事,朋友们就开始疏远他了。

ostrich [ˈɔstritʃ] *n.* 鸵鸟；自欺者

ostrich : bird = tiger : cat

otiose [ˈəuʃiəus] *a.* 无用的，多余的. ↔ functional

The enemy's attempts proved *otiose*.

敌人的企图证明是枉费心机的。

otitis [əu'taitis] *n.* 耳炎

参考：rhinitis（鼻炎），arthritis（关节炎）

otter ['ɔtə] *n.* 水獭

参考：carp（鲤鱼），perch（鲈鱼）

oust [aust] *v.* 驱逐. expel

The world wondered if Aquino would be able to *oust* his lover from office.

众人都想知道阿基诺是否能把他的情人赶出办公室。

outface [aut'feis] *v.* 无畏面对

outgoing ['aut͵gəuiŋ] *a.* 友善的；即将离去的

He was a *outgoing* fellow, always ready to lend a helping hand when needed.

他是个友善之人，随时预备伸出援助之手。

outing ['autiŋ] *n.* 远足，旅行. excursion

outlandish [aut'lændiʃ] *a.* 古怪的；笨拙的 eccentric；boorish

His suggestion was so *outlandish* that I couldn't see what he meant.

他的建议太古怪了，我都弄不懂他是什么意思。

outlying ['autlaiiŋ] *a.* 边远的. ↔ indwelling

outré ['uːtrei] *a.* 越轨的；过分的. deviant

outright ['aut-rait] *a.* 完全的；全然的

outset ['aut-set] *n.* 开始，开头. onset

out + set → set out → 开始

比较记忆：upset（颠覆）

outskirts ['aut-skəːts] *n.* 郊区，郊外. environs

outspoken [aut'spəukən] *a.* 坦率的. candid, blunt

The candidate was too *outspoken* to be a successful politician, he had not yet learned to weigh his words carefully.

这个候选人太过坦白，成不了成功的政治家，他还没学会（开口前)仔细掂量掂量他的话的分量。

outstrip [aut'strip] *v.* 超过，越过. surpass，outdo

Owens easily ***outstripped*** his competitors to win the gold medal at the Olympic Game.

欧文斯轻松超过所有对手,在奥运会上获得金牌。

outwit [aut'wit] *v.* 以机智胜过. outfox

ovation [əu'veiʃən] *n.* 热烈欢迎，鼓掌. acclamation

When Liu Xiaoqing came on stage in the first act of Queen Wu Zetian he was greeted by a tremendous ***ovation***.

刘晓庆在舞台上出现在《武则天》的第一幕里,受到观众长时间的鼓掌欢呼。

overawe [ˌəuvər'ɔ:] *v.* 威慑；吓住 (restrain or subdue by awe)

overbearing [ˌəuvə'bɛəriŋ] *a.* 专横的，傲慢的. arrogant

The man's ***overbearing*** behavior embarrassed his wife.

这个人专横的行为使他妻子感到困窘。

overcast ['əuvə-kɑ:st] *a.* (天)阴沉的；忧郁的. melancholy

比较记忆：outcast (遗弃者)

overdose ['əuvədəus] *n.* (药物)过度剂量

over + dose → 过度剂量

overhaul [ˌəuvə'hɔ:l] *v.* 彻底检查；大修；赶上

The startling finding that variations in the rate of the Earth's rotation depend to an unexpected degree on the weather has necessitated a complete ***overhaul*** world's time-keeping methods.

地球自转率的误差从很意外的程度上讲取决于气候条件,这一惊人发现势必导致世界上时间测定方法的彻底改变。

overhear [ˌəuvə'hiə] *v.* 偷听；无意中听到. eavesdrop

I ***overheard*** him saying that he was closing down his shop.

找偶然听说他要关了店。

overlap [ˌəuvəˈlæp] *v.* (部分地)重叠

overplus [ˈəuvə-plʌs] *n.* 剩余. odds

比较记忆：nonplus（左右为难）

overreach [ˌəuvəˈriːtʃ] *v.* 做事过头

override [ˌəuvəˈraid] *v.* 搁置；凌驾，践踏

The tyrant flagrantly *overrided* the people's right.

暴君昭然若揭地践踏人民的权利。

overriding [ˌəuvəˈraidiŋ] *a.* 凌驾于一切之上的. predominant

overrule [ˌəuvəˈruːl] *v.* 统治；否决；驳回. veto

The senator was *overruled* by the committee chairman.

议员受委员会主席支配。

oversee [ˈəuvəˈsiː] *v.* 监督. supervise

比较记忆：overseer（监工）

overshadow [ˌəuvəˈʃædəu] *v.* 遮暗；遮蔽. veil

She *overshadowed* the birdcage with a light cloth to quiet the bird.

她用一块薄布盖在鸟笼上挡住光，让鸟儿安静下来。

overt [ˈəuvəːt] *a.* 公开的. ↔ covert

According to the United States Constitution, a person must commit an *overt* act before he may be tried for treason.

根据《美国宪法》，要判一个人有叛国罪，他一定要有公开背叛行为。

overweening [ˌəuvəˈwiːniŋ] *a.* 自负的. ↔ humble

His *overweening* pride in his accomplishments was not justified.

他对自己成就那自负的骄傲是没有道理的。

overwrought [ˈəuvəˈrɔːt] *a.* 神经质的；歇斯底里的. hysterical

ovoid [ˈəuvɔid] *a.* 卵形的. oval

At Easter, she had to cut out hundred of brightly colored *ovoid* shapes.

复活节的时候，她剪了几百个颜色鲜艳的蛋形饰物。

ovule [ˈəuvjuːl] *n.* （植物）胚珠

owl [aul] *n.* 猫头鹰

比较记忆：awl（尖钻）

oxidize [ˈɔksidaiz] *v.* 氧化；生锈

比较记忆：oxide（氧化物）

oxymoron [ˌɔksiˈmɔːrɔn] *n.* 矛盾修饰法

ozone [ˈəuzəun] *n.* 臭氧

参考：carbohydrate（碳水化合物）

pabulum [ˈpæbjuləm] *n.* 食物；精神粮食. victuals

I am very delighted to be able to provide you with these *pabulum*.

我很高兴能给你提供这些食物。

pachyderm [ˈpækidəːm] *n.* 厚皮动物；厚颜无耻者

packy (thick) + derm (skin) → 厚皮动物

pachydermatous [ˈpækidəːmætəs] *a.* 厚脸皮的；神经麻木的. callous

pacifier [pəˈsifiə] *n.* 平定者. referee

pacifi (pacify) + er → 平定者

比较记忆：pacifist（反战主义者）

packed [ˈpækid] *a.* 拥挤的. brimful

They've had a *packed* theater for every performance.

他们的每场演出，剧场都挤得满满的。

pact [pækt] *n.* 契约，条约

Even if a peace *pact* is signed, neither nation will be in a position to honor it.

即使两国签署了一项和平条约，双方也是不会采取维护尊重这一条约的立场的。

pad [pæd] *n.* 垫； *v.* 装垫

padding : damage = disguise : recognize

paddle ['pædl] *n.* 桨； *v.* 荡桨；涉水. wade

We returned to shore after a brief *paddle* on the lake.

我们在湖上泛舟一小会儿之后又回到岸边。

paddock ['pædək] *n.* 驯马场

The *paddock* is located directly in front of the grand-stand so that all may see the horse being saddled and the jockeys mounted.

驯马场就座落在正面看台的正前方,这样所有人都可以看见如何给马备鞍,骑师又是如何上马的情形了。

paean ['pi:ən] *n.* 赞美歌,颂歌. hymn

Paeans celebrating the victory filled the air.

空中到处飘荡着庆祝胜利的颂歌声。

pagan ['peigən] *n.* 不信教者；异教徒. infidel

They were sickened by the immolation of animals in the *pagan* temple.

他们看见异教徒庙中的动物祭品,感到恶心。

pageant ['pædʒənt] *n.* 壮观的游行；露天表演

The *pageant* started at one end of town and ended at the other.

游行在镇子一端开始,到另一端结束。

painstaking ['peinsteikiŋ] *a.* 费力的. arduous, strenuous

pains + tak (take) + ing → taking pain of → 费力的

比较记忆：painkiller（止痛药）

palanquin [pælən'ki:n] *n.* 花轿

In India, a wealthy person may travel in a *palanquin* borne by means of resting on men's shoulders.

在印度,一个有钱人可以乘坐轿夫扛在肩上的轿子旅行。

palatable ['pælətəbl] *a.* 美味的；愉快的. delicious

Paying taxes can never be made *palatable*.

纳税永远也不会是愉快的。

96

palate ['pælit] *n.* 上腭；口味

    palate : month = ceiling : room

palatial [pə'leiʃəl] *a.* 宫殿般的，宏伟的. luxurious

    In this large, *palatial* home, he was able to sequester himself from the rigors of urban life.

    在这所宫殿般的大房子里，他可以远离城市生活的艰苦。

palaver [pə'lɑːvə] *v.* 商谈；闲谈；奉承. parley

    After years of futile *palaver*, Latin America's coffee-producing nations are finally getting together in a hard-boiled cartel to hold up the price of coffee.

    几年毫无效果的商谈后，拉丁美洲的咖啡生产国最终团结起来结成了一个强硬的同盟以支撑咖啡的价格。

paleography [pæliəu'grəfi] *n.* 古文书学

    paleo (archaic) + graphy (write) → 古文书学

Paleolithic [ˌpæliəu'liθik] *a.* 旧石器时代的. ↔ Neolithic

    paleo (archaic) + lith (rock) + ic → 旧石器的

paleontology [pæliɔn'tɔlədʒi] *n.* 古生物学

    The professor of *paleontology* had a superb collection of fossils.

    这位古生物学教授收藏有一批极好的化石。

palette ['pælit] *n.* 调色板

    At the present time, art supply stores are selling a paper *palette* which may be discarded after use.

    现在，艺术用品商店在卖一种纸调色板，用过就可以扔掉了。

palimpsest ['pælimpsest] *n.* 羊皮纸

    Using chemical reagents, scientists have been able to restore the original writings on many *palimpsests*.

    使用化学试剂，科学家复原了许多羊皮纸上原来的笔迹。

paling ['peiliŋ] *n.* 篱笆，木栅栏. palisade

palingenesis [ˌpælin'dʒenisis] *n.* 再生，轮回. ↔ stability

pall [pɔːl] *n.* 幕; *v.* 生厌. cloy

The study of word lists can eventually *pall* and put one to sleep.

学习生词表最终会让人厌烦地睡着。

pallet ['pælit] *n.* 简陋的床

The weary traveler went to sleep on his straw *pallet*.

疲惫的旅行者躺在他用草铺就的简陋的床上睡了。

palliate ['pælieit] *v.* 减轻(痛苦); 掩饰(罪行). abate

If we cannot cure this disease at present, we can, at least, try to *palliate* the symptoms.

我们目前要是治不了这种病的话,至少可以尽力减轻症状的痛苦吧。

pallid ['pælid] *a.* 苍白的,没血色的. ashen, waxen

Because his occupation required that he work at night and sleep during the day, he had an exceptionally *pallid* complexion.

他的工作要求他白天睡觉,晚上工作,因此他的脸色异常地苍白。

pallor ['pælə] *n.* 苍白,虚弱

palmistry ['pælmistri] *n.* 手相术

比较记忆: palmist (看手相者)

palpable ['pælpəbl] *a.* 明显的; 易觉察的. tangible

I cannot understand how you could overlook such a *palpable* blunder.

我无法理解你怎么会忽视了这么显而易见的错误。

palpable : touch = pliable : mold

palpate ['pælpeit] *v.* 用手触摸

palpitate ['pælpiteit] *v.* 悸动. throb, flutter

As he became excited, his heart began to *palpitate* more and more erratically.

他激动起来,心也开始越来越狂乱地悸动。

比较记忆：palpitant（悸动的）

palsy ['pɔ:lzi] *n.* 麻痹；瘫痪. paralysis

He has had cerebral *palsy* ever since he was eight years old.

他8岁时就患上了脑瘫。

paltry ['pɔ:tri] *a.* 可鄙的；微不足道的. mean；petty

This is a *paltry* sum to pay for such a masterpiece.

对于这么一件杰作，出这些钱微不足道。

pamper ['pæmpə] *v.* 纵容，娇惯. humor

Your *pampering* his lust may lead to his wanton life.

你纵容他的欲望可能会导致他（过上一种）放荡的生活。

pan [pæn] *n.* 平底锅； *v.* 严厉批评. rap

pan : culinary = nautical : astrolabe

panacea [pæn'siə] *n.* 万应药

There is no easy *panacea* that will solve our complicated international situation.

没有什么灵丹妙药能用来解决我们复杂的国际局势。

pan (all) + acea (heal) → 灵丹

panache [pæ'næʃ] *n.* 羽饰； *v.* 炫耀. verve

Many performers imitate Noel Coward, but few have his *panache* and sense of style.

许多人模仿诺埃尔·科沃德的表演，但几乎没有人具有他那样的羽饰和气派感。

pancreas ['pæŋkriəs] *n.* 胰(腺)

参考：kidney（肾），insulin（胰岛素）

panda ['pændə] *n.* 小熊猫

参考：sable（黑貂），puma（美洲狮）

pandemic [pæn'demik] *a.* (病)大范围流行的

pan (all) | dem (people) + ic → 涉及全部民众的 → 大范围流行的

比较记忆：epidemic（传染的），endemic（内部的）

pandemonium [pændi'məunjəm] *n.* 地狱，大混乱. hell

　　pan (all) + demon + ium → 地狱

　　比较记忆：demon（魔鬼）

pander ['pændə] *v.* 迎合

　　The reviewer accused the makers of *Lethal Weapon* of
　　pandering to the masses taste for violence.

　　评论家指责《致命武器》的创作者是要迎合大众对于暴力的口味。

　　比较记忆：ponder（苦思苦想）

pane [pein] *n.* 窗格玻璃

　　Hailstones as big as eggs broke several ***panes*** of glass.

　　像鸡蛋那么大的冰雹砸碎了好几块玻璃。

panegyric [pæni'dʒirik] *n.* 颂词，颂扬. encomium

　　The modest hero blushed as he listened to the ***pane-***
　　gyrics uttered by the speakers about his valorous act.

　　谦逊的英雄在听着讲话人对他的英雄壮举大加颂扬的时候脸都
　　红了。

panel ['pænl] *n.* 讨论小组；仪表盘

pang [pæŋ] *n.* 一阵剧痛

　　Except for a small ***pang***, his headache was gone.

　　他的头疼基本好了，只是还有一小阵的剧痛。

panoply ['pænəpli] *n.* 全副甲胄

　　pan (all) + oply (armor) → 全副装备

panorama [pænə'raimə] *n.* 全景，概观. purview

　　pan (all) + orama (sight) → 所见全部 → 全景，全貌

pant [pænt] *v.* 气喘；悸动. throb

　　After jogging a quarter of a mile he was sweating and
　　panting.

　　跑了四分之一英里之后，他就汗流满面，气喘吁吁的了。

pantheon [pæn'θi(:)ən] *n.* 万神殿，众神

100

pan (all) + theo (god) + on → 万神殿

pantomime ['pæntəmaim] *n.* 哑剧；哑剧演员

panto (all) + mime → 全哑 → 哑剧

pantry ['pæntri] *n.* 食品室. larder

比较记忆：pant（喘息）

A *pantry* adjoins the kitchen.

食品室紧挨着厨房。

papyrus [pə'paiərəs] *n.* 纸莎草，纸莎草纸

比较记忆：papyrology（纸草学）

papyrus：paper = daguerreotype：photograph（早期产品）

par [pɑ:] *n.* 同等；平价

比较记忆：pal（好朋友）

parable ['pærəbl] *n.* 寓言. comparison

Let us apply to our own conduct the lesson that this *parable* teaches.

让我们把这个寓言中教导我们的训诫应用到我们自己的行动中去。

paradigm ['pærədaim] *n.* 范例

In the study of grammatical forms, the *paradigm* is very helpful.

在学习语法形式时,使用范例很有帮助。

paradox ['pærədɔks] *n.* 谬论；似矛盾而正确的说法

para (abnormal) + dox (think) → 不正规的观点

比较记忆：orthodox（正统的）

paragon ['pærəgən] *n.* 模范，典型

para (beyond) + gon (whetstone) → 模范

比较记忆：trigon（三角形）, polygon（多角形）

paralyze ['pærəlaiz] *v.* 使瘫痪

The nation was *paralyzed* by a seizure of terror follow-

101

ing the assassination.

整个国家在暗杀事件后被一种恐惧的情绪紧紧抓住，从而陷入（一种）瘫痪（状态）。

比较记忆：paralysis（瘫痪，中风）

paramount [ˈpærəmaunt] *a.* 最重要的；最高权力的

para（beyond）+ mount → 最重要的

paramour [ˈpærəmuə] *n.* 情夫（妇）

参考：mistress（情妇）

paranoia [ˌpærəˈnɔiə] *n.* 偏执狂；妄想狂

Suffering from ***paranoia***, he claimed everyone was out to get him; ironically, his claim was accurate even paranoids have enemies.

他患有多疑症，言称所有人都一心要抓住他；具有讽刺意味的是，他所说的很准确，因为即便偏执狂也是有敌人的。

paranoid [ˌpærəˈnɔid] *a.* 患妄想狂（或偏执狂）的

parapet [ˈpærəpit] *n.* 栏杆；护墙

The best way to attack the soldiers fighting behind the ***parapets*** on the roof is by bombardment from the air.

打击在房顶护墙后作战的士兵的最好办法是从空中轰炸他们。

paraphernalia [pærəfəˈneiliə] *n.* 随身用具；设备

His desk was cluttered with paper, pen, ink, dictionary and other ***paraphernalia*** of the writing craft.

他桌上堆满纸，笔，墨水、字典及其他随手用得着的写作用品。

paraphrase [ˈpærəfreiz] *v.* 意译

paraphrase : translate = free : lateral

parasite [ˈpærəsait] *n.* 寄生虫；依人为生者

The tapeworm is an example of the kind of ***parasite*** that may infest the human body.

绦虫是能寄生于人体内的寄生虫的一种。

parch [pɑːtʃ] *v.* 烘烤，干透. dehydrate

102

The lack of rain had *parched* the land.

（干旱）少雨（的天气）烘烤着大地。

比较记忆：perch（栖息）

parched [ˈpɑːtʃid] *a.* 干枯的 (extremely dry)

The *parched* desert landscape seemed hostile to life.

干枯的沙漠地貌看上去对生命不那么友善（有利）。

parchment [ˈpɑːtʃment] *n.* 羊皮纸；羊皮纸手稿

源自羊皮纸产地 Parthian

pare [pεə] *v.* 削去，剥去. scrape, peel

Pare the potatoes into medium-size pieces.

把土豆削成中等大小的片。

paregoric [ˌpærəˈgɔrik] *n.* 镇痛药

The doctor prescribed a *paregoric* to alleviate his suffer

ing.

医生给他开了镇痛药以减缓他的痛苦。

parenthesis [pəˈrenθisis] *a.* 插入语；圆括号

parenthesis：enclose = colon：explain

pariah [ˈpæriə] *n.* 贱民. ↔ cynosure

源自 Pariah，印度南部和缅甸的贱民

I am not a *pariah* to be shunned and ostracized.

我不是个可以规避或摈弃的贱民。

parlance [ˈpɑːləns] *n.* 说法，用语

All this legal *parlance* confuses me；I need an inter-

preter.

这些法律用语令我迷惑，我需要个翻译（给我解释解释）。

parley [ˈpɑːli] *v.* 谈判；会谈.

The peace *parley* has not produced the anticipated

truce.

和平谈判没有取得预期的停战协定。

parlous [ˈpɑːləs] *a.* 不易对付的；危险的

103

In these ***parlous*** times, we must overcome the work of saboteurs and propagandists.

在这些危险的时刻,我们必须摆脱阴谋破坏者和宣传家们的控制。

parochial [pə'rəukjəl] *a.* 思想狭隘的

Although Jane Austen writes novels set in small rural communities, her concerns are universal, not ***parochial***.

尽管简·奥斯丁写的小说多发生在乡下的小社区内,但她所关心的话题却很普遍,并不狭隘。

来自: parish（教区）

parody ['pærədi] *n.* 嘲弄文章;拙劣的模仿

We enjoyed the clever ***parodies*** of popular songs which the chorus sang.

我们喜欢合唱团演唱的对流行歌曲聪明的滑稽模仿曲目。

参考: mimicry（模仿）, burlesque（讽刺）, travesty（滑稽模仿）

parole [pə'rəul] *n. & v.* 有条件释放（罪犯）

His ***parole*** from jail came unexpectedly.

他有条件地假释出狱来得出人意料。

参考: acquit（无罪释放）

paroxysm ['pærəksizəm] *n.* 突发,阵发. fit

When he heard of his son's misdeeds, he was seized by a ***paroxysm*** of rage.

当他听说他儿子的罪行时,被一阵突来的愤怒给抓住了。

parquet ['pɑːkei] *n.* 镶木地板

In laying the floor, the carpenters combined redwood and oak in an elegant ***parquet***.

铺地板时,木匠把红木和橡木混在一起铺成优美的镶木地板（图案）。

parquetry ['pɑːkitri] *n.* 镶木地板艺术或图案

104

parquetry : floor = fresco : wall

parricide ['pærisaid] *n.* & *v.* 杀父母. ↔ matricide

He hated his father so intensely that he committed *parricide*.

他如此强烈地恨他的父亲,以致他甚至犯下了杀父(的罪行)。

parrot ['pærət] *n.* 鹦鹉

参考: peacock (孔雀), magpie (喜鹊)

parry ['pæri] *v.* 挡开;避开

He was content to wage a defensive battle and tried to *parry* his opponent's thrusts.

他愿意打他一场防守战,而且尽力避开对手的打击。

parse [pɑːz] *v.* 从语法上分析

parsimonious [ˌpɑːsiˈməunjəs] *a.* 太节省的;小气的. ↔ lavish

My wealthy aunt exceeds the trait of being economical. She is so *parsimonious* that she washes paper plates to be used again.

我有钱的姑妈甚至胜过节俭一筹。她太节省了,连纸盘子也要洗洗再用。

parson ['pɑːsn] *n.* 牧师. pastor

bishop : parson = vicar : curate

particulars [pəˈtikjuləs] *n.* 详细情况,细节. ramification

partisan [ˌpɑːtiˈzæn] *n.* 党派支持者.

party + san (person) → 信徒, 党的支持者

partisan : objection = reprobate : temperate

parturition [ˌpɑːtjuəˈriʃən] *n.* 生产,分娩. labor

比较记忆: parturient (分娩的)

parvenu ['pɑːvənjuː] *n.* 暴发户. upstart

Although extremely wealthy, he was regarded as a *parvenu* by the aristocratic members of society.

尽管他极为富有,还是被社会中的贵族成员们看成是个暴发户。

比较记忆：parvenus（女暴发户）

passé ['pɑːsei] *a.* 过时的，已过盛年（妙龄）的

Her style is *passe* and reminiscent of the Victorian era.

她已过时的风格使人想起维多利亚时代。

pastel [pæ'sel] *n.* 彩色粉笔画；柔和的色彩

比较记忆：toothpaste（牙膏）

pasteurize ['pæstəraiz] *v.* 以高热杀菌，消毒

来自人名 Pasteur（巴斯德），发明巴氏消毒法

参考：fumigate（以烟熏消毒）

pastiche [pæs'tiːʃ] *n.* （音乐等）混成曲

He cannot even say that his music is a *pastiche* of this composer or that; it is, rather, reminiscent of many musicians.

他甚至不能说他的作品是这位或那位作曲家（作品主题）的混合之作，因为事实上它使人想起许多位作曲家（的作品）。

pastor ['pɑːstə] *n.* 牧师；牧人

来自：pasture（牧草，牧场），poster（态度）

pastoral ['pɑːstərəl] *a.* 田园生活的

In these stories of *pastoral* life, we find an understanding of the daily tasks of country folk.

在这些田园生活的故事里，我们可以对乡下人的日常生活事务有所了解。

pastry ['peistri] *n.* 糕点，点心. refreshment

pasty ['peisti] *a.* 浆糊的；苍白的

That frightening experience left a *pasty* expressions on her face.

那可怕的经历在她脸上留下了一个苍白的表情。

patch [pætʃ] *n.* 补丁，一小片（土地）. ↔ tract

We chased the rabbits out of the cabbage *patch*.

我们把兔子赶出了白菜地。

patchwork [ˈpætʃwək] *n.* 拼缝物

pate [peit] *n.* 头顶

> He wears a hat to conceal his bald *pate*.
> 他戴了顶帽子以掩住他的秃头。

Unit Twenty-Six

patent [ˈpeitənt, ˈpætənt] *a.* 显而易见的； *n.* 专利权（证书）.
manifest

It was *patent* to everyone that the witness spoke the truth.

显而易见，证人讲的是实话。

paternal [pəˈtəːnl] *a.* 父亲的

Everyone has two *paternal* grandparents and two maternal grandparents.

每个人都有两位（父亲那边的）祖父母和两位（母亲那边的）外祖父母。

pathology [ˌpəˈθɔlɔdʒi] *n.* 病理学

path (illness) + ology → 病理学

pathology : disease = meteorology : weather

pathos [ˈpeiθɔs] *n.* 哀婉，悲怆

A quiet tone of *pathos* ran through the novel.

一种静静的悲怆的语调贯穿小说的始终。

比较记忆：pathetic（引起怜悯的）

patina [ˈpætinə] *n.* 绿锈；任何外面之物

bronze : patina = iron : rust

patio [ˈpætiəu, ˈpɑːtiəu] *n.* 庭院；天井

patois [ˈpætwɑː] *n.* 方言；行话. dialect；cant

His years of study of the language at the university did not enable him to understand the *patois* of the natives.

他在大学里多年的语言研究也不能使他理解这些土著人的方言。

patriarchy [peitriˈɑːki] *n.* 家长政治；父系社会

108

patri (father) + archy (state) → 家长政治

patrician [pə'triʃən] *n.* 贵族. peer

We greatly admired her well-bred, *patrician* elegance.

我们对她良好的教养,贵族的优雅大加赞赏。

patrimony ['pætriməni] *n.* 遗产. heritage

As predicted by his critics, he spent his *patrimony* within two years of his father's death.

就像批评他的人们所预言的那样,他父亲死后两年他就花光了遗产。

patriot ['peitriət, 'pætriət] *n.* 爱国者

patronage ['pætrənidʒ] *n.* 赞助;惠顾

比较记忆: patron (赞助人)

patter ['pætə] *n.* 喋喋不休的废话;行话. lingo

They took a tedious *patter* about the cold weather and high inflation.

他们进行了一场有关寒冷的天气和高通货膨胀率的无聊的谈话。

paucity ['pɔːsiti] *n.* 小量;缺乏. meagerness

In economics, scarcity is defined as *paucity* of amount or supply in relation to demands or wants.

在经济学中,不足被定义为量上的缺乏或有关需求或要求的供给上的缺乏。

pauper ['pɔːpə] *n.* 贫民,乞丐. panhandler

Though Widow Brown was living on a reduced income, she was by no means a *pauper*.

尽管说寡妇布朗靠大为减少了的收入生活,但不管怎么说她也算不上个贫民。

pavilion [pə'viljən] *n.* 大帐篷 (tent used for entertainment or exhibits)

A huge *pavilion* was built for the city fair.

为了城市商品展览会用建了个大帐篷。

pawn [pɔːn] *n.* 走卒; *v.* 典当,抵押. hock

He raised money by *pawning* his watch.

他典当了手表换来些钱。

pawnbroker ['pɔːnbrəukə] *n.* 典当商

组合词：pawn + broker → 典当商

peach [piːtʃ] *v.* 揭发，检举. prosecute

The arrested culprit *peached* against all accomplices.

被捕的罪犯检举了所有的同谋。

peak [piːk] *v.* 憔悴，消瘦. pine

比较记忆：peaky（消瘦的）

pebble ['pebl] *n.* 小卵石，石子

pebble：landslide = droplet：deluge

pecan [pi'kæn] *n.* 美洲山核桃(树)

pecan：shell = wheat：chaff

peccadillo [ˌpækə'diləu] *n.* 小过失

pecca (mistake) + dillo (little) → 小过失

比较记忆：peccable（易犯罪的），peccant（有罪的），
impeccable（没有瑕疵的）

peckish ['pekiʃ] *a.* 饿的

Famine ravaged the countryside and left the people
peckish.

饥荒摧残着乡村，使人们挨饿。

pectoral ['pektərəl] *a.* 胸部的，胸的

I lift weights to develop my arms and *pectoral* muscles.

我通过举重增强我臂部和胸部的肌肉。

参考：thorax = bosom（胸膛）

peculate ['pekjuleit] *v.* 挪用(公款). embezzle（盗用）

His crime of *peculating* public funds entrusted to his
care is especially damnable.

他挪用他托管的公款的罪行特别可恶。

比较记忆：peculium（私有财产）

110

pecuniary [piˈkjuːnjəri] *a.* 金钱上的，金钱的. monetary

I never expected a *pecuniary* reward for my work in this activity.

我从没指望我在这项活动中(所做出)的工作会得到什么金钱上的报偿。

pedagogue [ˈpedəgɔg] *n.* 教师. demagogue

pedagogy [ˈpedəgɔgi] *n.* 教育学，教学法

ped (child) + agog (lead) + y → 引导儿童 → 教学法

pedant [ˈpedənt] *n.* 迂腐之人. ↔ pluralist

Her insistence that the book be memorized marked the teacher as a *pedant* rather than a scholar.

她坚持让背下那本书表明了这老师不是位饱学之士，而只是迂腐之人。

pedantry [ˈpedəntri] *n.* 迂腐

peddle [ˈpedl] *v.* 沿街叫卖

peddler [ˈpedlə] *n.* (沿街叫卖的)商贩

Tourists are advised not to purchase cameos from the street *peddlers* of Rome who sell poor specimens of the carver's arts.

建议游客不要在罗马的街头小贩那里购买石雕,因为他们卖的都是些雕刻工制作的拙劣艺术品的样品。

比较记忆：pedlar（小贩）

pedestal [ˈpedistl] *n.* (柱石或雕像的)基座

pedestrian [piˈdestriən] *a.* 徒步的；缺乏想像力的；　*n.* 行人. hiker

Unintentionally boring, he wrote page after page of *pedestrian* prose.

他一页一页地写着缺乏想像力的散文,但并非他有意想如此地乏味。

pediatrics [ˌpiːdiˈætrik] *n.* 小儿科

比较记忆：podiatrics（足病学），psychiatrics（精神病

111

学）

pedigree ['pedigri:] *n.* 家谱

Her *pedigree* dates back to the first settlers in this country.

她的家谱一直追溯到(这一家族)在这个国家的第一代定居者。

peek [pi:k] *v.* 偷看. peep

The little boy promised not to *peek* at his Christmas presents while his parents were gone.

小男孩保证在父母离开时不偷看他的圣诞礼物。

peer [piə] *n.* 同等之人；贵族； *v.* 凝视

He *peered* surreptitiously into his wallet to see if he had enough money to pay the bill.

他偷偷摸摸地往钱包里看看,看他的钱是不是够付账单的。

peerless ['piəlis] *a.* 无与伦比的. superlative

They are the first-place team because their team members are *peerless*.

他们是一流的队伍,因为他们的队员都是无与伦比的。

peevish ['pi:viʃ] *a.* 坏脾气的，易怒的. crusty

He was very *peevish* when he found out he had failed the test.

当他发现考试没有通过时,脾气很坏。

peg [peg] *a.* 栓

peg ∶ whole = picture ∶ frame

peignoir ['peinwɑ:] *n.* 妇女浴袍

参考：brassiere（乳罩），cape（披肩），brooch（胸针）

pejorative ['pi:dʒərətiv] *a.* 贬低的. opprobrious

Instead of criticizing Clinton's policies，the Republicans made *pejorative* remarks about his character.

共和党不是批评克林顿的政策,而是贬低他的品格。

pelagic [pə'lædʒik] *a.* 远洋的

112

比较记忆：archipelago（群岛）

pelf [pelf] *a*. 财富，钱

Your possessions are only *pelf*; they will give you no lasting pleasure.

你拥用的只是钱，它们不会给你(带来)长久的快乐。

pell-mell ['pel'mel] *a*. & *adv*. 混乱(的)地；匆促(的)地. headlong

Intellectual restlessness and flight from boredom have caused him to rush *pell-mell* into situations that less adventurous spirits might hesitate to approach.

思想上的不安分及对枯燥乏味的逃避使他进入了一种不太富有冒险精神的人也许会有所迟疑而去靠近的境地。

pellucid [pe'lju:sid] *a*. 清晰的；清澈的. limpid

After reading these stodgy philosophers, I find his *pellucid* style very enjoyable.

读过这些墨守成规的哲学家们的作品后，我发现清晰的风格十分令人愉快。

pen [pen] *n*. 围栏； *v*. 监禁. incarcerate

We have built several *pens* to hold our harvest of corn.

我们建了几处围栏来装我们丰收的玉米。

penalize ['pi:nəlaiz] *v*. 置(某人)于不利地位；处罚

penance ['penəns] *n*. 自我惩罚

His *penance* for behaving badly was to go without supper.

他对自己举止恶劣的惩罚是不吃晚饭。

penchant ['pentʃənt] *n*. 爱好，嗜好. bent

Although retiring, almost self-effacing in his private life, he displays in his plays and essays a strong *penchant* for publicity and controversy.

尽管过着一种几乎埋没于自己的私生活中的退隐生活，他在其剧作及文章中还是表现出一种对出风头和论战的嗜好。

113

pendant ['pendənt] *n.* 垂饰，坠子； *a.* 悬垂的

The grateful team presented the coach with a silver chain and ***pendant*** engraved with the school's motto.

满怀感激的队伍送给教练一条银链子，链坠上刻有这所学校的座右铭。

pendent ['pendənt] *a.* 吊着的；下垂的. dangling

A ***pendent*** balcony overlooked the garden.

花园上方耸着一悬空的阳台。

pending ['pendiŋ] *a.* 即将发生的；未决的. impending

The entire country was saddened by the news of his ***pending*** death.

整个国家为他将死的消息而悲哀。

pendulous ['pendjuləs] *a.* 悬垂的. drooping

比较记忆：pendulum（钟摆）

penetrating ['penitreitiŋ] *a.* 敏锐的，尖锐的. astute

The ***penetrating*** analysis of the play's weakness was unsparing in the harshness of its criticism.

对这部戏弱点那尖锐的分析，其批评的苛刻是毫不留情的。

比较记忆：penetrate（戳穿）

penguin ['peŋgwin] *n.* 企鹅

参考：swan（天鹅），peacock（孔雀）

penicillin [ˌpeni'silin, pe'nisilin] *n.* 青霉素

penicillin : chemical = chimerical : dragon

peninsula [pi'ninsjulə] *n.* 半岛

peninsula : land = bay : sea

penitent ['penitənt] *a.* 后悔的，忏悔的. repentant

When he realized the enormity of his crime, he became remorseful and ***penitent***.

当他意识到他是多么罪大恶极时，变得后悔了。

penitentiary [ˌpeni'tenʃəri] *n.* 监狱，感化院；教养所

114

Criminals are locked up in the *penitentiary* until their sentence is over.

罪犯在判决结束前,被关押在感化院。

penmanship ['penmənʃip] *n*. 书法. calligraphy

组合词：pen ＋ men ＋ ship → 书法

pennant ['penənt] *n*. (船上的)信号旗,三角旗

pennate ['peneit] *a*. 羽状的

The *pennate* leaves of the sumac reminds us of feathers.

漆树的羽状叶使我们联想到羽毛。

penniless ['penilis] *a*. 穷困潦倒的. destitute

penny 为英国辅币单位便士

pensile ['pensail] *a*. 悬着的. pendant

pensive ['pensiv] *a*. 沉思的,愁眉苦脸的

The *pensive* youth gazed at the painting for a long time and then signed.

愁眉苦脸的年轻人盯着画看了好长一段时间,而后签了字。

pentagon ['pentəgən] *n*. 五角形

参考：octagon (八角形), triangle (三角形)

penultimate [pi'nʌltimeit] *a*. 倒数第二的

pen (almost) ＋ ultimate → 倒数第二的

penumbra [pi'nʌmbrə] *n*. 半明半暗之处；边缘部分；半影

pen (almost) ＋ umbra (shadow) → 明暗交界处

比较记忆：adumbrate (预示)

penurious [pi'njəriəs] *a*. 贫困的；吝啬的. meager；stingy

penury ['penjuri] *n*. 赤贫,缺乏

In this land of plenty, we must be ashamed of the *penury* and suffering that still exists in the slum areas.

在这个富庶的国家的贫民区里,还存在贫穷和苦难,我们真该为此而羞愧。

peon [pjuːn, 'piːən] *n.* 劳工；苦工；短工；抵债奴. serf

    We find much ***peon*** and suffering in this slum area.

    在这个贫民区我们发现有许多农场工人和受苦人。

peony ['piəni] *n.* 牡丹

    参考：narcissus（水仙花），orchid（兰花）.

pep [pep] *n.* 锐气；   *v.* 激励. goad

    The speech was designed to ***pep*** the nation on towards
its goal of a just peace.

    演讲是为了激励这个国家向着公正的、和平的目标（而努力）而
设计的。

peppery ['pepəri] *a.* 辛辣的；暴躁的. piquant；testy

    来自：pepper（胡椒）

pepsin ['pepsin] *n.* 胃蛋白酶

    参考：enzyme（酶）

peptic ['peptic] *a.* 助消化的

perambulate [pə'ræmbjuleit] *v.* 巡行；漫步. amble

    per（throughout）+ ambul（amble）+ ate → 巡视

perceptible [pə'septəbl] *a.* 可以感觉到的

perceptive [pə'septiv] *a.* 感觉敏锐的

    Although Maud was a generally ***perceptive*** critic, she
had her blind sports, she could never see flaws in the
work of her friends.

    尽管一般地讲莫德是个感觉敏锐的批评家，她也有弱项，她从来
也看不见她朋友们作品中的缺点。

perceptual [pə(ː)'septjuəl] *a.* 知觉的；感性的

    The functions of the hands, eyes, and brain are so in-
tertwined that using the hands during early childhood
helps to promote the child's entire ***perceptual*** development.

    手,眼睛和大脑的功能是相互交织在一起的,在儿童时代早期就

开始用手有助于促进孩子的整体知觉发展。

perch [pəːtʃ] *n*. 河鲈； *v*.（鸟）栖息

The pigeons *perched* on the telephone wire.

鸽子停落在电话线上。

percipient [pə(ː)'sipiəns] *a*. 洞察力强的

percolate ['pəːkəleit] *v*. 过滤出，渗透. filtrate

per (throughout) + colate (seize) → 过滤过去

参考：colander（滤器）

percolator ['pəːkəleitə] *n*. 咖啡壶

percussion [pəː'kʌʃən] *n*. 撞击，敲击

Sitting so close to the *percussion* section of the orches-
tra, I found that the incessant beating of drums gave
me a headache.

我坐得离交响乐团的打击乐部太近了，发现不断的击鼓声使我头
疼。

percussionist [pəː'kʌʃənist] *n*. 打击乐器敲打手

perdition [pəː'diʃən] *n*. 地狱，灭亡. hell; inferno

Praying for salvation, young Daedalus feared he was
damned to eternal *perdition*.

年轻的代达罗斯祷告得到拯救，他害怕会被诅咒永远下地狱。

perdurable [pə(ː)'djuərəbl] *a*. 耐久的. abiding

per (throughout) + durable → 持久的

peregrination [ˌperigri'neiʃən] *n*. 徒步旅行

Auntie Mame was a world traveler whose *peregrina-
tions* took her from Tiahuanaco to Timbuctoo.

马姆姨妈是个环游世界的人，她徒步从蒂亚瓦纳科旅行到廷巴克
图。

peregrine ['perigrin] *a*. 外来的. extraneous

peremptory [pə'remptəri] *a*. 专横的. masterful

per (throughout) + empt (take) + ory → 专横的

参考：preempt（优先取得）

perennial [pə'renjəl] *a.* 终年的，永久的. ↔ evanescent

The ***perennial*** questions that consistently structure the study of history must be distinguished from merely ephemeral questions, which have their day and then pass into oblivion.

一贯构成历史研究的永久性问题必须同只是短暂性的问题加以区别，后者有其（存在的）时代而后就被人遗忘了。

perfectionist [pə'fekʃənist] *n.* 力求完美者，吹毛求疵者

来自：perfect（完美的）

perfidious [pəː'fidiəs] *a.* 背信弃义的. traitorous

When Caesar realized that Brutus had betrayed him, he reproached his ***perfidious*** friend.

当恺撒意识到布鲁图背叛了他时，责备了他那背信弃义的朋友。

perforate ['pəfəreit] *v.* 打洞

per + forate（= pierce）→ 全部刺穿 → 打洞

perforce [pə'fɔːs] *adv.* 必然地，必要地；不得已地

I must ***perforce*** leave as my train is about to start.

我的火车要开了，我必须得离开了。

perfunctory [pə(ː)'fʌŋktəri] *a.* 草率的，敷衍的

Because the inspector gave the plant a ***perfunctory*** examination, he overlooked many defects.

检查人员对工厂只是敷衍了事地检查了一下，忽视了许多缺陷。

pergola ['pəːgələ] *n.* 棚架；凉棚

参考：byre（牛棚）

perigee ['peridʒiː] *n.* 近地点. ↔ apogee

The rocket which was designed to take photographs of the moon was launched as the moon approached its ***perigee***.

当月亮（运行）到其近地点附近时，发射了那颗设计用来给月球拍

摄照片的火箭。

perilous ['periləs] *a.* 危险的，冒险的. precarious

Although the acrobat's performance seemed very *perilous*, it was not as dangerous as it looked.

尽管杂技演员的表演看上去十分危险，（事实上）它并没有看起来的那么危险。

perimeter [pə'rimitə] *n.* 周长；环形防线

peri (around) + meter → 周长

peripatetic [ˌperipə'tetik] *a.* 巡游的

I am not attracted by the *peripatetic* life of the vagabond, always wandering through the country-side, begging for charity.

我一点不为总在乡间四处游荡,乞求别人的施舍怜悯的巡游式的漂泊生活所吸引。

peripheral [pə'rifərəl] *a.* 边缘的；周围的. marginal

Victims of glaucoma find that their *peripheral* vision is impaired and that they can no longer see objects not directly in front of them.

青光眼患者发现他们视线边缘减弱了,若不站在物体正对面就再也看不见物体了。

periphrasis [pə'rifrəsis] *n.* 迂说法；迂回曲折的词句. circumlocution

periphrastic [ˌperi'fræstik] *a.* 迂回曲折的；迂说法的

peri (around) + phrase + tic → 绕圈子说话

periscope ['periskəup] *n.* 潜望镜 (view objects above the direct sight)

比较记忆：telescope（望远镜），microscope（显微镜）

perishable ['periʃəbl] *a.* （食物)易坏的

perishing ['periʃiŋ] *a.* 极不舒服的；致命的

来自：perish（死亡，枯萎）

perjure ['pəːdʒə] *v.* 作伪证；发假誓

The witness *perjured* himself by lying about what he did on the night of the crime.

证人作了伪证，对他在案发的那晚在做什么说了谎。

perjury ['pəːdʒəri] *n.* 伪证；假誓

When several witnesses appeared to challenge his story, he was indicted for *perjury*.

当出现几个证人对他讲的故事提出质疑时，他被指控作了伪证。

perks [pəːks] *n.* 津贴

perky ['pəːki] *a.* 活泼的；傲慢的. brisk；jaunty

He always spoke to his subordinates in a *perky* tone.

他总用傲慢的语调对他的下属讲话。

permeable ['pəːmjəbl] *a.* 可渗透的

A sponge is *permeable* by water.

海绵让水浸透了。

permeate ['pəːmieit] *v.* 渗透

Water will easily *permeate* a cotton dress.

棉布裙子很容易让水湿透。

permissive [pə(ː)'misiv] *a.* 纵容的；容许的

来自：permission（允许）

permutation [pə(ː)'mjuːteiʃən] *n.* 彻底改变

per（throughout）＋ mutation → 彻底改变

比较记忆：mutation（变迁）

pernicious [pə(ː)'niʃəs] *a.* 致命的. baneful

He argued that these books had a *pernicious* effect on young and susceptible minds.

他认为这些书对年轻易感的头脑有着致命的影响。

peroration ['perəreiʃən] *n.* 结论

per ＋ oration → 结论

比较记忆：oration（演讲）

perpetrate ['pə:pitreit] *v.* 犯(罪). commit

Only an insane person could *perpetrate* such a horrible crime.

只有疯子才会犯下这么可怕的罪行。

perpetuate [pə(:)'petjueit] *v.* 使不朽

perpetual [pə'petjuəl] *a.* 永恒的

Nothing can obstacle the *perpetual* flow of the Long River.

什么也阻挡不了长江永不停息地奔流。

perpetuity [ˌpə(:)pi'tju(:)iti] *n.* 永恒. eternity, endurance

比较记忆：perpetual（永恒的）

perquisite [pə'kwizit] *n.* 津贴，福利

The *perquisites* attached to this job make it even more attractive than the salary indicates.

这份工作所提供的福利待遇比它的薪水本身还要吸引人。

persevere [ˌpə:si'viə] *v.* 坚韧不拔

It was the unflagging faith that had *persevered* him

他不变的信念使他坚韧不拔。

比较记忆：severe（严厉的）

persiflage [ˌpɛəsi'flɑ:ʒ] *n.* 嘲弄. jest

This *persiflage* is not appropriate when we have such serious problems to discuss.

在我们讨论这么严肃的问题的时候,这种嘲弄是不合适的。

persnickety [pə(:)'snikiti] *a.* 苛求的；难应付的. fastidious；snobbish

personable ['pə:snəbl] *a.* 英俊的. handsome

The man I am seeking to fill this position must be *personable* since he will be representing us before the public.

我要为这一职位物色的人选必须英俊萧洒,因为他要代表我们在

公众面前出现。

personage ['pə:sənidʒ] *n.* 权贵；（戏剧）角色. mogul

比较记忆：personnel（全体职员）

personification [pə(:)ˌsɔnifiˈkeiʃən] *n.* 典型；化身. incarnation

Many Americans believe that individual initiative epitomized the 1890's and see the entrepreneur as the ***personification*** of that age.

许多美国人认为 19 世纪 90 年代的典范是个人创造精神，而且把企业家看作是那一时代的化身。

perspective [pə(:)ˈspektiv] *n.* 正确的眼光；观点

She is unable to see things in proper ***perspective***.

她不能从恰当的角度来看待事物。

比较记忆：prospective（未来的）

perspicacious [ˌpə:spiˈkeiʃəs] *a.* 独具慧眼的；敏锐的

per ＋ spic (look) ＋ acious → 一眼全部看到的 → 独具慧眼的

perspicuity [ˌpə:spiˈkju(:)iti] *n.* 清晰. lucidity

One of the outstanding features of this book is the ***perspicuity*** of its author, her meaning is always clear.

这本书最为突出的特色之一是清晰，作者（要表达的意义）总是清楚的。

perspiration [ˌpə:spəˈreiʃən] *n.* 出汗. sweat

比较记忆：inspiration（灵感）

pert [pə:t] *a.* 冒失的；活泼的. saucy

I think your ***pert*** and impudent remarks call for an apology.

我认为你得为你粗鲁莽撞的话道歉。

pertain [pə(:)ˈtein] *v.* 属于，关于

I was busy in filing the documents ***pertaining*** to the lawsuits.

我忙着把有关诉讼案件的文件归档。

122

pertinacious [ˌpəːtiˈneiʃəs] *a.* 顽固的. obstinate

He is bound to success because his ***pertinacious*** nature
will not permit him to quit.

他注定会成功,因为他顽强的天性使他不会(中途)放弃。

peruke [pəˈruːk] *n.* 长假发. wig

peruse [pəˈruːz] *v.* 细读. scrutinize

perverse [pə(ː)ˈvəːs] *a.* 刚愎自用的;堕落的. headstrong

Because of your ***perverse*** attitude, I must rate you as
deficient in cooperation.

因为你刚愎自用的态度,我只能说你是缺少(合作)精神。

perversion [pə(ː)ˈvəːʃən] *n.* 堕落;滥用;歪曲. abuse

Inasmuch as he had no motive for his crimes, we could
not understand his ***perversion***.

我们无法理解他的堕落,因为他没有犯罪动机。

pervert [pə(ː)ˈvəːt] *v.* 使堕落;滥用;曲解. distort

Do pornographic books ***pervert*** those who read them?

色情小说会不会使读者堕落?

pesky [ˈpeski] *a.* 讨厌的. vexatious

It is very ***pesky*** for me to interrogate the suspects day
after day.

整天地审问嫌疑犯令我厌烦。

pester [ˈpestə] *v.* 纠缠. bother

The dog is ***pestering*** his owner for dinner.

狗缠着它主人要吃食。

pesticide [ˈpestisaid] *n.* 杀虫剂

参考:pest (害虫,害人虫)

pestiferous [pesˈtifərəs] *a.* 伤风败俗的;传播疾病的. contagious

pesti + ferous (bearing) → 引起疾病的

pestilence [ˈpestiləns] *n.* 瘟疫

Modern medicine has put an end to many ***pestilence***.

现代医学结束了许多(疾病作为)不治之症(的历史)。

pestilent ['pestilənt] *a.* 致命的；有害的. virulent
比较记忆：pestilence（瘟疫）

pestle ['pesl, 'pestl] *n.* 杵，碾槌；　*v.* 研碎
From the way in which the elderly pharmacist pounded the drug with his *pestle*, young George could tell that his employer was agitated about something.
从那个上了岁数的药剂师用槌捣药的方式上，年轻的乔治能看得出他老板正为什么事恼火呢。

pet [pet] *n.* 怒气；　*v.* 抚爱. caress
I tenderly *petted* my girlfriend once more before boarding the train.
上火车前我又一次温柔地抚爱我的女友。

peter ['pi:tə] *v.* 逐渐枯竭；逐渐消失
The tempest *petered* out and the whole world return to normal again.
暴风雨逐渐小下来，整个世界又恢复了正常。

petite [pə'ti:t] *a.* 娇小玲珑的
In exhibition she showed off the *petite* figure that she had earned by long time dieting.
她显示着自己通过长期节食而得来的娇小身材。

petrify ['petrifai] *v.* 石化；吓呆. ossify; paralyze
petrify：stone ＝ incinerate：cremains

petrology [pi'trɔlədʒi] *n.* 岩石学

pettish ['petiʃ] *a.* 易怒的. cross, irritable
比较记忆：petty（细小的；卑鄙的）

petulant ['petjulənt] *a.* 性急的，暴躁的. peevish, grumpy
The feverish patient was *petulant* and restless.
那个发着烧的病人暴躁不安。
比较记忆：pertinent（中肯的）

124

phalanx ['fælæŋks] *n.* 集团

Their clique was, in effect, a *phalanx*.

他们那个小团伙事实上是个集团。

phanerogam ['fænərəugæm] *n.* 显花植物. ↔ cryptogram

phantasmal [fæn'tæzməl] *a.* 幻影的，幽灵般的

phantom ['fæntəm] *n.* 鬼怪；幻象. apparition

The sudden *phantom* of a headless horseman frightened the villagers.

突然出现的一个无头骑士的鬼影吓坏了村里人。

pharisaic [ˌfæri'seiik] *a.* 伪善的. hypocritical

It is not *pharisaic* to compliment a mother on the beauty of her plain child; it is merely common sense.

对一个母亲讲些恭维她那平常的孩子的溢美之辞不算伪善，这只是常识。

pharmaceutic [ˌfɑːmə'sjuːtic] *a.* 制药的；药用的

pharmaceutist [ˌfɑːmə'sjuːtist] *n.* 药剂师

It took the *pharmaceutist* no time to make up the prescription.

药剂师一下子就配好了这个药方。

pharmacology [ˌfɑːmə'kɔlədʒi] *n.* 药理学

phase [feiz] *v.* 按计划进行

phial ['faiəl] *n.* 小瓶(药水瓶)

Even though it is small, this *phial* of perfume is expensive.

就是这么小的一小瓶香水也是很贵的。

philander [fi'lændə] *v.* 调戏女人. dally

philanderer [fi'lændərə] *n.* 追求女性者

Swearing he had never so much as looked at another woman, Jack assured Jill he was no *philanderer*.

杰克发誓说他从没有这样地看过一眼别的女人，让吉尔相信他不是好色之徒。

philanthropist [fi'lænθrəpist] *n*. 慈善家. ↔ misanthrope

    phil (love) + anthrop (person) + ist → 慈善家

    skinflint : philanthropic = mendicant : supercilious

philatelist [fi'lætəlist] *n*. 集邮家

    When she heard the value of the Penny Black stamp, Phyllis was inspired to become a ***philatelist***.

    当菲莉斯听说了黑便士票的价值后,大受鼓舞,要成为一个集邮家。

philately [fi'lætəli] *n*. 集邮

philippic [fi'lipik] *n*. 猛烈的抨击. tirade

    参考:harangue(长篇公开演说)

philistine ['filistain] *n*. 庸人(insensitive to intellectual or artistic values). ↔ aesthete

    We need more men of culture and enlightenment, we have too many ***philistines*** among us.

    我们需要更多有文化的头脑开通之士,我们之中有着太多的庸人。

philology [fi'lɔlədʒi] *n*. 语言学

phlegmatic [fleg'mætik] *a*. 冷淡的. stoic

    The nurse was a cheerful but ***phlegmatic*** person, unexcited in the face of sudden emergencies.

    这个护士是个外表冷淡、内心热忱的人,面对意外情况脸上一点儿不带激动(的表情)。

phobia ['fənbiə] *n*. 恐惧

    Her fear of flying was more than mere nervousness; it was a real ***phobia***.

    她对乘飞机的恐惧远远不是一般性的紧张,那可真是恐惧。

phoenix ['fi:niks] *n*. (传说中的)凤凰

    参考:dinosaur(恐龙), dragon(龙)

phonetics [fəu'netic] *n*. 语音学

phony ['fəuni] *a.* 假的，伪造的. fake

　　The *phony* piety was belied by their actual behavior.

　　他们的实际行为同他们那假虔诚并不相符。

photosynthesis [ˌfəutəu'sinθəsis] *n.* 光合作用

　　photo (light) + synthesis → 光合作用

phrenalgia [fri'nældʒiə] *n.* 精神痛苦

phrenetic [fri'netik] *a.* 发狂的. frenetic

　　The dogs ran around the house at a *phrenetic* pace.

　　狗绕着房子发疯地跑。

phrenology [fri'nɔlədʒi] *n.* 骨相学

　　A *phrenology* theory based on the belief that certain mental faculties and character traits are indicated by the configurations of the skull.

　　骨相学理论以这种信仰为基础，即一定的思维才能和性格特征会在头骨的构造上体现。

phylum ['failəm] *n.* (动、植物)门

　　参考：genre ((艺术)门类)

physiognomy [ˌfizi'ɔnəmi] *n.* 观相术；相貌

piano ['pjænəu, pi'ænəu] *a.* (音乐)轻柔的. ↔ forte

　　参考：fortissimo (最强音的), pianissimo (最弱音的)

piazza [pi'ætsə] *n.* 阳台. terrace；*pl.* 广场，市场. bazaar

　　来自意大利语，意为 marketplace (市场)

picador ['pikədɔ:] *n.* 骑马斗牛士

　　参考：circus (竞技场，马戏场)

picaresque [ˌpikə'resk] *a.* 流浪冒险的

　　The more lasting and important kind of novel of the open road in England and America is the modern *picaresque*, such as Kingsley Amis's "Lucky Jim" and Saul Bellow's "Adventures of Augie March".

　　英美小说中有关开阔地的更为重要而又持久的一种是像金斯利

·埃米斯的《幸运的吉姆》以及索尔·贝洛的《奥吉·马奇历险记》这样的流浪冒险故事。

picayune [ˌpikə'juːn] *a.* 微小的；微不足道的. minute

Any combination of *picayune* failings could yet add up to disaster.

千里之堤，溃于蚁穴。

picket ['pikit] *n.* 尖桩；哨兵. stake；sentinel

Post a *picket* at the front and back doors during the display of the valuable collection.

在展出这些珍贵的收藏品期间，前后门都要设警卫。

pictorial [pik'tɔːriəl] *a.* 绘画的

A film director may be strong in handling the *pictorial* elements but weak in giving his stout line any sense of momentum.

电影导演在处理画面因素方面也许很有力度，但在赋予台词以力度方面却显得力不从心。

picturesque [ˌpiktʃə'resk] *a.* 生动的；独特的. quaint

picture + esque (style) → 生动的

piecemeal ['piːsmiːl] *a.* 逐渐的

pied [paid] *a.* 杂色的. roan

The *Pied* Piper of Hamelin got his name from the multicolored clothing he wore.

"哈姆林杂色马"的名声得自于他穿的五彩缤纷的衣服。

pierce [piəs] *v.* 刺透，穿过. probe

sword：pierce = club：pound

piercing ['piəsiŋ] *a.* 刺耳的；敏锐的. grating；acute

piety ['paiəti] *n.* 虔诚

Mother Tersa exemplifies the true spirit of *piety*.

特尔莎妈妈是虔诚精神的典范。

来自：pious（虔诚的）

pigment ['pigmənt] *n.* 天然色素

128

比较记忆：pigmeat（猪肉，肉感女人）

pigment：color ＝ seasoning：flavor

pigsty [ˈpigsti] *n.* 猪圈

The piglets played in the *pigsty* with their mother.

小猪在猪圈里同母猪嬉戏。

比较记忆：sty（圈）

pilaster [piˈlæstə] *n.* 壁柱

Pilasters are rectangular in shape, not round.

壁柱不是圆形，是椭圆形状的。

pilfer [ˈpilfə] *v.* 偷窃. filch, snitch

Tom was fired because his boss caught him *pilfering* supplies from the storeroom.

汤姆被解雇了，因为他老板在他从仓库往外偷东西时抓住了他。

pilgrim [ˈpilgrim] *n.* 朝圣客，香客

参考：inferno（地狱），monk（僧侣），nun（修女）

Unit Twenty-Seven

pillage [ˈpilidʒ] *v.* 抢劫，掠夺. plunder, sack

The enemy ***pillaged*** the quiet village and left it in ruins.

敌人洗劫了宁静的村庄后,那里一片废墟。

pillory [ˈpiləri] *n.* 颈手枷; *v.* 示众;嘲弄

Even though he was mocked and ***pilloried***, he maintained that he was correct in his beliefs.

尽管人们嘲笑他,他坚持他的信念没有错。

比较记忆:pillar（支柱）

pincers [ˈpinsəz] *n.* 钳子;镊子

比较记忆:pinch（捏;一撮）

pine [pain] *v.* 憔悴;渴望. yearn

She missed her dead lover so much that she ***pined*** away and died.

她太怀念她死去的情人了,以致她也逐渐憔悴死去。

pinion [ˈpinjən] *v.* 绑住;束缚. fetter

They ***pinioned*** his arms against his body but left his legs free so that he could move about.

他们把他胳膊绑在身上,脚没有绑上,这样他可以自由地四下走动。

pinnacle [ˈpinəkl] *n.* 尖塔;山峰

We could see the morning sunlight illuminate the ***pinnacle*** while the rest of the mountain lay in shadow.

我们可以看见朝阳照亮了山巅,而山的其他部分还在暗影中。

pinpoint [ˈpinpoint] *a.* 精确的; *n.* 精确测定

130

pinup ['pin'ʌp] *a.* 迷人的，非常漂亮的. modish

The woman looks *pinup* in her chalk-white make-up and silver lame dresses.

那位女士脸上粉白的化妆和银光闪闪的裙子使她看上去非常漂亮。

piquant ['piːkənt] *a.* 辛辣的；开胃的. spicy

The *piquant* sauce added to our enjoyment of the meal.

辛辣的调味汁使我们这顿饭更有味道（锦上添花）。

pique [piːk] *n.* 不悦，愤怒

She showed her *pique* by her refusing to appear with the other contestants at the end of the contest.

她拒绝同其他选手一同在比赛结束时出场，以此表示她的不悦。

piracy ['paiərəsi] *n.* 非法翻印；海盗行为

pirate ['paiərit] *n.* 海盗

The boy's tale of meeting *pirate* on the deserted beach is simply not believable.

那男孩讲的在荒凉的海滩上遇见海盗的故事显然不可信。

参考同类词：bandit（歹徒），gangster（歹徒），brigand（土匪），pirate（海盗）

piscatorial [ˌpiskə'tɔːriəl] *a.* 捕鱼的；渔民的

His interest in *piscatorial* activities took him to islands in the Bahamas and to icy mountain streams.

他对捕鱼活动的兴致把他带到巴哈马群岛，带到冰冷刺骨的山涧小溪中去。

pistil ['pistil] *n.* 雌蕊

参考：stamen（雄蕊）

pitch [pitʃ] *n.* 沥青，柏油

pitch [pitʃ] *n.* 音高

color : wavelength = pitch : frequency

pitcher ['pitʃə] *n.* 有柄水罐

Will you give me one of your *pitchers*, one that you can spare?

你能不能给我个你用不着的闲水罐?

piteous ['pitiəs] *a.* 令人同情的;可怜的

来自:pity(同情)

pitfall ['pitfɔl] *n.* 陷阱;未料到的危险或困难. snare

pith [piθ] *n.* 精髓,要点. crux, gist

The *pith* of Plato's philosophy was his doctrine of the archetype.

柏拉图哲学的精髓在于其理想型的教义。

pithy ['piθi] *a.* 简练的. epigrammatic

I enjoy reading his essays because they are always compact and *pithy*.

我喜欢读这些文章,它们总是很精炼的。

pittance ['pitəns] *n.* 微薄的收入;少量. trifle

He could not live on the *pittance* he received as a pension and had to look for an additional source of revenue.

他无法靠他得到的微薄的津贴生活,因而他要寻找其他的收入来源。

pivot ['pivət] *n.* 枢轴,中心点; *v.* 在枢轴上旋转. swivel

The hands of the watch rotate on a *pivot*.

表针绕枢轴转动。

placate [plə'keit] *v.* 抚慰,平息. propitiate

比较记忆:implacable(难以平息的)

placebo [plə'si:bəu] *n.* 安慰剂;无效对照剂

placebo:painstaking = backdrop:vista

placid ['plæsid] *a.* 安静的,平和的. tranquil

After his vacation in this *placid* section, he felt soothed and rested.

在这样一个安静的地方度过假后，他感到得到了抚慰，很宁静。

plagiarism ['pleidʒərizəm] *n.* 剽窃，抄袭

The editor recognized the *plagiarism* and rebuked the culprit who had presented the manuscript as original.

编辑认出了剽窃作品，指责了那个把它作为原作手稿拿来的剽窃犯。

plague [plɛig] *n.* 瘟疫； *v.* 烦扰. harass

In the 14th century the *plague* killed one-third of the population of Europe.

14 世纪的时候，一场瘟疫夺去了欧洲三分之一人口的生命。

plaintiff ['pleintif] *n.* 原告. ↔ defendant

参考：bar（法院）

plaintive ['pleintiv] *a.* 悲哀的，伤心的. lugubrious

Plaintive cries were heard at the funeral.

葬礼上传来伤心的哭喊声。

比较记忆：plaint（哀诉，起诉）

plait [plæt] *n.* 发辫； *v.* 编成辫

Girls in that high school wear *plaited* skirts.

那所中学的女学生穿编织的裙子。

plane [plein] *n.* 刨子；平面； *v.* 刨

planetarium [ˌplæni'tɛəriəm] *n.* 天文馆

plank [plæŋk] *n.* 厚木板；要点

They intend to fight the next election on *plank* of developing the country's trade.

他们打算下次选举时努力的要点定为发展国家贸易。

plankton ['plæŋktən] *n.* 浮游生物

参考：reptile（爬行动物），protozoa（原生动物），amphibian（两栖动物）

plaque [plɑːk] *n.* 饰板，血小板；徽章

plash [plæʃ] *v.* 轻泼 (splash gently)

plasma ['plæzmə] *n.* 血浆

参考：lymph（淋巴）

plateau ['plætəu] *n.* 高原；平稳的状态

Business has now reached a *plateau*, but we hope it will begin to increase again soon.

商业已达到了一种平稳状态，但我们希望它很快会再次开始增长。

platitude ['plætitjuːd] *n.* 陈词滥调. cliche

The candidate's speech was filled with empty promises, *platitudes* and cliches.

候选人的讲话里充斥着空泛的许诺和各种陈词滥调。

platitudinous [ˌplæti'tjuːdinəs] *a.* 陈腐的. trite

platonic [plə'tɔnik] *a.* 纯精神的（爱情）

来自柏拉图 Plato ＋ nic 柏拉图式的恋爱

Accused of impropriety in his dealings with female students, the professor maintained he had only a *platonic* interest in the women involved.

教授受到对待女性学生不当的指责，而他坚持说他对那些女性怀有的只是一种纯友谊的兴趣。

plausible ['plɔːzəbl] *a.* 似乎合理的，嘴巧的. reasonable

来自：worthy of applause

比较记忆：plaudits（称赞），applause（鼓掌）

playwright ['pleirait] *n.* 剧作家

参考：cartwright（造车匠）

plaza ['plɑːzə] *n.* 广场，集市. bazaar

pleat [pliːt] *n.* & *v.* （衣服上的）褶；打褶

She wore a *pleated* miniskirt.

她穿了件带褶的迷你裙。

来自：plait（把……编成辫子）

plebeian [pli'biː(ː)ən] *n.* 平民； *a.* 粗俗的

134

His speeches were aimed at *plebeian* minds and emotions, they disgusted the more refined.

他的讲话是针对平民的思想感情的，他们厌恶反复推敲、咬文嚼字的文雅的演讲。

plebiscite ['plebisit] *n.* 公民投票

I think this matter is so important that it should be decided not by a handful of legislators but by a *plebiscite* of the entire nation.

我认为这件事太重要了，不该由一小撮立法者来决定，而是由全体国民投票表决。

plenilune ['pli:nəlu:n, 'plenəlu:n] *n.* 满月. ↔ crescent

plenipotentiary [ˌplenipə'tenʃəri] *n.* 全权大臣

He was not given *plenipotentiary* powers by his country without consulting his superiors.

他的国家没有授予他不向上级请示（就可以自行决定）的全权大臣的权力。

plenitude ['plentitju:d] *n.* 完全，充分. bounty

比较记忆：plenteous（丰富的），plenary（充满的）

pleonastic [ˌpli(:)ə'næstik] *a.* 冗长的； 赘语的. verbose

The essay is so *pleonastic* that it becomes almost impossible to grasp the points the author wishes to make.

这篇文章太啰嗦了，以致几乎无法抓住作者想要表达的要点。

参考：pleophagous（杂食性的）

plethora ['pleθərə] *n.* 过量，过剩. redundancy

Confronted by such a *plethora* of conflicting testimony, the jury was convinced that some of the witness must be guilty of perjury.

面对这么多互相抵触的证言，陪审团相信一定是有证人作了伪证。

pliable ['plaiəbl] *a.* 顺从的；易弯的. pliant

He used *pliable* wire to get into the sewer grating.

他用根易弯曲的电线伸进下水道（上的铁栅）中去。

plica ['plaikə] *n.* 褶. ruck

pliers ['plaiəz] *n.* 钳子. tongs

plight [plait] *n.* 困境. predicament

The *plight* of the people in the drought-stricken area has not improved.

遭受旱灾地区的人民的困境还没有得到改善。

plinth [plinθ] *n.* 柱脚，底座. pedestal

plod [plɔd] *v.* 重步走；吃力干. trudge；drudge

The youth just *plodded* along at his piano lessons.

这个年轻人只能勉强跟得上他的钢琴课。

plodding ['plɔdiŋ] *a.* 沉重的；乏味的. grinding

plot [plɔt] *n.* 情节；   *v. & n.* 阴谋. intrigue

Although a few of the *plot* twists in her novel were unexpected，overall，the major events which took place in the novel were predictable enough.

尽管她小说中也有几处情节上的跌荡,总体看来,她小说中发生的主要事件都足以预见。

ploy [plɔi] *n.* 花招，手段. tactic

plumb [plʌm] *v.* 用铅锤测量；查明

plumb [plʌm] *adv.* 精确地；垂直地. vertically

plumbing ['plʌmiŋ] *n.* （建筑物）水管装置

plume [plu:m] *n.* 羽毛；   *v.* 搔首弄姿；整理

plummet ['plimit] *v.* 垂直或突然地落下

waft：plummet ＝ meander：dash

plumule ['plu:mju:l] *n.* 胚芽；（鸟）绒毛

参考：ovule（胚珠）

plunk [plʌŋk] *v. & n.* 猛跌，突降

She *plunked* herself down on the seat.

她一屁股跌坐进椅子里。

136

pluralism [ˈpluərəlizəm] *n.* 兼职；（哲学）多元论

plutocracy [pluːˈtɔkrəsi] *n.* 富豪，财阀统治

        pluto（wealth）＋ cracy（state）→ 财阀统治

        plutocracy：wealth ＝ aristocracy：patrician

pluvial [ˈpluːviəl] *a.* 洪水（般）的

        参考：freshet（洪水）

ply [plai] *v.* （搬运工等）等候顾客；弯曲

pneumonia [njuːˈməunjə] *n.* 肺炎

        参考：asthma（气喘症），hepatitis（肝炎）

poach [pəutʃ] *v.* 偷猎

        As soon as he could build a fire, he skinned and cooked the hare that he had ***poached***.

        他一能生上堆火，就剥了他偷猎的那只野兔的皮烧（来吃）。

pod [pɔd] *n.* 豆荚；   *v.* 剥落（豆荚）

podiatry [pəˈdaiətri] *n.* 足病学

        pod（feet）＋ iatry（医学科）→ 足病学

podium [ˈpəudiəm] *n.* 讲坛；乐队指挥台. forum

        The audience applauded as the conductor made his way to the ***podium***.

        指挥往指挥台上走去时，观众鼓起掌来。

poetaster [ˈpəutæstə] *n.* 蹩脚诗人

        poet ＋ aster（小星星，小人物）→ 蹩脚诗人

pogrom [ˈpɔgrəm] *n.* 大屠杀. holocaust

        Herod ordered all infants in the land to be on ***pogrom***

        希律下令杀掉这个国家所有的婴孩。

poignant [ˈpɔinənt] *a.* 伤心的；尖锐的. pungent

        The critic wrote a ***poignant*** review of the movie.

        批评家给这部影片写了篇尖锐的评论。

pointed [ˈpɔintid] *a.* 坦率的，显然的

pointer [ˈpɔintə] *n.* 一种短毛猎犬；教鞭

They brought out *pointers* to track down the escaped convict.

他们领出猎犬来追踪逃掉的囚犯。

poise [pɔiz] *n.* 泰然自若； *v.* 使平衡

He has a great deal of *poise* for a boy of only 17.

对于一个 17 岁的男孩子来讲，他很泰然自若。

poky ['pəuki] *a.* (地方)狭小的；慢吞吞的

比较记忆：poke（刺，嘲弄）

polemic [pə'lemik] *n.* 争论，论战

Her essays were, for the main part, *polemic* to refuse this offer.

他文章的主体部分都是在论战如何拒绝这一提议。

polio ['pəuliəu] *n.* 小儿麻痹症

参考：typhoid（伤寒），diarrhea（泻肚）

pollen ['pɔlin] *n.* 花粉

参考：petal（花瓣）

pollinate ['pɔlineit] *v.* 给……授粉

pollster ['pɔlstə] *n.* 民意测验者

poll + ster (person) → 民意测验者

比较记忆：poll（民意测验）

poltroon [pɔl'truːn] *n.* 懦夫. coward

Only a *poltroon* would so betray his comrades at such a dangerous time.

只有懦夫才会在这么危险的时刻如此背叛他的同志。

polyandry ['pɔliændri] *n.* 一妻多夫制

poly (many) + andry (man) → 一妻多夫制

比较记忆：androphobia（恐男症），android（男性的）

polygamy [pɔ'ligemi] *n.* 一夫多妻制

poly (many) + game (marriage) → 一夫多妻制

polyglot ['pɔliglɔt] *n. & a.* 通晓多种语言的(人)

138

New York City is a *polyglot* community because of the thousands of immigrants who settle there.

纽约城中有成千上万来自各方的移民在那里定居,因而那里也成了个汇杂各种语言的社区。

polymath [ˌpɔliˈmæθ] *n.* 知识广博者

pomp [pɔmp] *n.* 盛况；炫耀. splendor; ostentation

pomposity [ˈpɔmpəsiti] *n.* 自大,傲慢. arrogance

Although the commencement speaker had some good things to say, we had to laugh at his *pomposity* and general air of parading his own dignity.

尽管毕业典礼上的发言人也讲了不少好看法,我们还是没法不笑他的傲慢自大及夸耀他自己的尊贵那种总体气氛。

pompous [ˈpɔmpəs] *a.* 自大的. bloated

The *pompous* professor strutted around his classroom.

骄傲自大的教授大摇大摆地在教室里四下走动。

poncho [ˈpɔntʃəu] *n.* 南美披风；雨披

ponderous [ˈpɔndərəs] *a.* 笨拙的；笨重的. unwieldy; cumbrous

比较记忆：ponder（仔细考虑）

poniard [ˈpɔnijəd] *n.* 匕首,短剑. dirk

pontiff [ˈpɔntif] *n.* 教皇

Christmas Mass was celebrated by the *pontiff*.

教皇参加了圣诞节弥撒庆典。

pontifical [pɔnˈtifikl] *a.* 自以为是的,武断的

pontificate [pɔnˈtifikeit] *n.* 教皇职位；居傲而言

pony [ˈpəuni] *n.* 小马. foal

Then there was a *pony* expressly for my riding, a chubby pony, with a short neck and a mane all over his eyes.

而后有一匹特意(准备好)给我骑的小马,这是一匹圆滚滚,短颈,眼睛上长满鬃毛的小马。

pooch [puːtʃ] *n.* 狗

参考：canine（犬的）

poodle ['puːdl] *n*. 鬈毛狗

populace ['pɔpjuləs] *n*. 民众

比较记忆：popularity（流行）

populous ['pɔpjuləs] *n*. 人口稠密的

porcelain ['pɔːslin] *n*. 瓷，瓷器

Cups and plates are often made of *porcelain*.

杯子,碟子常是瓷质的。

porcine ['pɔːsain] *a*. 猪的，似猪的

参考：pork（猪肉）

porcupine ['pɔːkjupain] *n*. 豪猪，箭猪

参考：hog（公猪），swine（猪）

pore [pɔː] *n*. 毛孔； *v*. 凝视，沉思

Determined to become a physician, Both spent hours *poring* over her anatomy text.

博特下决心成为医生,她几小时几小时地对着解剖课本沉思。

pornographic [ˌpɔːnəˈgræfik] *a*. 淫秽的. smutty, lewd

The lecherous old man is often seen in the company of *pornographic* women.

有人经常看见老色鬼混在淫荡的女人堆里。

porous ['pɔːrəs] *a*. 可渗透的，多孔的

Dancers like to wear *porous* clothing because it allows the ready passage of water and air.

舞蹈演员喜欢穿多孔的布料（做的衣服）,因为这布料透气透水。

porphyry ['pɔːfiri] *n*. 斑岩

参考：granite（花岗岩），shale（页岩）

porringer ['pɔrindʒə] *n*. 小汤碗

portable ['pɔːtəbl] *a*. 轻便的；手提式的

比较记忆：portage（搬运）

portend [pɔːˈtend] *v*. 预兆，预示. foreshadow

The king did not know what these omens might *portend* and asked his soothsayers to interpret them.

国王不明白这些征兆可能预示着什么,就请他的占卜师为他释译。

portent ['pɔ:tent] *n.* 凶兆;预兆

He regarded the black cloud as a *portent* of evil.

他认为这片黑云是邪恶的凶兆。

portentous [pɔ:'tentəs] *a.* 凶兆的,预兆的. ominous

I regard our present difficulties and dissatisfaction as *portentous* omens of future disasters.

我认为我们目前的困难和不满可能会是灾祸的征兆。

portfolio [pɔ:t'fəuljəu] *n.* 文件夹;证券. folder;stock

His *portfolio* presented a report of the company's activities in the past year.

他的文件夹里是一份要上呈的有关公司过去一年的活动的报告。

portico ['pɔ:tikəu] *n.* (有圆柱的)门廊

portly ['pɔ:tli] *a.* 庄重的;肥胖的;魁梧的. grand;beefy

The overweight gentleman was referred to as *portly* by the polite salesclerk.

礼貌的售货员把那位超重的绅士称为魁梧。

pose [pəuz] *v.* 摆姿势,造作;造成,形成. profess

The increase in student numbers *poses* many problems for the universities.

学生数量的增加给大学造成了许多问题。

poser ['pəuzə] *n.* 棘手的问题

poseur [pəu'zə:] *n.* 装模作样的人

posh [pɔʃ] *a.* 豪华的;漂亮的. luxurious;chic

Critics judged the *posh* new opera house to be an aesthetic disaster.

评论家评价说那所豪华的新歌剧院是一美学的灾难。

posit [pə'zit] *v.* 假定,认为

posse ['pɔsi] *n.* 警察部队

The *posse* tracked the outlaws to their hiding place and arrested them.

警队追踪那群亡命之徒到他们的藏身之所，逮捕了他们。

possessed [pə'zest] *a.* 疯狂的

posterior [pɔs'tiəriə] *a.* 较后的

The tail of an animal is on the *posterior* part of the body.

动物的尾巴长在身体的较后部位。

posterity [pɔs'teriti] *n.* 后代，子孙. descendant

We hope to leave a better world to *posterity*.

我们希望能给后人留下个更美好的世界。

posthumous ['pɔstjuməs] *a.* 死后的，遗腹的. postmortem

post + hum (humus) + ous → 入土以后 → 殆后的

postulate ['pɔstjuleit] *n.* 基本原理；　*v.* 假定. ↔ prove

We must accept these statements as *postulates* before pursuing our discussions any further.

我们进一步探索我们的讨论之前，得把这种说法作为公理先接受。

比较记忆：expostulate（告诫，警告）

posy ['pəuzi] *n.* 花束

She arranged the roses into a *posy* and gave it to her mother.

她把玫瑰整理成一束送给了她母亲。

potable ['pɔtəbl] *n.* 适于饮用的；　*pl.* 饮料

potamic [pəu'tænik] *a.* 河流的

比较记忆：potamology（河流学）

potation [pəu'teiʃən] *n.* 畅饮

potboiler ['pɔt'bɔilə] *n.* 为赚钱而粗制滥造的作品

potentate [pəu'tənteit] *n.* 统治者，当权者

142

The *potentate* spent more time at Monte Carlo than he did at time in his throne.

当权者在蒙特卡洛消磨的时光比在他王座上的还多。

pother ['pɔðə] *v.* & *n.* 烦恼；喧闹. bother

A great *pother* resulted when he lost his Rolex watch.

他丢了他的劳力士手表时，特别烦恼。

potion ['pəuʃən] *n.* 一服，一剂

Tristan and Isealt drink a love *potion* in the first act of the opera.

在歌剧的第一幕中，特里斯丹和绮瑟喝下了爱情药酒。

potpourri [pəu'puri(:)] *n.* 混杂物；杂文集

He offered a *potpourri* of folk songs from many lands.

他写了部收集有许多国家的民歌的杂集。

potshot ['pɔtʃɔt] *v.* 肆意抨击

poultice ['pəultis] *n.* 膏药；泥罨剂

He was advised to apply a flaxseed *poultice* to the inflammation.

有人建议他往发炎的部位涂亚麻籽油。

pounce [pauns] *n.* & *v.* 猛扑，突袭. swoop

The little boys planned a *pounce* on the neighbor's orchard.

小男孩们计划着对邻居的果园进行一场突袭。

practitioner ['præktiʃnə] *n.* 开业者(尤指医生，律师)

pragmatic [præg'mætik] *a.* 实用主义的

Some students are *pragmatic* and want to take only the courses for which they see immediate value.

有些学生很实用主义，他们只想学那些能立见功效的课程。

pragmatism ['prægmətizm] *n.* 实用主义

prance [prɑ:ns] *v.* (马)腾跃；(人)神气活现地走

prank [præŋk] *n.* 恶作剧，玩笑

143

On April Fool's Day, people like to play *pranks* on their friends.

在四月一日愚人节这天，人们喜欢跟朋友们开开玩笑，搞点恶作剧。

比较记忆：plank（厚木板）

prate [preit] *v.* 瞎扯，胡说. babble

Let us not *prate* about our qualities, rather, let our virtues speak for themselves.

咱们别为我们的素质瞎扯了，让我们用品德说话吧。

prattle ['prætl] *v.* 闲聊，瞎扯. prate

The children *prattled* endlessly about their new toys.

孩子们拿着他们的新玩具没完没了地胡闹着。

preamble [pri:'æmbl] *n.* 前言，序言

In the *Preamble* to the Constitution, the purpose of the document is set forth.

在《宪法》前面的序中，阐述了这一文件的宗旨目的。

precarious [pri'kɛəriəs] *a.* 危险的；可疑的. ↔ stable

I think this stock is a *precarious* investment and advise against its purchase.

我认为买这家股票是一危险的投资，我建议不要买它。

precedent ['presidənt] *n.* 先例，前例

This decision sets a *precedent* for future cases of a similar nature.

这一决定为将来的类似情形树立了先例。

precept ['pri:sept] *n.* 箴言，格言

"Love the neighbor as themselves" is a worthwhile *precept*.

"尊重邻居（别人）的方式"是一句很有意义的箴言。

preceptor ['pri:septə] *n.* 教师. pedagogue

比较记忆：except（摘录）

precinct ['pri:siŋkt] *n.* 范围；区域

144

Each salesperson was assigned to a different **precinct**.

推销员们被分派往各自的不同区域。

preciosity [ˌpreʃiˈɔsəti] *n.* 矫揉造作

For insisting on "it is I" instead of "it is me", he was charged with **preciosity**.

由于他坚持说"那是我",而不说"是我",而被责怪为骄揉造作。

precipitant [priˈsipitənt] *n.* 沉淀剂. ↔ solvent; *a* 鲁莽的

precipitate [priˈsipiteit] *a.* 匆忙的，鲁莽的; *v.* 加速. ↔ gradual

The removal of American political support appeared to have **precipitated** the downfall of the Marcos regime.

看来是美国撤回其政治上的支持加速了马科斯政权的垮台。

precipitation [priˈsipiteiʃən] *n.* 急躁；降雨（量）

precipitous [priˈsipitəs] *a.* 陡峭的；仓促的

This hill is difficult to climb because it is so **precipitous**.

这座山太陡峭了，很难爬。

précis [ˈpreisiːz] *n.* 摘要，大纲

precis：essential = resume：career（经历）

preclude [priˈkluːd] *v.* 预防，排除. exclude

pre (anterior) + clude (close) → 排除

比较记忆：occlude（堵塞）

precocious [priˈkəuʃəs] *a.* 早熟的. ↔ retarded

By her rather adult manner of discussing serious topics, the child demonstrated that she was **precocious**.

这个孩子在讨论严肃问题时表现得十分像个成年人,这表明她很早熟。

precognition [ˌpriːkɔgˈniʃən] *n.* 预知; 预见

pre (anterior) + cogn (recognize) + ition → 预知

preconception [ˈpriːkənˈsepʃən] *n.* 先入之见

比较记忆：conception（观念）

precursor [priˈkəːsə] *n.* 先驱；先兆. forerunner

 Gray and Burns were ***precursors*** of the Romantic Movement in English literature.

 格雷和彭斯是英国文学史上的浪漫主义运动的先驱。

predator [ˈpredətə] *n.* 食肉动物. carnivore

 The natural balance between prey and ***predator*** has been increasingly disturbed, most frequently by human intervention.

 由于人类日益频繁地横加干涉,捕食者同猎物间的自然平衡(的关系)日益受到影响。

predatory [ˈpredətəri] *a.* 掠夺性的；食肉的

 The pirates were ***predatory*** and unpredictable.

 海盗(极)具掠夺性,且防不胜防。

predestine [ˈpriːdestin] *v.* 注定

 pre (before) + destine → 注定

predicament [priˈdikəmənt] *n.* 困境, 危境. straits

 Mary was in a ***predicament*** when she missed the last train home.

 玛丽没有赶上回家的最后一班火车,陷入了困境。

predictable [priˈdiktəbl] *a.* 可预知的；墨守成规的

predilection [priːdiˈlekʃən] *n.* 偏好

 pre (anterior) + dilect (love) + ion → 偏好

 比较记忆：delectable (美味的)

predisposition [ˈpriːdispəˈziʃən] *n.* 倾向, 癖性

preeminent [priːˈeminənt] *a.* 出类拔萃的. eminent

 The king traveled to Boston because he wanted the ***preeminent*** surgeon in the field to perform the operation.

 国王前往波士顿,因为他想要让这一领域内出类拔萃的医生(给他)动手术。

preempt [priːˈempt] *v.* 以先买权取得；先占

146

Your attempt to *preempt* this land before it is offered to the public must be resisted.

你试图在把这片土地献给政府前先买下的企图一定会被拒绝的。

preen [pri:n] *v.* 整理羽毛；（人）打扮修饰. ↔ rumple

As Kitty *preened* before the mirror carefully, smoothing her shining hair, she couldn't help preening herself on her good looks.

基蒂在镜前小心梳理抚平她光泽的头发,情不自禁为自己的美貌而自得。

prefatory ['prefətəri] *a.* 序言的，开端的

The chairman made a few *prefatory* remarks before he called on the first speaker.

主席在请出第一位发言人前,先讲了几句开场白。

prefect ['pri:fekt] *n.* 高级干部；（学校）级长

Because of his high reputation, he was chosen as *prefect* of his country.

因他有较高的名望,被他的国家选拔为高级干部。

比较记忆：perfect（完美的）

prefigure ['pri:'figə] *v.* 预示；预想. augur

pre (anterior) + figure → 预想

pregnant ['pregnənt] *a.* 怀孕的；充满的. gravid; plenary

参考：gravida（孕妇）

prehensile [pri'hensail] *a.* 能握住的

Monkeys use not only their arms and legs but also their *prehensile* tails in traveling through the trees.

猴子在树间穿行时,不仅用胳膊和腿,也用它可以抓住东西的尾巴。

prejudicial [predʒu'diʃəl] *a.* 有害的；引起偏见的

比较记忆：judicial（法庭的；公正的）

prelate ['prelit] *n.* 高级教士. bishop

The archbishop of Moscow and other high-ranking *prelates* visited the Russian Orthodox seminary.

莫斯科的大主教和其他级别较高的主教参观了莫斯科东正教神学院。

preliterate [pri'litəreit] *a.* 无文字记录的；有文字以前的

prelude ['prelju:d] *n.* 序幕；前奏

pre + lude (play) → 序幕，前奏

premeditated [pri:'mediteitid] *a.* 预谋的；事先计划的

比较记忆：meditation（沉思）

premiére ['premiɛə] *n.* 首次公演

来自：premier（首要的，最早的）

premise ['premis] *n.* 前提

Because Jack had based his argument upon a faulty *premise*, his opponent cheerfully pointed out the holes in his logic.

因为杰克的论点建立在一错误的前提上，他的对手满心喜悦地指出了他逻辑上的漏洞。

premium ['pri:mjəm] *n.* 保险费；奖金

The *premium* for his car insurance was higher than the figure originally agreed.

他汽车保险的保险费比开始说好的的数目要高。

参考：subsidy（津贴），bounty（补助金），bonus（奖金），dividend（红利）

preponderate [pri'pɔndəreit] *v.* 压倒，超过. overwhelm

I feel confident that the forces of justice will *preponderate* eventually in this dispute.

我相信在这一争端中，正义的力量最终会压倒（邪恶）。

prepossessing [pri:pə'zesiŋ] *a.* （个性等）给人好感的

pre + possess + ing → 预先就拥有人的情感 → 有吸引力的

preposterous [pri'pɔstərəs] *a.* 荒谬可笑的. absurd

The excuse he gave for his lateness was so *preposterous* that everyone laughed.

他解释他迟到的借口也太荒谬了，大家都笑了。

prerequisite [pri:'rekwizit] *n.* 先决条件

比较记忆：perquisite（福利）

prerogative [pri'rɔgətiv] *n.* 特权. privilege

pre + rog (claim) + ative → 特权

presage ['presidʒ] *n.* 预感； *v.* 预示. forebode

比较记忆：sage（智者，智慧）

presbyter ['prezbitə] *n.* （基督教的）长老

The early Christian church was guided by a handful of *presbyter*.

早期基督教会由一小撮长老领导着。

prescient ['presiənt] *a.* 有先见之明的. ↔ myopia

比较记忆：omniscient（全知的）

Unit Twenty-Eight

prescript ['priːskript] *n.* 命令，规定

来自：prescribe (*v.* 命令，规定)

prescription [pri'skripʃən] *n.* 处方(上的药)

prescription : overdosed = duty : derelict

preservative [prezəː'veitiv] *a.* 防腐的；　*n.* 防腐剂

preside [pri'zaid] *v.* 负责；指挥. chair

pre + side (sit) → 坐在前面 → 指挥

press [pres] *v.* 挤压；进逼

You must ***press*** them to meet the deadline.

你必须加紧以赶得上最后期限。

prestidigitation ['prestididʒi'teiʃən] *n.* 变戏法，魔术

presto ['prestəu] *n.* 急板

presumption [pri'zʌmpʃən] *n.* 假定；冒昧

It took a great deal of ***presumption*** to insult the ambassador at his own party.

在大使他自己举办的晚会上侮辱他实在太过冒昧。

来自：presume（假定，假设）

presumptuous [pri'zʌmptjuəs] *a.* 自大的；傲慢的

presupposition [ˌpriːsʌpə'ziʃən] *n.* 预先假定；臆测

pretended [pri'tendid] *a.* 假的. bogus

pretense [pri'tens] *n.* 虚伪

pretension [pri'tenʃən] *n.* 自命

pretentious [pri'tenʃəs] *a.* 做作的；自负的. priggish

I do not feel that your limited resources will permit you to carry out such a ***pretentious*** program.

我感到你有限的财力无法支撑你实现这么自负的一个项目。

preternatural [ˌpretəˈnætʃrəl] *a*. 异常的；超自然的. supernatural

preter (above) ＋ natural → 超自然的

比较记忆：preterlegal（超越法律）

pretext [ˈpriːtekst] *n*. 借口. excuse

He looked for a good *pretext* to get out of paying a visit to his aunt.

他想找个好借口不去看他姑妈。

prevaricate [priˈværikeit] *v*. 支吾其词；说谎. equivocate

Some people believe that to *prevaricate* in a good cause is justifiable and regard the statement as a "white lie".

有些人认为出于善良的目的而说谎是情有可原的，把这种谎言叫作"善良的谎言"（无害的谎言）。

prevision [priːˈviʒən] *n*. 预见；预知

pre ＋ vision → 预先看到

prick [prik] *v*. 刺伤；戳（穿）. jab

She *pricked* blisters on my sole with a needle.

她用针戳破了我脚底板上的泡。

prickle [ˈprikl] *n*. 刺；棘

prickly [ˈprikli] *a*. 多刺的；易怒的. thorny

prig [prig] *n*. 自命不凡者

prim [prim] *a*. 端庄的，整洁的. ↔ informal

Many people commented on the contrast between the *prim* attire of the young lady and the inappropriate clothing worn by her escort.

许多人对那位年轻女士整洁的衣着和她护卫那不合适的穿戴间形成的鲜明对比颇有微辞。

primate [ˈpraimit，ˈpraimeit] *n*. 灵长类（动物）；大主教

参考：reptile（两栖动物）

prime [praim] *n.* 全盛时期；初期的. heyday

He's the *prime* suspect in the murder case.

他是这一谋杀案的第一嫌疑人。

primeval ['prai'mi:vəl] *a.* 原始的，早期的

prime + ev (age) + al → 原始的

primogeniture [praiməu'dʒenitʃə] *n.* 长子身份

By virtue of *primogeniture*, the first-born child has many privileges denied his brothers and sisters.

由于长子身份的功效，第一个降生的(男)孩子有许多其弟、妹得不到的特权。

primordial [prai'mɔ:diəl] *a.* 最初的；原始的

The Neanderthal Man is one our *primordial* ancestors.

尼安德特人是我们最早的祖先之一。

primp [primp] *v.* 刻意打扮

She *primps* for hours before a dance.

她在舞会前打扮了好几个钟头。

princely ['prinsli] *a.* 慷慨的；奢侈的. bounteous

来自：prince（王子）

prink [priŋk] *v.* 打扮；化妆

pristine ['pristain] *a.* 太古的；纯洁的；质朴的. chaste

This area has been preserved in all its *pristine* wildness.

在这片土地上的原始状态的原野都得以保留下来。

privation [prai'veiʃən] *n.* 丧失；贫困. destitution

Only the rich can save money without *privation*.

只有有钱人才能光攒(钱)不花(钱)。

privative ['privətiv] *a.* 剥夺的；缺乏的

privilege ['privilidʒ] *n.* 特权；特免. immunity

Psychology has slowly evolved into an independent scientific discipline that now functions autonomously with

152

the same *privileges* and responsibilities as other sciences.

心理学已发展成为一独立的学科,同其他学科一样具有同等的特权和义务,独自起作用。

privy ['privi] *a.* 秘密的. clandestine

We do not care for *privy* chamber government.

我们不喜欢秘密政府。

probation [prə'beiʃən] *n.* 试用期,检验

比较记忆:approbation (认可,批准)

probe [prəub] *v.* 探索;彻底调查

The surgeon *probed* the wound for foreign matter before suturing it.

外科医生在缝合伤口前,先探查了一下伤口,看有没有异物。

probity ['prəubiti] *n.* 刚直,正直

His imperturbability in the face of evidence indicating his deliberate fraud failed to reassure supporters of his essential *probity*; instead, it suggested a talent for guile that they had never suspected.

他在证据面前表现出的沉着冷静表明他的蓄意欺骗并没有说服他的支持者们相信他本质上的刚正,恰恰相反,这倒提醒了他们,他还有他们从不曾疑心过的狡猾的天分。

proboscis [prə'bɔsis] *n.* (象)长鼻,(昆虫等)喙

The elephant uses his *proboscis* to handle things and carry them from place to place.

大象用它的长鼻子应付东西,用鼻子把它们搬过来挪过去。

proceeds [prə'siːdz] *n.* 收入

比较记忆:procession (行列,前进)

proclivity [prə'kliviti] *n.* 倾向;癖性. inclination

比较记忆:acclivity (上斜坡) ↔ declivity (下斜坡)

procrastinate [prəu'kræstineit] *v.* 耽搁,拖延. ↔ expedite

It is wise not to *procrastinate*; otherwise, we find our-

selves bogged down in a mass of work which should
have been finished long ago.

拖延耽搁是不明智的,否则我们会发现自己陷入一摊我们早该完
成的工作中。

procreate ['prəukrieit] *v.* 生育. bear, propagate

pro (forward) + create → 生儿育女

Procrustean [prəu'krʌstiən] *a.* 强求一致的

源自 Procrustes,希腊神话中巨人,抓到人后,缚之床
榻,体长者截下肢,体短者拔之使与床齐长

proctor ['prɔktə] *n.* 代理人;学监

prod [prɔd] *v.* 刺激;激励. goad

If you *prod* him hard enough , he'll eventually clean his
room.

你要是使劲激励他,最终他也会清扫他的房间的。

prodigal ['prɔdigəl] *a.* 挥霍的; *n.* 挥霍者. extravagant

The *prodigal* son squandered his inheritance.

那个败家的儿子挥霍光了他继承的遗产。

prodigious [prə'didʒəs] *a.* 很大的,巨大的. ↔ minute

He marveled at her *prodigious* appetite when he saw all
the food she ate.

当他看见她吃了多少食物时,对她的巨大胃口惊叹不已。

prodigy ['prɔdidʒi] *n.* 奇事;天才

Menuhin was a *prodigy*, performing wonders on his vi-
olin when he was barely eight years old.

梅纽因是个天才,在他还只有 8 岁时,就能在小提琴上表演奇迹
了。

prodrome ['prəudrəum] *n.* 前驱症状. foretoken

pro (forward) + drome (running) → 症状

比较记忆:syndrome(并发症)

profane [prə'fein] *v.* 亵渎;玷污. blaspheme

154

Tourists are urged not to *profane* the sanctity of holy places by wearing on proper garb.

游客们被要求穿着得体,以便不要亵渎了这一神圣的地方(的圣洁)。

professed [prə'fest] *a*. 公开声称的;假装的. frankly; ostensible

He is only *professedly* poor.

他只是装穷。

proffer ['prɔfə] *v*. 提议. propound

proficient [prə'fiʃənt] *a*. 熟练的,精通的. crack

She is such a *proficient* typist that everyone prefers to hire her.

她是个熟练的打字员,大家都乐于雇用她。

profiteer ['prɔfitiə] *n*. 奸商; *v*. 牟取暴利

Profiteers made much money in World War I.

奸商在一战中牟取了大量暴利。

profligate ['prɔfligeit] *a*. 挥金如土的;淫荡的. profuse; lascivious

In this *profligate* company, he lost all sense of decency.

在这个挥金如土的公司里,他也丢掉了正派。

profundity [prə'fʌnditi] *n*. 深奥;深刻

来自:profound(深刻的)

profuse [prə'fju:s] *a*. 丰富的;浪费的. extravagant

A *profuse* spread of food covered the table.

桌上铺满丰富的食物。

progenitor [prəu'dʒenitə] *n*. 祖先,始祖. patriarch

We must not forget the teachings of our *progenitors* in our desire to appear modern.

我们不能为了表现得现代而忘记祖先的教诲。

progeny ['prɔdʒini] *n*. 子孙后代. offspring

He was proud of his *progeny* but regarded George as the

most promising of all his children.

他为他的儿孙们感到骄傲,但认为乔治是他们中最有前途的一个。

prognosticate [prəg'nɔstikeit] *v.* 预测,预示. forebode

pro (forth) + gnostic (know) + ate → 预测

比较记忆:diagnostic (诊断的),agnostic (不可知论者)

prohibitive [prə'hibitiv] *a.* 抑制的,价格昂贵的

projectile ['prɔdʒiktail] *n.* 抛射物,发射体

pro (forth) + ject (throw) + ile → 抛射物.

proletarian [prəule'tɛəriən] *n.* 无产阶级

The aristocrats feared mob rule and gave the right to vote only to the wealthy, thus depriving the ***proletarians*** of a voice in government.

贵族们很害怕下层民众掌权,因此只给予那些有钱的人投票权,从而剥夺了无产阶级在政府中的发言权。

proliferate [prəu'lifəreit] *v.* 激增;繁殖. engender

pro (forth) + lifer (life) + ate → 繁殖

prolific [prə'lifik] *a.* 多产的,多育的. fecund

Langston's creative works were the highlight, not the entirety of his writings; he was also a ***prolific*** writer of non-fiction and political commentary.

兰斯顿的创作作品(小说)是他写作的最重要的组成部分,但并不是全部,他也是个高产的写实作品(非小说作品)及政论作家。

prolix ['prəuliks] *a.* 啰嗦的,冗长的. diffuse

He is much too ***prolix*** in his writings; he writes a page when a sentence should suffice.

他的作品太过于啰嗦,一句话就够的地方,他也写上一页纸。

prolonged [prələŋd] *a.* 长时期的. lengthy

promenade [prɔmi'nɑːd] *v.* 散步;开车(兜风)

promiscuous [prə'miskjuəs] *a.* 滥交的;杂乱的. miscellaneous

promontory ['prɔməntri] *n.* 岬

> They erected lighthouse on the **promontory** to warn approaching ships of their nearness to the shore.
>
> 他们在海岬上建起一灯火通明的灯塔以警示靠近的船只，（它们）已靠近海岸了。

prompt [prɔmpt] *a.* 敏捷的；   *v.* 促使；激起. acute；inspire

> Whatever **prompted** you to ask for such a big piece of cake when you're on a diet?
>
> 是什么促使正在节食的你要这么一大块蛋糕?

prompting ['prɔmptiŋ] *n.* 激励，鼓舞

> Having no sense of moral obligation, Shiper was as little subject to the reproaches of conscience after he acted as he was motivated by its **prompting** before he acted.
>
> 希泼没有什么道德义务感，他在演出（这一角色）后，像在那之前一样几乎从不为道德心的自责受到激励，不受其约束。

promptness ['prɔmptnis] *n.* 敏捷，迅速

promulgate ['prɔməlgeit] *v.* 颁布

> As soon as the Civil Service Commission **promulgates** the names of the successful candidates, we shall begin to hire members of our staff.
>
> 行政委员会一颁布获胜的候选人的名字，我们就开始雇用我们的雇员。

prone [prəun] *a.* 俯卧的；易于……的

> She was **prone** to sudden fits of anger.
>
> 她很容易突然发脾气。

pronounced [prə'naunst] *a.* 明显的；（观点等）强硬的

> 来自：pronounce（宣称，发音）

proofread ['pru:fred] *v.* 校对

prop [prɔp] *n.* 支撑物；   *v.* 支持. bolster

> Beams were used as **props** to keep the wall from collapsing.

用横梁作支撑物以防墙倒塌。

propaganda [ˌprɔpə'gændə] *n.* 宣传机构

The debater's repetitious arguments approached the simple-mindedness of *propaganda*.

辩论选手的重复性论辩，近乎于宣传机构的头脑简单。

propel [prə'pel] *v.* 推进

pro (forth) + pel (pull) → 推进

pedal : propel = anchor : hold

propensity [prə'pensiti] *n.* 倾向

The poet Auden believed that the greatest poets of his age were almost necessarily irresponsible, that the possession of great gifts engenders the *propensity* to abuse them.

诗人奥登认为他那个时代最伟大的诗人几乎都注定了是不负责任的，拥有巨大的天分造成他们滥用天分的倾向。

prophylactic [ˌprɔfi'læktik] *a.* 预防(性)的； *n.* 预防法

Despite all *prophylactic* measures introduced by the authorities, the epidemic raged until cool weather set in.

尽管当局采纳了一些预防措施，天气变凉前，传染病还是到处肆虐。

propinquity [prə'piŋkwiti] *n.* 邻近；近亲关系

比较记忆：propinquant（接近的）

propitiate [prə'piʃieit] *v.* 抚慰；调解. appease

The natives offered sacrifices to *propitiate* the gods.

土著人晋献祭祀品以抚慰神灵们。

propitiatory [prə'piʃieitəri] *a.* 讨好的；劝解的

propitious ['prəpitiəs] *a.* 吉利的；慈悲的. auspicious；benevolent

I could not wish for a more *propitious* occasion on which to announce my plans for enlarging our establishment.

这是公布我扩展我们企业的计划的再吉利不过的场合了。

proponent [prə'pəunənt] *n.* 支持者，拥护者. ↔ opponent

After the bill had been amended and re-amended in committee，even its original ***proponents*** didn't want to vote in its favor.

委员会这一提案一改再改之后，即使是它最初的支持者们也不想给它投赞成票了。

proprietary [prə'praiətəri] *a.* 所有(人)的；专利的

来自：proprietor（所有人）

propriety [prə'praiəti] *n.* 礼貌；适当；   *pl.* 礼节. etiquette

I want you to behave at this dinner with ***propriety*** ：don't embarrass me.

我希望你在晚宴上举止得体，别让我难堪。

propulsion [prə'pʌlʃən] *n.* 推进力

比较记忆：repulse（驱逐，反击）

prorogue [prə'rəug] *v.* 休会；延期. table

It was agreed that the king could not ***prorogue*** parliament until it had been in session for at least fifty days.

国会至少要开五十天会议，在那之前国王不得(令其)休会，对此达成了一致。

prosaic [prəu'zeiik] *a.* 平凡的；乏味的. prosy

He felt the office routine was too ***prosaic*** for a man of his dreams.

他感到对于一个像他这样有梦想的人，办公室的日常事务太单调了。

proscenium [prəu'si:niəm] *n.* 舞台前部

In the theater-in-the-round，there can be no ***proscenium*** or proscenium arch.

在表演场设在观众座席中央的剧院里，不可能有舞台前部或舞台的前部圆弧。

proscribe [prəu'skraib] *v.* 禁止. inhibit

比较记忆：prescribe（开处方），circumscribe（限定）

prosecute ['prɔsikjuːt] *v.* 告发；检举. peach

prosecution [ˌprɔsi'kjuːʃən] *n.* 起诉；检举

Here is the gist of the *prosecution's* case against the accused.

这是不利于被告人的有关检举揭发案的证据。

比较记忆：persecute（迫害），prosecutor（检察官）

proselyte ['prɔsilait] *n.* 皈依者；改变宗教信仰者

proselytize ['prɔsilitaiz] *v.* 改变宗教信仰

To *proselytize* is to try to convert an individual.

皈依就是使一个人发生信仰上的改变。

prosody ['prɔsədi] *n.* 诗体学，韵律学

This book on *prosody* contains a rhyming dictionary as well as samples of the various verse forms.

这本有关韵律学的书包括一音韵词典，还有各种各样的诗句形式的例句。

prospect ['prɔspekt] *n.* 顾客

prospectus ['prɔspektəs] *n.* 发起书；内容简介

prostrate ['prɔstreit] *v.* 平卧；征服；使……衰竭

He *prostrated* himself before the idol.

在这个偶像面前，他彻底被征服了。

protagonist [prəu'tægənist] *n.* 提倡者；支持者

参考：antagonist（对抗者）

protean [prəu'tiːən] *a.* 变化多端的；多才多艺的. versatile

How can you depend upon a person who is so *protean*.

你怎么可以依靠这么个变化多端的人。

protégé ['prəuteʒei] *n.* 被保护者；门徒

The wealthy benefactor demanded nothing whatsoever in return for the money he gave to his *protégés*.

有钱的捐助人对他给予捐助对象的钱财不要求任何形式的回报。

Protestant [prɔtistənt] *n.* 新教徒

160

protestation [ˌprəutes'teiʃən] *n.* 声明；断言

protocol ['prəutəkɔl] *n.* 外交礼节；草约；议定书

        protocol : blunder = bumper : damage

prototype ['prəutətaip] *n.* 原型；典型

        The crude typewriter on display in this museum is the ***prototype*** of the elaborate machines in use today.

        展览馆中展出的原始的打字机是我们今天所使用的复杂的机器的原型。

Protozoa [prəutə'zəuə] *n.* 原生动物门

        比较记忆：protoplasm（原生质）

protract [prə'trækt] *v.* 延长，拖延. postpone

        pro (forth) + tract (draw) → 拖长

protrusive [prə'truːsiv] *a.* 伸出的，突出的

        参考：intrude（闯入）

protuberant [prə'tjuːbərənt] *a.* 突出的，隆起的

        比较记忆：tuber（块茎）

provenance ['prɔvinəns] *n.* （艺术等）出处，起源

        I am not interested in its ***provenance***; I am more concerned with its usefulness than with its source.

        我对其出处不感兴趣，我对其用途比其来源更关心些。

provender ['prɔvində] *n.* （牛马吃的）干草料，粮秣

        I am not afraid of a severe winter because I have stored a large quantity of ***provender*** for the cattle.

        我可不怕天气严酷的冬日，因为我贮存了一大批喂牛的草料。

proverbially [prə'vəːbiəli] *adv.* 无人不知地

        来自：proverb（谚语）

provident ['prɔvidənt] *a.* 深谋远虑的；节俭的. farsighted

        In his usual ***provident*** manner, he had insured himself against this type of loss.

        他以惯有的深谋远虑，投保以防备（出现）这种损失。

providential [ˌprɔviˈdenʃəl] *a.* 幸运的. auspicious

They saw the breaking of the hurricane as a ***providential*** blessing on their mission.

他们见到了飓风的发生，真是他们使命中的幸事。

provincial [prəˈvinʃəl] *a.* 偏狭的；粗俗的. homespun

We have to overcome their ***provincial*** attitude and get them to become more cognizant of world problems.

我们得克服他们偏狭的态度，使他们更多地认识到世界上的问题。

provision [prəˈviʒən] *n.* 供应；(法律等)条款

According to the ***provision*** of this agreement, you must continue to work for them another 2 years.

根据这项协议条款(的规定)，你必须继续为他们工作两年。

provisional [prəˈviʒənəl] *a.* 暂时的，临时的. transient

The appointment is ***provisional***, only on the approval of the board of directors will it be made permanent.

任命只是暂时性的，只有董事会的认可才可使之成为永久性的。

proviso [prəˈvaizəu] *n.* 附文；(附带)条件

I am ready to accept your proposal with the ***proviso*** that you meet your obligations within the next two weeks.

我准备有条件地接受你的提议，条件是下两周内你要尽职责。

provocateur [ˌprɔvəˈkeitə] *n.* 内奸

prowess [ˈprauis] *n.* 勇敢；杰出的才能. valor

Her racy, pungent speech and erotic ***prowess*** would have put me to shame.

她辛辣尖刻的言辞和挑逗的勇气使我惭愧。

proximate [ˈprɔksimit] *a.* 最接近的；近似的

比较记忆：approximate (大约的), proximity (附近)

prude [pruːd] *n.* 过分守礼的人

The X-rated film was definitely not for ***prudes***.

儿童不宜的影片不是给拘泥守礼的人看的。

162

prudence ['pru:dəns] *n.* 谨慎，慎重

prudent ['pru:dənt] *a.* 慎重的，谨慎的

> The doctor didn't think it ***prudent*** for his patient to make a long journey.
>
> 医生认为他的病人作长途旅行是不慎重的。

prudery ['pru:dəri] *n.* 过分守礼，假正经

> ***Prudery*** actually draws attention to the vice it is supposed to repress; the very act that forbids speech or prohibits sight dramatizes what is hidden.
>
> 假正经实际上恰好把注意力引到它本该加以约束的坏事上去了，不让看不让讲这一行动剧性地（导致了偏偏想看看）到底在隐藏什么（的念头）。

prudish ['pru:diʃ] *a.* 过分守礼的，假正经的

prune [pru:n] *n.* 梅干； *v.* 修剪. shear

> prune : shrub = trim : heir
>
> prune : plum = raisin : grape

prurient ['pruəriənt] *a.* 好色的，淫乱的. obscene, lascivious

> The police attempted to close the theater where the ***prurient*** film was being presented.
>
> 警察要关闭放映色情片的那家剧场。

pry [prai] *n.* 杠杆； *v.* 刺探；撬

> pry : inquiry = importune : request

psalm [sɑ:m] *n.* 赞美诗，圣诗

psephology [si'fɔlədʒi] *n.* 选举学

pseudonym ['psju:dənim] *n.* 假名，笔名

> pseudo (spurious) + nym (name) → 假名
>
> 比较记忆：pseudoscience（伪科学）

psyche ['saiki] *n.* 心灵，精神

> Psyche 是以少女形象出现的人类灵魂的化身
>
> It is difficult to delve into the ***psyche*** of a human being.

163

探究人类的精神是件难事。

psychedelic [ˌsaikiˈdelik] *a.* 引起幻觉的；

psyche + delic (visible) → 迷幻药

psychiatry [saiˈkaiətri] *n.* 精神病学

psyche + atry（病学科）→ 精神病学

psychoanalysis [saikəuəˈnæləsis] *n.* 精神分析

psyche + analysis → 精神分析

psychosis [saiˈkəusis] *n.* 精神病

We must endeavor to find an outlet for the patient's re-
pressed desires if we hope to combat this ***psychosis.***

我们要想制服这个精神病，得尽量找个能让他释放压抑的欲望的
发泄方式。

psychotic [saiˈkɔtik] *a.* 精神病的； *n.* 精神病患者

比较记忆：psychic（精神的）

pterodactyl [ˌterəˈdæktil] *n.* 飞龙目动物

pterodactyl：phoenix = dinosaur：dragon（虚实）

puberty [ˈpjuːbəti] *n.* 青春期

参考：pubescent（到达青春期的）

pucker [ˈpʌkə] *n.* 皱褶； *v.* 皱起

Worries ***puckered*** up his brows.

他忧愁地皱起眉头。

puddle [ˈpʌdl] *n.* 水坑，洼

pudgy [ˈpʌdʒi] *a.* 矮胖的. dumpy

Irving emphasized the ***pudgy*** governor by describing his
height and circumference.

欧文通过描绘州长的身高和体宽来突出矮胖的州长形象。

pudsy [ˈpʌdzi] *a.* 丰满的. buxom

The ***pudsy*** maid is a stock character in many plays.

丰满的女佣是许多剧目中都出现的人物形象。

puerile [ˈpjuərail] *a.* 幼稚的，儿童的

His *puerile* actions surprised his cohorts.

他幼稚的行为使他的同伴们吃惊。

比较记忆：puerpera（产妇）

puff [pʌf] *v.* 吹嘘. inflate

This much *puffed* project proved a disappointment when it collapsed.

大加吹嘘的工程的垮台证明事实上它令人大失所望。

pugilism [ˈpjuːdʒilizm] *n.* 拳击，搏击

pugilist [ˈpjuːdʒilist] *n.* 拳击手

A boxing match will be held today to determine the best *pugilist* here.

今天要举办一场拳击赛以确定谁是这里最好的拳击手。

pugnacious [pʌgˈneʃəs] *a.* 好斗的. belligerent

As a child he was *pugnacious* and fought with everyone.

他是个好斗的孩子，和谁都打架。

puissant [ˈpjuːisnt] *a.* 强有力的

We must keep his friendship for he will make a *puissant* ally.

我们要保持同他的友谊，因为他可以成为（我们）强有力的盟友。

puke [pjuːk] *v.* 呕吐. vomit

The foul smells make her *puke* continuously.

难闻的气味使她呕吐不止。

pulchritude [ˈpʌlkritjuːd] *n.* 美丽

I do not envy the judges who have to select this year's Miss America from this collection of female *pulchritude*.

我并不羡慕那些要从这么一大群美人里选出今年的美国小姐的评委们。

pulchritudinous [ˌpʌlkriˈtjuːdinəs] *a.* 美丽的. elegant, pin-up

pulley [ˈpulɪ] *n.* 滑轮

参考：cylinder（汽缸），crane（吊车）

pullulate ['pʌljuleit] *v.* 繁殖；剧增. procreate

比较记忆：pullus（幼，雏鸟）

pulmonary ['pʌlmənəri] *a.* 肺的

In his research on ***pulmonary*** diseases, he discovered many facts about the lungs of animals and human beings.

在他对肺病的研究中，发现了许多关于动物肺和人类肺的情况。

pulp [pʌlp] *n.* 果肉

pulpit ['pulpit] *n.* 布道坛，讲坛

参考：lectern（诵经台），altar（祭坛），forum（论坛）

pulsate [pʌl'seit] *v.* 有规律地震动；（心脏）跳动

We could see the blood vessels in his temple ***pulsate*** as he became more angry.

当他变得大怒时，我们（甚至）可以看见他太阳穴里的血管在跳动。

pulsating [pʌl'seitiŋ] *a.* 节奏强的；极为兴奋的

pulverize ['pʌlvəraiz] *v.* 压成细粉；彻底击败

The Kid ***pulverized*** Tom with a series of brutal lefts.

基德用一系列残忍的左手勾拳彻底地打垮了汤姆。

pummel ['pʌml] *v.* 打击. pommel

The severity with which he was ***pummeled*** was indicated by the bruises he displayed on his head and face.

他头上脸上的擦伤表明他受到的打击的严重性。

punch [pʌntʃ] *v.* 以拳猛击；打洞

All the nails have been ***punched*** in, so that the surface is quite smooth.

所有的钉子都砸进去了，表面很光滑。

punctilious [pʌŋk'tiliəs] *a.* 谨小慎微的. conscientious

比较记忆：punctual（准时的）

puncture ['pʌŋktʃə] *n.* 孔； *v.* 刺破

pundit ['pʌndit] *n.* 权威人士，专家. pandit

Even though he discourses on the matter like a ***pundit*** , he is actually rather ignorant about this topic.

尽管他像个权威人士似的对此发表讲话，而事实上他对这个话题很无知。

pungent ['pʌndʒənt] *a.* 刺鼻的；尖刻的. ↔ insipid

The ***pungent*** aroma of the smoke made me cough.

刺鼻的烟味使我咳嗽。

punitive ['pjuːnitiv] *a.* 惩罚性的. ↔ rewarding

He asked for ***punitive*** measures against the offender.

他要求对冒犯（他的人）采取惩罚措施。

puny ['pjuːni] *a.* 次要的；弱小的. ↔ robust

Our ***puny*** efforts to stop the flood were futile.

我们想阻止洪水那渺小的努力无济于事。

puppy ['pʌpi] *n.* 小狗. pup

参考：puppy love（初恋），pooch（狗）

purblind ['pəːblaind] *a.* 愚钝的；视力不佳的. myopic

In his ***purblind*** condition，he could not identify the people he saw.

在他视力不佳的情况下，辨别不出他看到的人。

purchase ['pəːtʃəs] *n.* 紧握，紧抓（防止下落）

The mountaineer struggled to get a proper ***purchase*** on the slippery rock.

登山运动员奋力紧抓滑溜溜的岩石（以防下滑）。

purebred ['pjuəbred] *a.* （动物）纯种的

比较记忆：lowbred（下贱的）

purgative ['pəːgətiv] *n.* 泻药. cathartic.

参考：laxative = aperient（轻泻药）

purgatory ['pəːgeitəri] *n.* 炼狱；暂时性苦难

167

In this ***purgatory***, he could expect no help from his comrades.

在这种苦难时刻,他指望不上同志们的帮助。

purge [pəːdʒ] *v.* 清洗,洗涤. elutriate

If you are to be ***purged*** of the charge of contempt of Congress, you must be willing to answer the questions previously asked.

你要想洗清(对你)不敬议会的指控,必须甘愿回答先前问过你的问题。

Puritan ['pjuəritən] *n.* 清教徒

puritanical ['pjuəri'tænikəl] *a.* 拘谨的;反享受的. ↔ salacious

purlieus ['pəːljuːz] *n.* 近郊;范围

purloin [pəː'lɔin] *v.* 偷窃. snitch

In the story "The ***Purloined*** Letter", Poe points out that the best hiding place is often the most obvious place.

在小说《被窃的信件》中,坡指出最好的藏匿地点往往是最醒目的地方。

purport ['pəːpət] *n.* 意义,涵义

If the ***purport*** of your speech was to arouse the rabble , you succeeded admirably.

你讲话的涵义如果是要煽动乱民,你令人钦佩地成功做到了。

purr [pəː] *v.* 猫叫声

参考：bellow (牛叫), grunt (猪叫)

purvey [pəː'vei] *v.* (大量)供给,供应

The neighbors ***purveyed*** food and clothing for the new tenants.

邻居给新房客提供了衣物和食品。

purveyance [pəː'veiəns] *n.* 供给的食物. commissariat

pusillanimous [ˌpjuːsi'læniməs] *a.* 懦弱的. dastard

168

You should be ashamed of your *pusillanimous* conduct during this dispute.

你该为自己在这一争论中(所表现)的懦弱行为而羞愧。

putrefy ['pjuːtrifai] *v.* (使)腐烂. decay

Salmon that had spawned and died now lay *putrefying* in the shallows of the stream.

大马哈鱼产卵过后躺在溪流的浅滩上死去了,逐渐腐烂。

putrescence ['pjuːtresns] *n.* 腐败

putrid ['pjuːtrid] *a.* 腐烂的

The gangrenous condition of the wound was indicated by the *putrid* smell when the bandages were removed.

拆去绷带,伤口发出腐臭味,表明了其形成坏疽的情况。

putsch [pʌtʃ] *n.* 起义,暴动. insurrection

Dictators fear *putsch*.

独裁者惧怕起义。

pygmy ['pigmi] *n.* 侏儒. ↔ giant

The *pigmy* made up for his lack of size with his might.

侏儒的能力弥补了其身材的不足。

pylon ['pailən] *n.* 塔门;架高压电缆的铁塔

guy : pylon = strut : wing

pyre ['paiə] *n.* 火葬柴堆

pyromania [paiərəu'meinjə] *n.* 纵火狂

pyro (fire) + mania → 纵火狂

Pyrrhonism ['pirənizəm] *n.* 极端怀疑主义

python ['paiθən] *n.* 蟒

参考:cobra (眼镜蛇), scorpion (蝎)

quack [kwæk] *n.* 冒充内行之人,骗子

When he was accused of being a charlatan, he retorted he was not a *quack*.

当有人指责他是个骗子时,他反驳说他并非冒充内行之人。

quadrangle [kwɔ'dræŋgl] *n.* 四边形

    quadr (four) + angle → 四边形

Unit Twenty-Nine

quadrant [ˈkwɔdrənt] *n.* 象限

  quadrant ∶ circle = hemisphere ∶ globe

quadrennial [kwɔˈdrenjəl] *a.* 四年一次的

  quadr (four) + ennial → 四年一次的

quadruped [ˈkwɔdruped] *n.* 四足动物

These tracks indicate they were made by a *quadruped*.

这些痕迹表明它们是一种四足兽留下的。

参考∶ biped（两足动物）

quaff [kwɑːf] *v.* 畅饮. swig

As we *quaffed* our ale, we listened to the gay songs of the students in the tavern.

我们在畅饮淡色啤酒时,听着小旅店里的学生们唱着欢快的歌。

quagmire [ˈkwægmaiə] *n.* 沼泽地；困境. bog

Our soldiers who served in Vietnam will never forget the drudgery of marching through the *quagmires* of the delta country.

我们在越战中服过役的士兵永远也忘不了行军穿越三角洲乡村的沼泽地时的艰苦。

quail [kweil] *v.* 畏缩. cow

He was afraid that he would *quail* in the face of danger.

他怕他在危险面前会畏缩。

quaint [kweint] *a.* 奇异的. odd

Her *quaint* clothes and old-fashioned language marked her as an eccentric.

她奇异的服装,老调的语言标志着她是个古怪的人。

171

qualitative [ˈkwɔlitətiv] *a.* 定性的. ↔ quantitative（定量的）

qualm [kwɔːm] *v.* 疑虑；一阵恶心

His *qualms* of conscience had become so great that he decided to abandon his plans.

良心上的疑虑变得如此之大,他决定放弃他的计划。

quandary [kwɔnˈdɛəri] *n.* 进退两难. dilemma

When the two colleges to which he had applied accepted him, he was in a *quandary* as to which one he should attend.

当他同时被他所申请的两所大学录取了时,他反而陷入了（选择）该去哪一所的两难境地。

quantum [ˈkwɔntəm] *n.* 定量

quarantine [ˈkwɔrəntiː] *n.* 检疫期；隔离

We will have to place this house under *quarantine* until we determine the exact nature of the disease.

我们在确定这种疾病的性质前,得先把这所房子隔离起来。

quarry [ˈkwɔri] *n.* 猎物；追求物

The police closed in on their *quarry*.

警察向他们的追捕对象围拢上来。

quarry [ˈkwɔri] *n.* 采石场； *v.* 采(石)

quarry : stone = fell : timber

quartet [kwɔːˈtet] *n.* 四重奏；四重唱

参考：trio（三重奏）, duet（二重奏）

quartz [kwɔːts] *n.* 石英

While hiking up the mountain, they found several pieces of *quartz*.

他们在山间徒步旅行时,发现了好几块石英。

quash [kwɔʃ] *v.* 取消，平息

The authorities acted quickly to *quash* the student rebellion, sending in tanks to cow the demonstrators.

当局对平息学生的反抗反应迅速,派出坦克去恐吓游行示威的人。

quatrain ['kwɔtrein] *n.* 四行诗

参考:triolet(八行二韵诗),limerick(五行打油诗)

quaver ['kweivə] *v.* 震颤. quiver

The earthquake caused the ground to *quaver* for several minutes.

地震引起大地震颤了几分钟。

quay [ki:] *n.* 码头. wharf, pier

Because of the captain's carelessness, the ship crashed into the *quay*.

由于船长的粗心,船撞上了码头。

queasy ['kwi:zi] *a.* 令人作呕的. squeamish

As the ship left the harbor, he became *queasy* and thought that he was going to suffer from seasickness.

船出港口时,他开始感到恶心,心想恐怕要遭受晕船(的折磨了)。

queer [kwiə] *a.* 奇怪的;古怪的. freakish; insane

Her *queer* way of dressing attracted the stares of passersby.

她奇异的着装方式吸引了过路人(的目光)。

quell [kwel] *v.* 平息;镇压

The police used fired hoses and tear gas to *quell* the rioters.

警方用火焰喷射器和催泪弹镇压暴民。

quench [kwentʃ] *v.* 熄灭(火),抑制(欲望). extinguish

We *quenched* our thirst with a cold glass of Lemonade.

我们用一杯冰凉的柠檬汁来解渴。

querulous ['kweruləs] *a.* 抱怨的;多牢骚的

His classmates were repelled by his *querulous* and complaining statements.

他的同学都反感他那些抱怨牢骚话。

query [ˈkwiəri] *v.* 质问；询问

> He *queried* whether he could sing.
>
> 他询问他能不能唱歌。

quest [kwest] *v.* 搜寻；探索

> The New York University research team is collaborating in its *quest* for a cure for arthritis.
>
> 纽约大学的研究小组在其关节炎治疗的探索中是通力合作的。

queue [kjuː] *v.* 排队

> They stood patiently in the *queue* outside the movie theater.
>
> 他们在电影院外耐心地排着队。

quibble [ˈkwibl] *n.* 遁辞；吹毛求疵的意见

> quip（妙语，借口）的变体
>
> quibble ∶ objection ＝ minutiae ∶ details

quickie [ˈkwiki] *n.* 草草完成的劣品

quiddity [ˈkwiditi] *n.* 本质

> The *quiddity* of war is death and cruelty.
>
> 战争的本质不过是死亡和残酷。

quiescent [kwaiˈesnt] *a.* 不动的，静止的

> 比较记忆：quietude（静止）

quietus [kwaiˈiːtəs] *n.* 清偿，解脱

> The cancerous man welcomed death a *quietus* from suffering.
>
> 那个癌症患者希望以死解脱（他遭受的）痛苦。

quill [kwil] *n.* （豪猪等的）刺

> She found several *quills* by the duck pond.
>
> 她在鸭塘旁发现了几根刺。

quintessence [kwinˈtesns] *n.* 榜样；精华

> quint（five）＋ essence → 原指（空气、火、水、土之外的）等五种基本物质

174

quirk [kwəːk] *n.* 嘲弄；怪癖

By a *quirk* of fate, he found himself working for the man whom he had discharged years before.

他发现自己在为几年前他解雇了的那个人工作，这真是命运的捉弄。

quisling ['kwislɪŋ] *n.* 卖国贼，内奸. provocateur

来自人名 Quisling，挪威政客，二战德国占领挪威期间任傀儡政府总理

In his conquest of Europe, Hitler was aided by the *quislings* who betrayed their own people and served in the puppet governments established by the Nazis.

希特勒在征服欧洲的过程中，得到了那些背叛自己的国家，为傀儡政府卖命的卖国贼们的帮助。

quittance ['kwitəns] *n.* 免除；赔偿

John received a *quittance* of military service on physical grounds.

约翰因身体原因而免服兵役。

quitter ['kwitə] *n.* 遇困难即放弃者；懦夫.

quiver ['kwivə] *n.* 箭筒；　*v.* 颤抖

Robin Hood reached back and plucked one last arrow from his *quiver*.

罗宾汉绕到后边，射出了箭筒中的最后一支箭。

quiver : arrow = holster : pistol

quixotic [kwik'sɔtik] *a.* 不切实际的，空想的

来自：Don Quixote（堂吉诃德）

His head is in the clouds; he is constantly presenting these *quixotic* schemes.

他直昂头脑发昏了，总拿出这么些不切实际的计划。

quizzical ['kwizikəl] *a.* 爱挖苦的；戏弄的

Will Rogers' *quizzical* remarks endeared him to his audiences?

罗杰斯的挖苦话会让他讨得听众的喜欢吗？

quondam ['kwɔndæm] *a.* 过去的

quorum ['kwɔːrəm] *n.* 法定人数

The senator asked for a roll call to determine whether a *quorum* was present.

议员要求点名看出席的人够不够法定人数。

quota ['kwəutə] *n.* 限额

The space *quota* permitted precis ruled out details of research project.

鉴于篇幅上的局限,研究项目的一些细节在摘要中可先略去不作考虑。

quotidian ['kwəutidiən] *a.* 每日的；平凡的

rabbit ['ræbit] *n.* 懦夫. milksop, poltroon

Only a *rabbit* would so betray his comrades at such a dangerous time.

只有一个懦夫才会在这么危险的时刻如此背叛他的同志。

rabble ['ræbl] *n.* 乌合之众

A *rabble* is gathering where the protesters are marching.

抗议者们行进之处聚起来一帮乌合之众。

rabid ['ræbid] *a.* 患狂犬病的；失去理性的

来自：rabies（狂犬病）

He was a *rabid* follower of the Dodgers and watched them play whenever he could go to the ball park.

他是道奇斯队的疯狂的追随者,只要一有机会去棒球场,就去看他们打球。

rack [ræk] *v.* 折磨；拷问. afflict; grill

racket ['rækit] *n.* 球拍；　*v.* 诈骗；喧闹. extort; fracas

Stop making such a *racket*! I can't sleep.

别胡闹了,我都睡不着觉了。

racketeer [ˌrækiˈtiə] *n.* 诈骗犯

参考：gangster（歹徒），recreant（懦夫），thug（凶手），mob（乌合之众）

raconteur [ˌrækɔnˈtəː] *n.* 讲故事的人

My father was a gifted *raconteur* with an unlimited supply of anecdotes.

我爸爸是个天才的讲故事的能手，他总有讲不完的奇闻轶事。

racy [ˈreisi] *a.* 猥亵的；充满活力的. risque

The gentleman exchanged *racy* jokes once the ladies had retired after dinner.

女士们从晚宴桌上一退下，先生们就开始讲些下流的笑话了。

radiance [ˈreidjəns] *n.* 亮光；喜悦的神色

比较记忆：radiator（散热器）

raffish [ˈræfiʃ] *a.* 轻浮的，放荡的. libidinous

It was once thought *raffish* for a woman to dine alone with a man in his flat.

从前一位女士同一个男子在他家里单独进餐被当成（举止）轻浮。

raft [rɑːft] *n.* 木筏

All my goods began to fall off the end of the *raft*.

我的东西全从木筏后头掉下去了。

rafter [ˈrɑːftə] *n.* 椽子

rafters : roof = ribs : umbrella

ragamuffin [ˈrægəˌmʌfin] *n.* 衣衫褴褛者

He felt sorry for the *ragamuffin* who was begging for food and gave him money to buy a meal.

他为那讨饭的破衣烂衫的人感到难过，给了他钱让他去像样地吃上一顿。

ragged [ˈrægid] *a.* 破烂的；（表面）凹凸不平的

ragtag [ˈrægtæg] *n.* 乌合之众. rabble

The *ragtag* poured into the frontier in search of gold.

乌合之众蜂拥而至,到边疆来找金子。

raid [reid] *n*. & *v*. 突然袭击. foray

    In an air ***raid*** last night, enemy aircraft bombed the city.

    昨夜的空袭中,敌机轰炸了这个城市。

rail [reil] *n*. 栏杆; *v*. 猛烈指责. castigate

    You may ***rail*** him all you want; you will never change him.

    你可以想怎么说就怎么说他,但你永远别想改变他。

raillery ['reiləri] *n*. 善意嘲弄

    His humorous ***raillery*** was not well received by his friends.

    他善意幽默的嘲弄却不为他的朋友们所接受。

raiment ['reimənt] *n*. 衣服

    "How can I go to the ball?" asked Cinderella, "I have no ***raiment*** fit to wear."

    "我怎么去参加舞会呢?"灰姑娘说"我没有合适的衣服穿呀。"

rainbow ['reinbəu] *n*. 彩虹;幻想. daydream

    Many believe that a ***rainbow*** is auspicious, a sign of good luck.

    许多人相信彩虹是吉兆,会带来好运。

raisin ['reizn] *n*. 葡萄干

    参考:plum(梅干),grape(葡萄)

rake [reik] *n*. 耙子;浪子. philanderer

rakish ['reikiʃ] *a*. 漂亮的,时髦的. sporty

    He wore his hat at a ***rakish*** and jaunty angle.

    他以一种活泼时髦的角度戴帽子。

rally ['ræli] *v*. 召集. convoke; *n*. 集会

    The teacher ***rallied*** the group before setting out for the museum.

    出发去博物馆前,老师先集合起了学生。

ram [ræm] *n.* 公羊； *v.* 压；冲撞. cram

    n. A *ram* is a full-grown uncastrated male sheep.

    公羊是一未阉割的成年羊。

    v. He *rammed* down the soil round the newly planted bush with his boots.

    他用靴子猛踩刚种下的灌木周围的泥土。

rambunctious [ræm'bʌŋkʃəs] *a.* 粗暴的，蛮横的. rowdy；unruly

    Not many people can handle her *rambunctious* behavior.

    没有几个人能对付得了她放纵的行为。

ramification [ˌræmifi'keiʃən] *n.* 分枝；支流；细节

    Unfortunately，his damaging attacks on the *ramifications* of the economic policy have been undermined by his wholehearted acceptance of that policy's underlying assumptions.

    不幸地是，他对这一经济政策毁灭性的攻击却被他对构成这一政策的假设（前提）的全盘接受暗中损害了。

ramify ['ræmifai] *v.* 分枝，分叉

ramp [ræmp] *n.* 斜坡

    The house was built with *ramps* instead of stairs in order to enable the man in the wheelchair to move easily from room to room and floor to floor.

    房子里不建楼梯而代之以斜坡，这样可以使坐在轮椅里的人在房间、楼层间自由行动。

rampage [ræm'peidʒ] *v. & n.* 暴跳；横冲直撞. rage

    The untamed dogs went on a *rampage* throughout the countryside.

    野狗在乡间到处横冲直撞。

rampant ['ræmpənt] *a.* 蔓生的；猖獗的

    The *rampant* weeds in the garden killed all the flowers which had been planted in the spring.

    春天种下的花都让蔓延开来的野草杀死了。

rampart ['ræmpɑːt] *n.* 壁垒；城墙. barrier, citadel

"From the *ramparts* we watched" as the fighting continued.

战斗在继续，我们从城墙上看着。

ramshackle ['ræmʃækl] *a.* 摇摇欲坠的；要倒塌的. rackety

The boys propped up the *ramshackle* clubhouse with a couple of boards.

男孩子们用几块木板加固了一下要倒塌的更衣室。

rancid ['rænsid] *a.* 不鲜的，变味的. stale

A *rancid* odor filled the ship's galley and nauseated the crew.

甲板上有股不新鲜的(霉)味，令船员们作呕。

rancor ['ræŋkə] *n.* 深仇，怨恨

Let us forget our *rancor* and cooperate in this new endeavor.

让我们忘却我们之间的仇恨，在这一新的努力中携手合作。

rancorous ['ræŋkərəs] *a.* 怨恨的，憎恨的. vicious

randy ['rædi] *a.* 淫荡的，好色的. sexual

The *randy* monarch helped bring about his country's downfall.

淫荡的君王加速了他王国的陷落。

range [reindʒ] *n.* 山脉

ranger ['reindʒə] *n.* 森林看守员

ranger : tree = custodian : prisoners

rank [ræŋk] *a.* 茂盛的；臭名昭著的. luxuriant；notórious

The *rank* system of bribery should have reeked of foul play to any impartial investigator.

那个臭名昭著的行贿网在任何一个公正的调查人员眼里都充满罪恶的气息。

rankle ['rækl] *v.* (导致)痛苦；发怒. ↔ pacify

180

The memory of having been jilted *rankled* him for years.

被抛弃的记忆折磨了他好几年。

ransom ['rænsəm] *n.* 赎金； *v.* 赎回

They took away the boy and held him to *ransom*.

他们绑走男孩(以他为人质)讨要赎金。

rant [rænt] *v.* 咆哮. yell

As we heard him *rant* on the platform，we could not understand his strange popularity with many people.

我们听着他在台上咆哮,不理解怎么会有那么多的人喜欢他。

rap [ræp] *v.* 严厉指责；叩击；敲击. rebuke

Nervous，he *rapped* the table top with his knuckles until they were sore.

他紧张地用指关节敲打桌面,结果敲得关节都酸疼。

rapacious [rə'peiʃəs] *a.* 极其贪婪的

Hawks and other *rapacious* birds may be killed at any time.

任何时候都可以杀死老鹰及其他(类似的)极为贪婪的鸟。

rape [reip] *n.* 油菜； *v.* 强奸；抢夺. deflower

参考：barley（大麦），maize（玉米）

rapids ['ræpidz] *n.* 急流，湍流

rapine ['ræpain] *n.* 劫掠. pillage

Bands of teenagers broke the shop windows and took a frenzied *rapine* on the displays.

成群结队的少年砸碎玻璃窗疯狂洗劫展览品。

rapport [ræ'pɔ:] *n.* 关系，联系

In team teaching, it is important all teachers in the group have good *rapport* with one another.

在分科教学中,所有教师彼此协调一致很重要。

rapprochement [ræ'prɔʃmɑ̃:ŋ] *n.* 和睦状态

181

Both sides were eager to effect a ***rapprochement*** but did not know how to undertake a program designed to bring about harmony.

双方都迫切希望和平,却不知道怎么才能实现一个带来和睦的项目安排。

rapt [ræpt] *a.* 专注的;狂喜的. engaged; ravished

There was a ***rapt*** look on his face whenever he looked at his sweetheart.

他一见他的恋人,脸上就出现一种狂喜的表情。

raptor ['ræptə] *n.* 猛禽

rapturous ['ræptʃərəs] *a.* 狂喜的. ecstatic

rarefy ['rɛərifai] *v.* 稀薄化;净化

She ***rarefied*** the room with a thorough cleaning.

她搞了个彻底的大扫除,弄干净了房间。

rasp [rɑ:sp] *n.* 锉刀;刺耳声;   *v.* 锉. file

A ***rasp*** escaped from her throat as she endured the fifth day of her flu.

她忍受了五天流感的折磨之后,嗓子不再沙哑了。

raspy ['rɑ:spi] *a.* 刺耳的. cacophonous

The sergeant's ***raspy*** voice grated on the recruits' ears.

中尉刺耳的声音刺激着新兵的耳朵。

rat [ræt] *v.* 背叛. apostatize

ratiocination [ˌrætiɔsiˈneiʃən] *n.* 推理,推论

ratiocination : thinking = articulation : talking

ration ['ræʃən] *n.* 定量,配给量

Each flood victim was provided with a stated daily ***ration***.

每个洪水受害者,每天都得到一份规定的定量配额。

rationale [ˌræʃiəˈnɑ:li] *n.* 基本原理

比较记忆:rational(合理的)

182

rattle ['rætl] *v.* 喋喋不休. gossip

比较记忆：rattlesnake（响尾蛇）

raucous ['rɔːkəs] *a.* 声音沙哑的；喧闹的. strident；boisterous

His *raucous* laughter irritated me and grated on my ears.

他沙哑的笑声令我烦，刺激着我的耳朵。

ravage ['rævidʒ] *v.* 毁坏. demolish

The conquering army *ravaged* the whole country.

征服者的军队毁灭了整个国家。

rave [reiv] *n.* 痴心；一派胡言

ravel ['rævəl] *v.* （编织物）散开；使混乱；解开 (out). ↔ knit

A single thread pulled loose, and the entire scarf started to *ravel*.

一根线松脱了，整条围巾开始散开。

ravenous ['rævinəs] *a.* 饿极了的；贪婪的. voracious

The *ravenous* dog upset several garbage pails in its search for food.

饿极了的狗在找食吃时弄翻了几只垃圾桶。

ravine [rə'viːn] *n.* 深谷，峡谷

Steeper than a gully, less precipitous than a canyon, *ravine* is, like them, the product of years of erosion.

深谷比溪谷深，但没有峡谷陡峭，也是长期腐蚀的产物。

ravish ['ræviʃ] *v.* 迷住；强夺. enchant；rape

比较记忆：lavish（浪费）

ravishing ['ræviʃiŋ] *a.* 令人陶醉的

rawhide ['rɔːhaid] *n.* 生牛皮

组合词：raw + hide → 生牛皮

raze [reiz] *v.* 夷平；抹掉. demolish

The construction crew had to *raze* the old building before laying the foundation for the new one.

建筑队在打地基，建新楼之前，得先夷平旧楼。

比较记忆：razor（剃刀）

razzle ['ræzl] *n.* 狂欢. bacchanal

reactionary ['riː'ækʃnəri] *a.* 保守的；反动的

re（against）＋ action ＋ ary → 反动的

比较记忆：reactor（反应堆）

reactivate ['riː'æktiveit] *v.* 恢复活动

re（again）＋ activ（active）＋ ate → 重新活跃

ready ['redi] *a.* 聪慧的

reagent [ri'eidʒənt] *n.* 试剂（导致化学反应）

reagent : reaction ＝ explosive : destroy

realtor ['riəltə] *n.* 房地产经纪人

When we wanted to move to a larger home, the same *realtor* sold our house and found us a new one.

我们想搬到所大点的房子时，还是那个房地产经纪人给我们卖掉旧房子，又找了幢新的。

realty ['riəlti] *n.* 不动产（real estate）

He receives a large income from his *realty*.

他的不动产给他带来一大笔收入。

ream [riːm] *n.* 令（纸张的计数单位）

reaper ['riːpə] *n.* 收割者

reaper : scythe ＝ barber : razor

reassure [riːə'ʃuə] *v.* 使安心，宽慰

rebarbative [ri'bɑːbətiv] *a.* 令人讨厌的，冒犯人的. repellent

re（against）＋ barb（beard）＋ ative → 冒犯人的

rebate ['riːbeit] *v.* 折扣，回扣. discount

When he canceled his travel plans, the travel agent sent him a *rebate*.

当他取消旅行计划时，放行社按折扣退还了他的钱。

比较记忆：abate（减轻）

rebellious [ri'beljəs] *a.* 反抗的；难对付的. defiant；refractory

rebuff [ri'bʌf] *v.* 断然拒绝. snub

> She *rebuffed* his invitation so smoothly that he had been snubbed.
>
> 她这么直截了当地拒绝了他的邀请,让他感到像是受到了故意怠慢。
>
> 比较记忆：buff（迷；皮肤）

rebus ['ri:bəs] *n.* 字谜，画谜

> rebus：symbols ＝ jigsaw puzzle：pieces

rebut [ri'bʌt] *v.* 反驳. refute

> Each team will have a final opportunity to *rebut* before the debate is judged.
>
> 在辩论决断之前,每队还有一个反驳的最后机会。

rebuttal [ri'bʌtəl] *n.* 反驳

> The defense lawyer confidently listened to the prosecutor sum up his case，sure that she could answer his arguments in her *rebuttal*.
>
> 辩护律师自信地听着公拆人总结他的案件(陈述),相信她能在反驳中回击了他的论点。

recalcitrant [ri'kælsitrənt] *a.* 固执的；顽抗的. ↔ unruly

> Donkeys are reputed to be the most *recalcitrant* of animals.
>
> 驴以最为顽固的动物而著称。

recant [ri'kænt] *v.* 撤回声明；放弃(信仰). renounce

> Unless you *recant* your confession，you will be punished severely.
>
> 除非你放弃你的信仰声明,否则会被严厉地惩罚。

recapitulate [ˌri:kə'pitjuleit] *v.* 扼要重述

> Let us *recapitulate* what has been said thus far before going ahead.
>
> 让我们扼要地重述一下上面讲到的,而后再往下进行。

比较记忆：capitulate（投降）

recede [ri'si:d] *v.* 后退，收回（诺言）. ↔ redeem

re（back）+ cede（go）→ 后退

receptacle [ri'septəkl] *n.* 容器

You will find a *receptacle* in the corner for your left-overs.

你会在角落找到个盛剩饭用的容器。

receptive [ri'septiv] *a.* 善于接受的

Adventure-loving Huck Finn proved a *receptive* audience for Tom's tales of buried treasure and piracy.

爱冒险的哈克·费恩证明真有乐于接受汤姆那些关于海盗和埋藏的宝藏的故事的听众。

recess [ri'ses] *n.* （墙壁、山脉）凹进处；深处；　*v.* 休假. furlough

Outwardly he appeared forgiving，but in the *recesses* of his mind he planned revenge.

外表看来他宽容大度，而内心深处却在算计着复仇。

recession [ri'seʃən] *n.* 衰退；后退

The slow *recession* of the flood waters created problems for the crews working to restore power to the area.

洪水慢慢地退去，给要恢复这一地区的电力供应的工作人员制造了问题。

recessive [ri'sesiv] *a.* 衰退的；隐性的. ↔ dominant（显性的）

recherché [rə'ʃɛəʃei] *a.* 精选的；珍贵的

His language was peculiarly literary；he avoided common expressions and used *recherch*é terminology as often as possible.

他的语言特别书面化，他避免使用任何常见的词藻，只要可能就用些精雕细琢反复推敲的术语。

recidivism [ri'sidivizm] *n.* 累犯，重犯

Recidivism is a phase of the study of penology.

重犯是刑罚学研究的一个方面。

recidivism：rehabilitate ＝ relapse：convalesce

reciprocate [ri'siprəkeit] *v.* 答谢，回报. requite

If they attack us, we shall be compelled to *reciprocate* and bomb their territory.

要是他们袭击我们，我们就不得不回击，轰炸他们的领土。

比较记忆：reciprocal（＝ mutual）（互惠的）

recital [ri'saitl] *n.* 独奏会；吟诵

来自：recite（背诵）

recitative [resi'teitiv] *n.* （歌剧中的）宣叙部

Their high school glee club had little interest in the passage of *recitative*.

他们中学的合唱队对宣叙部分的段落没有什么兴致。

reclaim [ri'kleim] *v.* 纠正；开垦（土地）

We *reclaimed* land from the sea on which to build an airport.

我们填海开出片地要建个机场。

recline [ri'klain] *v.* 躺；依赖. repose

比较记忆：decline（衰败），incline（倾向于）

recluse [ri'klu:s] *n.* 隐士；　*v.* 隐居. anchorite

The *recluse* lived in a hut in the forest.

隐士住在森林中的一座小屋子里。

recoil [ri'kɔil] *v.* 退却；退缩. flinch

She *recoiled* at the sight of the snake.

她一看见蛇直往后缩。

recollection [rekə'lekʃən] *n.* 回忆. remembrance

When we questioned him about the accident, he did not seem to have any *recollection* of what had happened.

当我们询问他有关事故的事时，他看上去好像一点儿也不记得曾发生过什么事了。

recompense ['rekəmpens] *n. & v.* 报酬；赔偿. offset

比较记忆：compensate（补偿）

recondite [ri'kɔndait] *a.* 深奥的；难解的. abstruse

He read many ***recondite*** books in order to obtain the material for his scholarly statement.

他为了获取他的学术报告用的材料，读了许多深奥难解的书。

reconnaissance [ˌri'kɔnisəns] *n.* 侦察

Cezanne's delicate watercolor sketches often served as a ***reconnaissance*** of a subject, a way of gathering fuller knowledge before the artist's final engagement of the subject in an oil painting.

塞尚精致的水彩素描常被用作对某一主题的草测，是一个艺术家最终进入油彩主题之前取得更全面的知识的一种方式。

reconnoiter [ˌrekə'nɔitə] *v.* 侦察

Before deciding on the place of construction, a team of engineers ***reconnoitered*** the field.

在决定建造地点前，一队工程师勘测了这块地。

recount [ri'kaunt] *v.* 描述，叙述

recoup [ri'kuːp] *v.* 重获；补偿. retrieve

He ***recouped*** his extravagance at the racecourse by embezzling funds from his bank.

他补回了他在赛马上挥霍掉的盗用的银行款项。

recreant ['rekriənt] *n.* 懦夫；叛徒. apostate

The religious people ostracized the ***recreant*** who had abandoned their faith.

那群教徒逐放了那个放弃他们信仰的懦夫。

比较记忆：miscreant（坏蛋）

recriminate [ri'krimineit] *v.* 反责；反（控）诉

re (against) + crimin (crime) + ate → 反告别人有罪

比较记忆：discriminate（辨别），incriminate（牵连）

188

recrudesce [ri'kru:'des] *v.* (病)复发

re (again) + crude + esce (begin) → 复发

recruit [ri'kru:t] *n.* 新兵；新成员； *v.* 征募

recruit：veteran = rookie：professional

rectitude ['rektitju:d] *n.* 诚实，正直. uprightness

He was renowned for his *rectitude* and integrity.

他以其诚实正直闻名。

比较记忆：rectify（改正，调正）

recumbent [ri'kʌmbənt] *a.* 侧卧的；休息的. supine

比较记忆：incumbent（任职者）

recuperate [ri'kju:pəreit] *v.* 恢复（健康），复原. regain

The doctors were worried because the patient did not *recuperate* as rapidly as they had expected.

医生们有些担忧,因为病人没有他们预期中恢复得那么快。

recurrent [ri'kʌrənt] *a.* 重现的；周期性发生的. intermittent

These *recurrent* attacks disturbed us and we consulted a physician.

这种周期性的发作令我们苦恼,我们就此咨询了医生。

recusant ['rekjuzənt] *a.* 不服从权威的； *n.* 不服从权威的人

People who refused to belong to the Church of England were once called *"recusants"*.

那些拒绝归从英国圣公会的人曾一度被称为不服从权威的人。

redeem [ri'di:m] *v.* 赎罪，赎回；实践(诺言). ↔ pawn

He willed to pay any price to *redeem* his kidnapped daughter.

他愿意付出任何代价赎回他被绑架的女儿。

比较记忆：deem（相信）

redemption [ri'dempʃən] *n.* 赎罪

比较记忆：preempt（优先取得），peremptory（断然的）

redolent ['redələnt] *a.* 芬芳的，芳香的. fragrant

The air is ***redolent*** of rape flowers.

空气中有油菜花的芬芳。

比较记忆：indolent（懒惰的）

redoubtable [ri'dautəbl] *a.* 可敬畏的

The neighboring countries dare not offend the Russians because they could be ***redoubtable*** foes.

邻国不敢冒犯俄罗斯，因为他们是可敬畏的敌手。

redound [ri'daund] *v.* 促进；增加. aggrandize

Car safety was ***redounded*** by the addition of seat belts and collapsible steering columns.

汽车的安全性由于有了座椅安全带和可折叠操纵杆而大大增加了。

redress [ri'dres] *v.* 改正. remedy, rectify

比较记忆：dress（整理）

redundancy [ri'dʌndənsi] *n.* 过多；冗长

redundant [ri'dʌndənt] *a.* 累赘的. superfluous

Your composition is ***redundant***；you can easily reduce its length.

你的作文实在啰嗦了，明显地可以删短。

reedy ['ri:di] *a.* 尖声的；细长的. slender；frail

He awakened by the ***reedy*** sound of the chickens.

他被小鸡尖细的叫声惊醒了。

reef [ri:f] *n.* 礁；   *v.* 收缩；缩(帆). curtail

reek [ri:k] *n.* 浓烈的臭味；   *v.* 发臭气. stink

The room ***reeked*** with stale tobacco smoke.

屋里弥漫着陈烟草味。

refection [ri'fekʃən] *n.* 点心；便餐；恢复体力. refreshment

In our anxiety to reach our destination as rapidly as possible，we stopped on the road for only a slight ***refection***.

我们迫切想尽快抵达目的地，路上只停留一下吃了点东西。

refectory [ri'fektəri] *n.* 餐厅

> In this huge **refectory**, we can feed the entire student body at one sitting.
>
> 这个大餐厅可容纳所有学生同时就餐。

refinement [ri'fainmənt] *n.* 提取；文雅. cultivation

> 比较记忆：refined（高雅的）

reflect [ri'flekt] *v.* 反射；仔细考虑. contemplate

> The book **reflected** the author's own thoughts on the matter.
>
> 这本书反映了作者对这一问题的个人观点。

reflective [ri'flektiv] *a.* 深思熟虑的. pensive

refractory [ri'fræktəri] *a.* 难驾驭的；(病)难治的. stubborn

> Being **refractory**, the child was not permitted to have his supper.
>
> 因为不听话，不让这个孩子吃晚饭了。

refrain [ri'frein] *n.* 迭句； *v.* 抑制，避免. abstain

> Wherever he heard a song with a lively chorus, Sol could never retrain from joining in on the **refrain**.
>
> 不管在哪儿听到有活泼的合唱歌声，索尔都要情不自禁地加入进去，跟着合唱。

refulgent [ri'fʌldʒənt] *a.* 辉煌的，灿烂的. fulgurant

> We admired the **refulgent** moon and watched it for a while.
>
> 我们惊羡于月亮的灿烂，看了好大一会儿。

refund ['ri:fʌnd] *v.* 归还；偿还(债务)

> If these shoes did not wear well, the shop will **refund** your money.
>
> 这些鞋子若穿着不合适，商店会退还给你钱的。

refurbish ['ri:'fə:biʃ] *v.* 刷新. renovate，furbish

> The flood left a deposit of mud on everything; it was

necessary to *refurbish* our belongings.

洪水退去，所有东西上都留有淤泥，我们必须刷洗一下。

regal ['ri:gəl] *a.* 帝王的；华丽的

His status requires that he act in a *regal* manner.

他的身份要求他有帝王般的举止。

比较记忆：regale（款待），gale（盛会）

regale [ri'geil] *v.* 款待；使喜悦

John *regaled* us with tales of his adventures in Africa.

约翰用讲他在非洲的历险故事来款待我们。

regatta [ri'gætə] *n.* 划船比赛；赛船会

Many boating enthusiasts followed the *regatta* in their own yachts.

许多热心于赛船的人，驾着自己的游艇参加赛船会。

regenerate [ri'dʒenəreit] *v.* 改过自新

regent ['ri:dʒənt] *n.* 摄政者（代国王统治者）

regicide ['redʒisaid] *n.* 弑君者；弑君

The beheading of many Queen of Scots was an act of *regicide*.

杀苏格兰女王的头是弑君行为。

regime [rei'ʒi:m] *n.* 政权；社会制度

When a Frenchman mentions the Old *Regime*, he refers to the government existing before the revolution.

当一个法国人提及古老的政体时，他指的是大革命前的政府存在形式。

regimen ['redʒimən] *n.* 养生法

I doubt whether the results warrant our living under such a strict *regimen*.

我怀疑在这种严格的养生办法下，其结果是否真的可以保证我们的生命（长寿）。

regiment ['redʒimənt] *v.* 管辖

regimentation [ˌredʒimən'teiʃən] *n.* 管辖

192

A war, even of fighting for individual liberty and democratic rights, usually requires that these principles be suspended, for they are incompatible with the *regimentation* and discipline necessary for military efficiency.

即使为一个自由或民主权利而进行的战争，通常也要求这些信条推后实现，因为它们同必要的军事效果的严格控制互不相容。

Unit Thirty

regressive [ri'gresiv] *a.* 退步的；退化的. retrograde

  re（back）+ gress（go）+ ive → 退步的

regurgitate [ri(ː)'gəːdʒiteit] *v.* 反胃；呕吐. vomit, disgorge

  Many type of animals, such as bull, ***regurgitate*** their food.

  许多像牛这样的动物都反刍食物。

rehabilitate [ˌriːhə'biliteit] *v.* 修复；恢复. ↔ relapse

  比较记忆：habilitate（穿衣；取得资格），habiliments（衣服；设备）

rehash ['riː'hæʃ] *v.* 改头换面地重复

  比较记忆：hash（切碎；谈论）

reimburse [riːim'bəːs] *v.* 偿还. refund

  比较记忆：purse（钱包）

reincarnate [riː'inkɑːneit] *v.* 使转世化身

  比较记忆：incarnate（化身）

reinforce [ˌriːin'fɔːs] *v.* 加强；增援

  比较记忆：enforce（实施；强制）

reinstate [ˌriːin'steit] *v.* 恢复（原职）

reiterate [riː'itəreit] *v.* 重申. iterate

reiteration [riːˌitə'reiʃən] *n.* 反复；重申

  The playwright was known not for his original ideas but for his ***reiteration*** of ideas that had been propounded by others.

  剧作家不是以他的原创思想，而是他对其他作家已提出的问题的重申而著名。

rejoin [ri'dʒɔin] *v.* 回答，答辩

比较记忆：enjoin（吩咐）

rejoinder [ri'dʒɔində] *n.* 回答

When someone has been rude to me, I find it particularly satisfying to come up with a quick *rejoinder*.

有人粗暴对待我时,我发觉用一个简短的回答效果特别令人满意。

rejuvenate [ri'dʒuːvineit] *v.* 返老还童

比较记忆：juvenile（年青的）

relapse [ri'læps] *v.* 旧病复发；恶化

比较记忆：lapse（过失）

relegate ['religeit] *v.* 降级，贬谪

比较记忆：delegate（代表）

relent [ri'lent] *v.* 怜悯；减弱. slacken

When her stern father would not *relent* and allow her to marry Robert Browning, Elizabeth Barrett eloped with her suitor.

当伊丽莎白·巴雷特严厉的父亲不怜悯她,不允许她同罗伯特·布朗宁结婚时,她同她的求婚者私奔了。

relic ['relik] *n.* 遗物；遗迹. site

In the attic, we found *relics* of Grandmother's childhood.

在阁楼里,我们找到老祖母孩提时代遗留下来的物品。

relict ['relikt] *n.* 残存物；寡妇

relief [ri'liːf] *n.* 浮雕

参考：cameo（浮雕宝石）

relinquish [ri'liŋkwiʃ] *v.* 放弃；撤回. forgo

I will *relinquish* my claims to this property if you promise to retain my employees.

你要是保证留用我的雇员,我可以放弃对这一领地的拥有权。

remainder [ri'meində] *n.* 剩余物

　　　　比较记忆：remains（遗址；遗体）

reminisce [ˌremi'nis] *v.* 回忆，怀旧地说（或写）. recall

reminiscences [ˌremi'nisns] *n.* 回忆录

　　　　Her *reminiscences* of her experiences are so fascinating
　　　　that she ought to write a book.

　　　　她有关自己经历的回忆录太吸引人了，该写成本书。

remiss [ri'mis] *a.* 疏忽的，粗心的. negligent

　　　　He was accused of being *remiss* in his duty when the
　　　　prisoner escaped.

　　　　当狱犯逃跑了时，他受到玩乎职守的指责。

remission [ri'miʃən] *n.* 减轻；宽恕；赦免. exemption

　　　　Though Senator Tsongas had been treated for cancer,
　　　　his symptoms were in *remission*, and he was considered
　　　　fit to handle the strains of a Presidential race.

　　　　议员聪格斯的癌证得到了治疗，症状有所减轻，（医生）认为他的
　　　　身体情况可以应付竞选总统的紧张。

remit [ri'mit] *v.* 免除；汇款. exculpate

　　　　The cold wave finally *remitted* its icy grip on the city.

　　　　寒流最终撤回了它打击这个城市的冰凉的铁拳。

remittance [ri'mitəns] *n.* 汇款

　　　　Only after he had sent his *remittance* did the mail-order
　　　　house forward the suit he had ordered.

　　　　只有在他寄出汇款后，函购公司才寄出他订的西装。

remittee [riˌmi'tiː] *n.* 收款人

remittent [ri''mitənt] *a.* （病）间歇性的，忽好忽坏的

remnant ['remnənt] *n.* 残余物；零头布料

　　　　I suggest that you wait until the store places the *rem-*
　　　　nants of these goods on sale.

　　　　我建议你等到商店甩卖这些零布头时（再买）。

remonstrance [ri'mɔnstrəns] *n.* 抗议；规劝

The parents' *remonstrance* against the teacher's treatment was over-whelming.

家长对教师(对待孩子的)办法的抗议势不可挡。

比较记忆：monster（怪物）

remonstrate [ri'mɔnstreit] *v.* 抗议，规劝

remorse [ri'mɔ:s] *v.* 懊悔. repent

The murderer felt no *remorse* for his crime.

杀人犯对他的罪行不思改悔。

remunerate [ri'mju:nəreit] *v.* 报酬，补偿. reimburse

remuneration [ri,mju:nə'reiʃən] *n.* 报酬，补偿

Are you receiving adequate *remuneration* for the work you are doing?

你做的工作得到了足够的报偿吗？

renaissance [rə'neisəns] *n.* 复兴；新生

re (again) + naiss (born) + ance → 新生

renal ['ri:nəl] *a.* 肾脏的

参考：gastric（胃的），kidney（肾脏）

renascent [ri'næsnt] *a.* 新生的. nascent

rend [rɛnd] *v.* 撕碎；割裂. rip

In his grief, he tried to *rend* his garments.

他悲痛地猛扯他的袍子。

rendering ['rendəriŋ] *n.* 演出；翻译

比较记忆：render（给与）

rendezvous ['rɔndivu:] *n.* 约会；约会地点

The two fleets met at the *rendezvous* at the appointed time.

两支舰队在约定时间约定地点会聚了。

renegade ['renigeid] *n.* 背教者，叛徒. apostate

Because he refused to support his fellow members in

their drive, he was shunned as a *renegade*.

因为他拒绝支持他同伴的努力,被当成一个叛徒一样地回避着。

renege [re'niɡ] *v.* 背信,违约. transgress

re (back) + neɡe (deny) → 反过来不承认 → 背信

参考:negate(否定)

renounce [ri'nauns] *v.* 放弃,抛弃. abandon

比较记忆:denounce(指责),enounce(发音,表达)

renown [ri'naun] *n.* 名望,声誉. reputation

Ladies and gentlemen, I am very privileged to present to you the *renowned* star of stage and screen, John Wayne.

女士们,先生们,我特别荣幸地向你们推出著名影视名星约翰·韦恩。

rent [rent] *n.* 裂缝;(意见)分歧. breach

The conflict over abortion threatens to spilt our nation creating a *rent* in the social fabric that it will be difficult to mend.

威胁着我们国家的对堕胎这一问题的冲突,在社会结构中造成了一条无法弥补的裂痕。

renunciation [ri͵nʌnsi'eiʃən] *n.* 放弃,抛弃. abnegation

Do you sign this *renunciation* of your right to sue until you have consulted a lawyer?

你是不是征询你律师的意见后,再签署这项放弃起诉权的协议?

renvoi [ren'vwɑː] *n.* 驱逐(外交官)出境. oust

reparable ['repərəbl] *a.* 能补救的,可挽回的. ↔ irreparable

Fortunately, the damages we suffered in the accident were *reparable* and our car looks brand new.

幸运地是,车祸中遭受的损坏可以补救,我们的车看上去又像是崭新的了。

repartee [͵repɑː'tiː] *n.* 巧妙的回答

He was famous for his witty *repartee* and his sarcasm.

他以其机智灵活的回答及其挖苦话而闻名。

repast [ri'pɑːst] *n.* 饮食

On the eve of Chinese Lunar New Year, we usually have a rich *repast*.

在除夕夜,我们通常要吃一顿丰盛的饭。

repatriate [riː'pætrieit] *v.* (自异国)遣返

re (back) + patr (country) + iate → 遣返回国

repellent [ri'pelənt] *a.* 令人厌恶的. foul

比较记忆:repel (击退;反感)

repentance [ri'pentəns] *n.* 悔恨. penitence

来自:repent (后悔)

repercussion [ˌriːpə(ː)'kʌʃən] *n.* 反应;深远影响. reverberation

比较记忆:percussion (震动)

repertoire ['repətwɑː] *n.* (剧团)保留剧目

The opera company decided to include Madame Butterfly in its *repertoire* for the following season.

歌剧团决定把《蝴蝶夫人》包括进下一演出季节的保留剧目。

repine [ri'pain] *v.* 不满;抱怨. mope

There is no sense *repining* over the work you have left undone.

抱怨你剩下没做完的工作没有意义。

比较记忆:pine (憔悴), rapine (劫掠)

replenish [ri'pleniʃ] *v.* 补充;再装满

The end of rationing enabled us to *replenish* our supply of canned food.

配给制结束了,我们用罐头食品补充了我们的给养。

replete [ri'pliːt] *a.* 饱满的;塞满的. fraught

比较记忆:expletive (多余的), deplete (倒空)

replica ['replikə] *n.* 复制品

Are you going to hang this *replica* of the Declaration of

Independence in the classroom or in the auditorium?

你要把这个《独立宣言》的复制品挂在教室里还是挂在礼堂里?

replicate ['replikeit] *v.* 重复；复制

To the chagrin of the scientists they were unable to *replicate* the results of their controversial experiment.

科学家们的苦恼是他们无法重现他们自相矛盾的实验结果。

reportorial [ˌrepə'tɔːriəl] *a.* 报告文学的；记者的. ↔ imaginative

参考：correspondent（记者）

repose [ri'pəuz] *v.* 躺着休息；安置. ensconce

After lunch, father *reposed* in the hammock.

午饭后,父亲躺在吊床上歇息。

reposeful [ri'pəuzful] *a.* 从容的；镇静的. self-possessed

repository [ri'pɔzitəri] *n.* 贮藏室，仓库. depot

Libraries are *repositories* of the world's best thoughts.

图书馆是保存世界上最优秀的思想的宝库。

reprehend [ˌrepri'hend] *v.* 谴责，责难. censure

She gently *reprehended* her husband for having forgotten their wedding anniversary.

她温柔地责备她丈夫忘了结婚纪念日。

比较记忆：comprehend（综合，理解）

reprieve [ri'priːv] *v.* 缓刑；暂减

During the twenty-four-hour *reprieve*, the lawyers sought to make the stay of execution permanent.

在二十四小时的缓刑期内,律师们寻求办法使执行延缓变成永久性的。

reprimand ['reprimɑːnd] *v.* 训诫，严厉谴责. castigate

I am afraid that my parents will *reprimand* me when I show them my report card.

我担心给父母看我的报告单时,他们会惩罚我的。

reprisal [ri'praizəl] *n.* （政治或军事的）报复

I am confident that we are ready for any *reprisals* the enemy may undertake.

我相信我们可以对付敌人可能发动的任何报复性（行动）。

reprobate ['reprɔbeit] *a*. & *n*. 堕落的(人)；   *v*. 谴责. degenerate

The judge sharply *reprobated* the witness for being evasive and unco-operative.

法官尖锐地谴责了证人的逃避责任及不合作。

比较记忆：approbation（赞扬）

reptilian ['reptiliən] *a*. (像)爬行动物的，卑下的. menial

来自：reptile（爬行动物）

repudiate [ri'pju:dieit] *v*. 拒绝；抛弃. disavow

He announced that he would *repudiate* all debts incurred by his wife.

他宣布他拒绝(偿付)她妻子招致的一切债务。

repugnant [ri'pʌgnənt] *a*. 令人厌恶的. obnoxious

re (against) + pugn (fight) + ant → 反过去打 → 令人厌恶的

比较记忆：pugnacious（好打斗的）

repulse [ri'pʌls] *v*. & *n*. 拒绝；击退. reject

re (back) + pulse (pull) → 击退

比较记忆：compulsion（强迫），impulse（推动），expulse（放逐），pulse（跳动）

repulsive [ri'pʌlsiv] *a*. 令人厌恶的；排斥的. disgusting

reputable ['repjutəbl] *a*. 名誉好的，有声望的. notable

He is a man of *reputable* character.

他是个好名声的人。

requiem ['rekwiem] *n*. 安灵弥撒；挽歌

They played Mozart's *Requiem* at the funeral.

他们在葬礼上演奏莫扎特的《安魂曲》。

requisition [ˌrekwi'ziʃən] *n.* 要求，请求

　　　　比较记忆：requisite（必需品，必要的）

requital [ri'kwaitl] *n.* 酬劳，报答

requite [ri'kwait] *v.* 酬答；报答

　　　　The wretch *requited* his benefactors by betraying them.

　　　　这个卑鄙小人用背叛来报答他的恩人。

rescind [ri'sind] *v.* 废除；取消. abolish

　　　　re (back) + scind (cut) → 砍掉 → 废除

rescript ['riːskript] *n.* 法令；重抄

　　　　re + script (write) → 重抄

reserved [ri'zəːvd] *a.* 说话不多的. ↔ blatant

reservist [ri'zəːvist] *n.* 后备役军人

　　　　参考：regular（常备兵），volunteer（志愿兵）

reservoir ['rezəwɑː] *n.* 水库，蓄水池

reshuffle ['riː'ʃʌfl] *v.* 重新洗牌；改组

　　　　比较记忆：shuffle（洗牌）

residue ['rezidjuː] *n.* 剩余（财产）

　　　　比较记忆：residual（残余的）

resign [ri'zain] *v.* 听从；辞职. quit

　　　　You must *resign* yourself to the fact that you'll never be
　　　　rich or famous.

　　　　事实就是你永远也发不了财，出不了名，因而你必须顺应这一现
　　　　实。

resigned [ri'zaind] *a.* 屈从的，顺从的

　　　　Bob Cratchit was too *resigned* to his downtrodden exis-
　　　　tence to protest when Scrooge bullied him.

　　　　鲍勃·克拉特切特太温顺了，斯克鲁奇欺负他时，在那种被蹂躏
　　　　的境遇中，他都不反抗。

resilience [ri'ziliəns] *n.* 弹性；弹回

　　　　来自：resile（弹回，恢复活力）

resonance ['rezənəns] *n.* 回声；共鸣. ↔ dissonance

resound [ri'zaund] *v.* 回荡；引起回响. sensation

Our helmsman's name, Deng Xiaopin, ***resounds*** in the pages of history.

我们伟大舵手的名字——邓小平在历史的篇章中回荡。

resourceful [ri'sɔːsful] *a.* 机智的. ready

The ***resourceful*** castaway will make everything he needs from the materials he can find.

机智的船上遇难幸存下来的人,用他找得到的材料制作了他所需要的所有东西。

来自：resource（机智）

respective [ris'pektiv] *a.* 分别的；各自的

比较记忆：respecting（关于）

respire [ris'paiə] *v.* 呼吸

re (again) + spire (breathe) → 呼吸

参考：aspire（渴望）

respite ['respait] *n.* 暂息(时间)；中止. ↔ exertion

The judge granted the condemned man a ***respite*** to enable his attorneys to file an appeal.

法官准予被告中间休息,以使他的律师可以做好提出上诉(的准备)。

resplendent [ris'plendənt] *a.* 华丽的, 辉煌的. refulgent

The toreador wore a ***resplendent*** costume called a suit of fights.

斗牛士穿一种华丽的叫作战斗制服的服装。

respondent [ris'pɔndənt] *n.* 被告. ↔ plaintiff

比较记忆：corespondent（记者）

responsive [ris'pɔnsiv] *a.* 敏感的, 反应快的

restitute ['restitjuːt] *v.* & *n.* 归还；赔偿. compensate

比较记忆：destitute（贫穷的）

restive ['restiv] *a.* 难驾驭的；浮躁的. refractory；nervous

We must quiet the *restive* animals.

我们得平息这些浮躁的动物。

restorative [ris'tɔrətiv] *a.* 恢复健康的，恢复的

resumption [ri'zʌmpʃən] *n.* 重新开始

During the summer break，Don had not realized how much he missed university life；at the *resumption* of classes，however，he felt marked excitement and pleasure.

在暑假期间，马克并没有意识到他有多么怀念大学生活；然而新学期开始的时候，他明显地感到兴奋愉快。

来自：resume（恢复）

resurgent [ri'sədʒənt] *a.* 恢复活力的；复活的

re（again）+ surg（surge）+ ent → 浪潮再起 → 复兴的

resurrect [ˌrezə'rekt] *v.* 使复活；恢复

The paramedic *resurrected* the man who was overcome by gas.

医务人员救活了那个煤气中毒的人。

resuscitate [ri'sʌsiteit] *v.* （使）复活；（使）苏醒

The lifeguard tried to *resuscitate* the drowned child by applying artificial respiration.

卫兵试图给溺水的孩子做人工呼吸来救活他。

retail ['ri:teil] *v.* 零售

This dress *retails* for ＄100 but the manufacturer only charged the store ＄25 for it.

这条裙子的零售价是 100 美元,但生产商只要商店 25 美元。

比较记忆：entail（需要）

retaliate [ri'tælieit] *v.* 报复，反击。avenge

When one of their soldiers was killed，the occupation

army *retaliated* by killing hostages.

当他们的一个士兵被杀时,占领军以杀死人质加以报复。

retaliatory [ri'tæliətəri] *a*. 报复性的

The repudiation of Puritanism in seventeenth century England expressed itself not only in *retaliatory* laws to restrict Puritans, but also in a general attitude of contempt for Puritan.

在 17 世纪的英国,对清教主义的报复不仅体现在禁止清教徒的报复性法律条文的规定,还体现在对清教徒的一种总体上蔑视的态度中。

retarded [ri'tɑːdid] *a*. 迟钝的

He is in such limited ability that he is *retarded* to understand the simplest direction.

他的能力太差了,就是听懂最简单的说明也很迟钝。

retention [ri'tenʃən] *n*. 保留,保持

retentive [ri'tentiv] *a*. 记忆力强的

The pupil did not need to spend much time in study as he had a *retentive* mind.

这个小学生记忆力特别好,因此不用在学习上花费很多时间。

reticent ['retisənt] *a*. 沉默不语的. taciturn

Hughes preferred *reticent* employees to loquacious ones, nothing that the formers' dislike of idle chatter might ensure their discretion about his affairs.

休斯喜欢沉默不语的雇员,不喜欢话多的,这种人没有什么他们不喜欢拿来闲聊的,这很难保证他们对他事务的谨慎性。

reticulation [ri͵tikju'leiʃən] *n*. 网纹;网状

retinue ['retinjuː] *n*. 侍从;随员

The queen's *retinue* followed her down the aisle.

王后的随从跟着她走下过廊。

retiring [ri'taiəriŋ] *a*. 孤独的,不爱社交的. withdrawn

Given Susan's *retiring* personality, no one expected her

to take up public speaking; surprisingly enough, she became a star of the school debate team.

由于苏珊不爱社交的性格,没人认为她会从事公共讲演;然而令人吃惊的是,她居然成了校辩论队里的明星。

retrace [ri'treis] *v.* 回顾,回想

re (back) + trace → 找回踪迹 → 回顾

retract [ri'trækt] *v.* 缩回;收回(声明). ↔ allege

re (back) + tract (draw) → 缩回

retreat [ri'tri:t] *v.* 撤退;隐居. seclude

retrench [ritrentʃ] *v.* 节省;削减. abate

retribution [ˌretri'bju:ʃən] *n.* 报应

re (against) + tribut (render) + ion → 反过来给予 → 报应

比较记忆:contribution (贡献),attribute (把…归因于)

retrieve [ri'tri:v] *v.* 取回,纠正(错误)

re (again) + trieve (find) → 寻回

retriever [ri'tri:və] *n.* 猎犬. pointer, hound

When I hunted, I brought my *retriever* to track the quarry.

我打猎时,带着猎犬追踪猎物。

retroactive [ˌretrəu'æktiv] *a.* 有追溯效力的

Because the law was *retroactive* to the first of the year, we found he was eligible for the pension.

因为这项法律可追溯到今年初(开始生效),我们发现他符合发给补助金的条件。

retrograde ['retrəugreid] *a.* 后退的; *v.* 倒退

retro (back) + grade (go) → 后退

retrogress ['retrəugres] *v.* 退化

retro (back) + gress (go) → 倒退

retrospect ['retrəuspekt] *v.* 反顾，回顾. ↔ anticipate

retro (back) + spect (look) → 回顾

Students of the Great Crash of 1929 have never understood why even the most informed observers did not recognize and heed the prior economic danger signals that in ***retrospect*** seem so apparent.

学生们在研究 1929 年的大崩溃时，怎么也理解不了为什么即使最为见多识广的观察家在当时也没有留意到、认识清经济危机的前兆信号，而今回顾起来，这些信号是那么地显而易见。

revamp ['riː'væmp] *v.* 翻新，修改. revise

We have decided to ***revamp*** the entire nation's foreign policy.

我们决定修改整个国家的外交政策。

revelation [ˌrevi'leiʃən] *n.* 显示；被揭示的真相

sibyl : revelation = seamstress : gown

revelry ['revlri] *n.* 狂欢. spree

New Year's Eve is a night of ***revelry***.

除夕之夜是狂欢之夜。

来自；revel（陶醉，狂欢）

revenant ['revinənt] *n.* 归来之人

revenue ['revinjuː] *n.* 收入；国家税收

State universities get most of their ***revenue*** from taxes.

州立大学的收入主要来源于税收。

reverberate [ri'vəːbəreit] *v.* 回响，反响

re (back) + verber (lash) + ate → 反响

比较记忆：verberate（振动）

revere [ri'viə] *v.* 崇敬，敬畏. ↔ profane

One of the Ten Commandments enjoys us to ***revere*** our parents.

《十诫》中的一条要我们孝敬父母。

reverend ['revərənd] *a.* 值得尊敬的； *n.* 牧师

reverent ['revərənt] *a.* 恭敬的；虔诚的. devout

His *reverent* attitude was appropriate in such question.

他在这样一个问题上的虔诚的态度很恰当。

reverie ['revəri] *n.* 幻想，梦幻曲

Did you have *reveries* about what you'd do when you grew up?

你对长大后做什么有什么梦想吗？

revile [ri'vail] *v.* 辱骂. abuse

比较记忆：vile（卑鄙的，恶的）

revitalize [riː'vaitəlaiz] *v.* 使复活

比较记忆：vitality（生命力，活力）

revocation [ˌrevə'keiʃən] *n.* 取消. invalidation

revoke [ri'vəuk] *v.* 废除，取消. repeal, annul

The authorities will *revoke* your license if you get another speeding ticket.

要是你再得一张超速罚款单的话,有关当局会吊销你的执照的。

revolt [ri'vəult] *v.* 叛乱；反感. mutiny; nauseate

When an oppressed group *revolts* against a society, one must look for the underlying forces that led to the group's alienation from that society.

一个被压迫的群体反抗一个社会时,我们必须寻找导致这一群体背离那一社会的深层的力量。

revolting [ri'vəultiŋ] *a.* 令人作呕的. nauseating

It is impossible to be polite when confronted with his *revolting* impertinence.

面对他令人作呕的傲慢,没法子礼貌。

rhapsody ['repsədi] *n.* 狂想曲；叙事诗；狂言

rhetoric ['retərik] *n.* 修辞学；浮夸语言；雄辩（术）

Rhetoric often seems to triumph over reason in a heated

debate, with both sides engaging in hyperbole.

在一场激烈的辩论中，双方都很夸张，看起来往往是演讲术战胜了推理。

rhinal ['rainəl] *a.* 鼻的. nasal

参考：ventral（腹部的），pectoral（胸部的）

rhinestone ['rainstəun] *n.* 莱茵石

rhubarb ['ru:bɑ:b] *n.* （植物）大黄；　*v.* 喧闹. racket

参考：barley（大麦），beet（甜菜）

rhythmic ['riðəmik] *a.* 有节奏的. ↔ arrhythmic

rib [rib] *n.* 肋骨；伞骨

参考：clavicle（锁骨），skull（颅骨），spine（脊柱）

ribald ['ribəld] *a.* 下流的，粗鄙的. salacious

He sang a *ribald* song that offended many of the more prudish listeners.

他唱了首下流歌曲，惹恼了许多假正经的人。

rickety ['rikiti] *a.* 摇摇晃晃的，不牢固的. wobbly

riddance ['ridəns] *n.* 清除

来自：rid（扫除）

riddle ['ridl] *n.* 谜；筛. enigma；sieve

rider ['raidə] *n.* 补充条款；附录；附加条款

Senator Foghorn said he would support Senator Filibuster's tax reform bill only if Filibuster agreed to add an antipollution *rider* to the bill.

福格霍恩议员说，如果菲利巴斯特议员同意在税收改革提案中加上反对污染的附加条款，就支持他（这一提案）。

ridge [ridʒ] *n.* 脊（如屋脊，山脊等），隆起部

He walked along the mountain *ridge*.

他沿着山脊走。

rife [raif] *a.* 流行的，普遍的. prevalent

In the face of the many rumors of scandal, which are

rife at the moment, it is best to remain silent.

面对当前四处流传的许多有关丑闻的传言,最好是保持沉默。

rifle ['raifl] *n.* 步枪;   *v.* 洗劫. loot

He *rifled* other writers and appropriated whole passages.

他把其他作者的文章整段整段地挪为己用。

rift [rift] *n.* 裂缝,缝隙. cleft

The plane was lost in the stormy sky until the pilot saw the city through a *rift* in the clouds.

飞机在暴雨的天空迷失了方向,直到飞行员从云缝间看见了这座城市。

rig [rig] *v.* 舞弊;装配;操纵

"Victory" has nearly finished *rigging* and will sail tomorrow.

"胜利号"差不多装配好了,明天就要出航。

rigmarole ['rigmərəul] *n.* 冗长的废话

When too many phrases interrupt the normal flow from subject to verb, a *rigmarole* can result.

当正常的主谓语间连接短语过多时,其结果可能就是废话连篇。

rigorous ['rigərəs] *a.* 严厉的;(气侯)严酷的. rigid

In contrast to physicists who base their procedures on scientific theory, he modeled his procedure on strict observation; so despite the fact that his method was less *rigorous*, his results were factually sound.

同物理学家以科学理论为基础的做法不同的是,他的做法建立在严格的观察的模式上,因此尽管他的方法不那么严格,但事实上结果却很有道理。

rile [rail] *v.* 恼怒. exasperate

Red had a hair-trigger temper; he was an easy man to *rile*.

雷德的脾气一触即发,很容易就会惹恼了他。

rill [ril] *n.* 小溪

rind [raind] *n.* 果(或蔬菜)皮

        rind : colon = apple : peel

ringlet ['riŋlit] *n.* 卷发

        ring (卷) + let (little) → 小卷发

riotous ['raiətəs] *a.* 暴乱的，放纵的. unruly, tempestuous

        来自：riot（暴乱）

rip [rip] *v.* 撕裂，撕破. slit

        The sail *ripped* under the force of the wind.

        风扯破了船帆。

risible ['rizibl] *a.* 可笑的，引人发笑的

        比较记忆：derisive（嘲笑的）

risque ['riːskei] *a.* 淫猥的，伤风败俗的. lewd

        Please do not tell your *risque* anecdotes at this party.

        在这个晚会上可别讲你那伤风败俗的轶事。

rite [rait] *n.* (宗教的)仪式. ↔ improvisation

        He died after receiving the *rites* of the church, the Holy

        Sacrament.

        他接受了教会的洗礼圣事仪式后死去了。

        liturgy : rite = lullaby : song

ritual ['ritjuəl] *n.* 仪式，习惯； *a.* 仪式的. ↔informal

        The Catholic Mass is a *ritual* practiced in countries all

        over the world.

        世界上许多国家举行天主教弥撒仪式。

ritzy ['ritsi] *a.* 豪华的；时髦的. posh

        The *ritzy* symphony ran on more than two hours and

        captivated all of us.

        优美的交响乐演奏了两个小时,迷住了我们所有的人。

rive [raiv] *v.* 裂开，撕开. slice；strew

riven ['rivən] *a.* 裂开的. ↔ intact

rivet [ˈrivit] *n.* 铆钉； *v.* 吸引(注意力)；系牢

Rivet yourself to the seat before takeoff.

起飞前，(用座椅安全带)把自己系牢在椅子上。

riveting [ˈrivitiŋ] *a.* 非常精彩的

The reviewer described Byatt's novel *Possession* as a **riveting** tale absorbed in the story, he had finished it in a single evening.

评论家把拜厄特的小说《财产》描述为一篇精彩的故事,他沉浸在故事里,一晚上一气读完了。

rivulet [ˈrivjulit] *n.* 小溪, 小河. brook, rill

rivu (= river) + let (little) → 小河

roan [rəun] *a.* 杂色的

You can distinguish this horse in a race because it is **roan** while all the others are bay or chestnut.

你在比赛中可以辩认出这匹马,因为只有它是杂色的,其他马都是栗色的。

robe [rəub] *n.* 长袍；礼服

参考：toga（官服）

robin [ˈrɔbin] *n.* 知更鸟

参考：parrot（鹦鹉）, magpie（喜鹊）

robust [rɔˈbʌst] *a.* 健壮的. stalwart

The candidate for the football team had a **robust** physique.

橄榄球队员的候选人体魄健壮。

rococo [rəˈkəukəu] *a.* 高度装饰的. baroque

At the present time, architects avoid **rococo** designs.

当前,建筑师回避装饰过多的设计。

rodent [ˈrəudənt] *n.* 啮齿类动物

Dental patterns often enable the taxonomist to distinguish members of one **rodent** species from those of another.

牙齿的模式常常可以让分类学家区分开几种不同的啮齿类动物的成员。

roe [rəu] *n.* 鱼卵. spawn

比较记忆：rue（后悔）

rogue [rəug] *n.* 无赖. knave

The *rogue* ruined her virtue and then refused to marry her.

那个无赖毁了她的名声，然后又拒绝娶她。

roguish ['rəugiʃ] *a.* 捣蛋的，无赖的

roil [rɔil] *v.* 搅浑；激怒

Be careful when you pour not to *roil* the wine; if you stir up the sediment you'll destroy the flavor.

倒葡萄酒时小心别搅浑了酒，要是把底上的沉淀物搅起来，味道就坏了。

roll call ['rəul kɔ:l] *n.* 点名

rollicking ['rɔlikiŋ] *a.* 欢乐的，愉快的. jaunty

He struggled to look *rollicking* and interesting in his yachting outfit.

他穿着驾快艇的衣服，尽力表现得愉快风趣。

rood [rud] *n.* 十字架. crucifix

" By the *rood*" used to be a strong oath.

"以十字架的名义"曾是十分强烈的誓言。

rookie ['ruki] *n.* 新兵；新球员

roost [ru:st] *v.* 栖息. perch

The ogre comes home to *roost* and ruins the life every day.

女妖每天回家来休息，毁了一天的生活。

比较记忆：rooster（公鸡）

roseate ['rəuziət] *a.* 愉快的；乐观的

I am afraid that you will have to alter your *roseate*

views in the light of the tragic news that had just arrived.

恐怕据刚刚得到的坏消息，你得变一变你乐观的看法了。

roster [ˈrəustə] *n.* 值勤表；花名册. rota

They print the *roster* of player in the season's program.

他们在赛季安排中印了选手(运动员)名册。

比较记忆：rooster（公鸡）

rostrum [ˈrɔstrəm] *n.* 演讲台

The crowd murmured angrily and indicated that they did not care to listen to the speaker who was approaching the *rostrum*.

人们愤怒地咕哝着，表明他们不喜欢听那个走向演讲台的讲演人的发言。

参考：pulpit（布道坛），altar（祭坛）

rotary [ˈrəutəri] *a.* 旋转的，转动的. gyral

比较记忆：rotate（旋转）

rote [rəut] *n.* 死记硬背

When he recited the passage by *rote*, he revealed that he was reproducing sounds without understanding their meaning.

他背诵死记硬背下来的那一段时，表明他根本不懂其意义，只是重复那声音。

参考：endorse（背书）

rotund [rəuˈtʌnd] *a.* （人）圆胖的；（声音）洪亮的. ↔ angular

rouge [ruːʒ] *n.* 胭脂 (cosmetic used to give a red color to checks)

roundabout [ˈraundəbaut] *a.* 绕道的；转弯抹角的

rout [raut] *n.* 大败，溃败. debacle

The reinforcements were able to *rout* the enemy.

增援部队大败敌人。

rove [rəuv] *v.* 流浪，漂泊

Always restless, he *roved* from one woman to another, never satisfied for long.

他很不安分，从一个女人的怀抱投向另一个女人的怀抱，从没有满足过多长时间。

row [rəu] *v.* 喧闹；划船

After the *rowing* of the city, he welcomed the tranquillity of the state park where he camped for two weeks.

经历够城市的喧嚣，他倒宁愿到宁静的州立公园里去露宿上两个星期。

Unit Thirty-One

rowdy ['raudi] *a.* 吵闹的；粗暴的. turbulent；fierce

The class fell into *rowdy* laughter over the professor's Freudian slip.

教授漫不经心说走了嘴，全班哄堂大笑。

royalty ['rɔiəlti] *n.* 皇室；版税（付给著作人的钱）

rubbery ['rʌbəri] *a.* 坚韧的

比较记忆：robbery（抢劫）

rubble ['rʌbl] *n.* （一堆）碎石. detritus

Ten years after World War II, some of the *rubble* left by enemy bombings could still be seen.

二战后十年仍可见敌人轰炸留下的碎石废墟。

rubicund ['ruːbikənd] *a.* （脸色）红润的

Her *rubicund* complexion was the result of an active outdoor life.

她红润的脸色得自于活跃的户外生活。

参考：ruby（红宝石）

ruck [rʌk] *n.* 皱褶. crease；普通群众；一群（人）

rucksack ['ruksæk] *n.* （旅行等的）背包

组合词：ruck + sack

rudder ['rʌdə] *n.* 船舵；指导原则

His ideas provided a *rudder* for the new company.

他的想法给这个新公司提供了一个指导。

ruddy ['rʌdi] *a.* （脸色）红润的，红色的

His *ruddy* features indicated that he had spent much time in the open.

他红润的脸色表明他长时间呆在户外。

rudimentary [ru:di'mentəri] *a*. 初步的；未充分发展的

She needs to complete her *rudimentary* education before entering college.

她上大学前,得先完成初等教育。

rudiments ['ru:dimənts] *n*. 基础知识,入门

比较记忆：erudite（深奥的）

rue [ru:] *n*. & *v*. 后悔. ↔ satisfaction

He'll *rue* his angry words when he sees what they have cost him.

当他看到得为他那愤怒的话语付出什么样的代价时,会后悔（说了那些话的）。

ruffian ['rʌfjən] *n*. 恶棍. rascal; *a*. 残暴的

The *ruffians* threw stones at the police.

恶棍冲警察扔石头。

ruffle ['rʌfl] *n*. 褶皱; *v*. 弄皱；激怒. rumple; agitate

ruffle : shirt = molding : cabinet

ruminant ['ru:minənt] *a*. （动物）反刍的；沉思的

We cannot afford to wait while you are *ruminant* upon these plans.

我们可等不起你(在这里)对着这些计划深思。

ruminate ['ru:mineit] *v*. 反刍；沉思. muse

We cannot afford to wait while you *ruminate* upon these plans.

我们可等不起你(在这里)对着这些计划反复思考。

ruminative ['ru:mineitiv] *a*. 沉思默想的；反复思考的

rummage ['rʌmidʒ] *n*. & *v*. 翻寻

When we *rummaged* through the trunks in the attic, we found many souvenirs of our childhood days.

我们在阁楼上翻木箱子时,找到许多我们童年时代的纪念品。

rumormonger ['ru:mə'mʌŋgə] *n*. 散布谣言者. talebearer

组合词：rumor ＋ monger

rumple ['rʌmpl] *v.* 弄皱；弄乱. tousle

The gale *rumpled* her frizzing hair.

大风吹乱了她的卷发。

rumpus ['rʌmpəs] *n.* 吵闹，喧闹. fracas

There was a terrible *rumpus* going on upstairs.

楼上有可怕的吵闹声。

runic ['rʌnik] *a.* 神秘的. arcane

rupture ['rʌptʃə] *n.* & *v.* 破裂，断裂. breach

The balloon *ruptured* into several pieces when it struck the pin.

气球一撞上针,爆碎成了几片。

比较记忆：erupt（喷发），corrupt（腐败的），rapture（狂喜）

ruse [ruːs] *n.* 诈术，谋略. machination

You will not be able to fool your friends with such an obvious *ruse*.

你这个显而易见的骗术怎么能骗得过你那些朋友。

rustic ['rʌstik] *a.* 乡村的，乡土的

The backwoodsman looked out of place in his *rustic* attire.

那个贵族穿了乡下人的衣服看上去很别扭,不对劲。

比较记忆：rusticity（乡村风味，笨拙）

rusticate ['rʌstikeit] *v.* 过乡间生活

I like city life so much that I can never understand how people can *rusticate* in the suburbs.

我太喜欢城市生活了,永远也理解不了怎么有人过得了那样的郊外生活。

rustler ['rʌslə] *n.* 偷牲口贼

rut [rʌt] *n.* 常规

218

Poet's chimerical stories are sometimes morbid and out of *rut*.

诗人那些爱空想的故事有时是病态地标新立异的。

saber['seibə] *n*. 军刀；（击剑用的）长剑

saber∶fence ＝ pencil∶mark

sable['sebl] *n*. 黑貂；黑色

参考：puma（美洲狮），hyena（土狼）

参考：vermilion（朱红色），tawny（茶褐色）

sabotage['sæbətɑːʒ] *n*. 颠覆活动

As a reprisal for the act of *sabotage*, the invaders wiped out an entire village.

作为对抵抗运动的报复，侵略者扫平了整个村庄。

比较记忆：saboteur（破坏者）

saccharin['sækərin] *n*. 糖精

saccharine ['sækərain] *a*. 过甜的；奉承的. ↔ crabbed

She tried to ingratiate herself, speaking sweetly and smiling a *saccharine* smile.

她甜甜地讲话，脸上挂着奉承的微笑，表现出一副讨好的样子。

sacerdotal [ˌsækə'dəutl] *a*. 圣职的；僧侣的. ↔ lay（凡俗的）

Regina took on the job of tending the church alter and the *sacerdotal* robes.

雷金娜担当照看教堂圣坛和整理僧衣的工作。

sachem ['seitʃəm] *n*. 大亨，首领. tycoon

sachet ['sæʃei] *n*. 小袋，小香袋

sack [sæk] *n*. 粗布袋； *v*. 掠夺. plunder, pillage

Armies *sacked* mansion after mansion along the route of their march.

军队行军途中，洗劫了 座又一座城堡。

sacrament ['sækrəmənt] *n*. 圣礼

sacrilege ['sækrilidʒ] *n*. 渎圣

The primitive tribe considered it a *sacrilege* to utter the sacred name.

原始部落把说出那些神圣的名字看成是一种亵渎神灵的行为。

sacrilegious [ˌsækriˈlidʒəs] *a.* 亵渎神圣的. blasphemous

sacri (sacred) + leg (steal) + ious → 窃取圣物

sacrosanct [ˈsækrəusæŋkt] *a.* 神圣不可侵犯的. inviolable

Her husband respected her *sacrosanct* faith and did not try to change her manner of living

她丈夫很尊重她那神圣不可侵犯的忠贞信仰,一点也不想改变她的生活方式。

参考:sanctity (圣洁,神圣)

saddle [ˈsædl] *n.* 鞍,马鞍

After we reached the railroad terminus, we continued our journey into the wilderness on *saddle* horses.

我们乘火车抵达终点后,换乘马匹在原野上继续我们的行程。

saddle : horse = mattress : bed

sadism [ˈseidizəm] *n.* 虐待狂

比较记忆:sadist (虐待狂者)

sadistic [ˈsædistik] *a.* 虐待狂的. ↔ masochistic

If we are to improve conditions in this prison, we must first get rid of the *sadistic* warden.

我们要想改变这所监狱的条件,首先就得消灭看守虐待(狱犯的现象)。

safari [səˈfɑːri] *n.* 狩猎旅行

sag [sæg] *v.* 下陷;下垂. droop

My spirits *sagged* when I saw the amount of work I had to do.

一看到我得干多少活儿,我的情绪开始下沉。

saga [ˈsɑːgə] *n.* 英雄传奇;长篇故事

This is a *saga* of the sea and the men who risk their

lives on it.

这是一个人们怎样在海上冒险的英雄故事。

sagacious [sə'geiʃəs] *a.* 精明的. shrewd

He is much too *sagacious* to be fooled by a trick like that.

他太精明了，那么个小把戏怎么会骗得了他呢。

sage [seidʒ] *a.* 智慧的；   *n.* 圣贤

Hearing tales of a mysterious Master of All Knowledge who lived in the hills of Tibet, Sandy was possessed with a burning desire to consult the legendary *sage*.

听到这个有关一位住在西藏的无所不知圣人的故事后，桑迪有种想去找这位圣贤讨教的疯狂欲望。

salacious [sə'leiʃəs] *a.* 好色的，淫荡的. lewd, lascivious

Disturbed by the *salacious* nature of the plays being presented, the Puritans closed the theaters in 1642.

为上演的色情剧所困扰，清教徒们 1642 年关闭了这家剧院。

salient ['seiljənt] *a.* 显著的. noticeable

Another *salient* function of the political institution is the protection of the society from external forces.

政治机构的另一显著功能是保护社会不受外部力量（干涉）。

saline ['seilain] *a.* 似盐的；盐的

She uses *saline* solution to cleanse her contact lenses.

她用（生理）盐水洗隐形眼镜。

参考：desalinization（脱盐）

saliva [sə'laivə] *n.* 唾液，口水

salivate ['sæliveit] *a.* 流涎

Pavlov's experiment in which he trains a dog to *salivate* on hearing a bell is a paradigm of the conditioned responded experiment in behavioral psychology.

巴甫洛夫训练一条狗一听到铃声就会流口水的实验是行为心理学有关条件反射实验的一个例子。

saliva : secretion = yam（地瓜）: tuber

sallow [ˈsæləu] *n.* 柳树； *a.* 灰黄色的. ↔ rubicund

We were disturbed by his *sallow* complexion，which was due to jaundice.

我们很讨厌他由于黄疸性肝炎而造成的灰黄色肤色。

sally [ˈsæli] *n.* & *v.* 突围；远足. excurse

We *sallied* to the beach，completing with hampers and flasks of cool drinks.

我们远足到海滨，以食物篮（里丰盛的食品）和细颈瓶中的饮料（结束了这次远足）。

salmon [ˈsæmən] *n.* 鲑

参考：herring（鲭鱼），carp（鲤鱼）

saloon [səˈluːn] *n.* 客舱；大厅

saltatory [ˈsæltətəri] *a.* 跃进的；舞蹈的

The male members of the ballet company were renowned for their *saltatory* exploits.

芭蕾舞团中的男演员们以其舞蹈成就而闻名。

salubrious [səˈljuːbriəs] *a.* 有益健康的. wholesome

Many people with hay fever move to more *salubrious* sections of the country during the months of August and September.

许多患有花粉热病的人，在八九月间都要到这个国家更有益于健康的地区去。

salutary [ˈsæljutəri] *a.* 有益的；有益健康的. nutritious

The punishment had a *salutary* effect on the boy，as he became a model student.

惩罚对这个小男孩产生了有益的影响，他成了个模范生。

salutation [ˌsæljuːˈteiʃən] *n.* 致敬，（信开头）称呼

salutatory [səˌluːtətəri] *a.* （在毕业典礼上）致欢迎词的. ↔ valedictory

salve [sælv] *n.* 药膏；   *v.* 拯救；缓和. salvage；assuage

        salve：unctuous = placebo：innocuous

salver ['sælvə] *n.* 盘

salvo ['sælvəu] *n.* (礼炮)齐鸣；(火炮)齐射

sampler ['saimplə] *n.* 刺绣样品；取样员

sanctimonious ['sæŋkti'məuniəs] *a.* 伪装虔诚的. hypocritical

        You do not have to be so ***sanctimonious*** to prove that
        you are devout.

        你用不着故作虔诚以证明你是虔诚的。

sanctimony ['sæŋktiməni] *n.* 伪装虔诚

sanction ['sæŋkʃən] *v.* 批准；制裁. endorse

        sanction：foster = recommend：laud

sanctuary ['sæŋktjuəri] *n.* 圣殿；避难所. asylum

        参考：chapel（小礼拜堂），inferno（地狱）

sanctum ['sæŋktəm] *n.* 圣所. shrine

sandal ['sændəl] *n.* 拖鞋；凉鞋

sandwich ['sændwitʃ, 'sænwidʒ] *n.* 三明治；   *v.* 挤入. ↔ milk

sane [sein] *a.* 神志清楚的. ↔ insane

        The killer was declared sufficiently ***sane*** to stand trial.

        杀人凶手被证实头脑十分清醒，完全可以承受审判。

sangfroid [sɔŋ'frwɑ:] *n.* 沉着. poise

        The captain's ***sangfroid*** helped to allay the fears of the
        passengers.

        船长的沉着有助于缓和乘客们的恐惧心理。

sanguinary ['sæŋgwinəri] *a.* 血淋淋的；血腥的. truculent

        The battle of two groups was unexpectedly ***sanguinary***
        with many casualties.

        两个集团之间的战斗打得出人意料的血腥，造成大批伤亡。

sanguine ['sæŋgwin] *a.* 充满希望的，乐观的. buoyant

        Since you have failed three of the last four tests, you

cannot afford to be *sanguine* about passing for the term.

鉴于四次考试中你有三次不及格,对于你通过这一学期(进入下一学期)实在是不容乐观的。

sanitarium [ˌsæni'tɛəriəm] *n.* 疗养院,休养所

Following her long illness, she went off to a *sanitarium* to recover her strength.

大病一场后,她去了疗养院(疗养)以恢复体力。

sanitary ['sænitəri] *a.* 清洁的. hygienic

In the chocolate factory we work under very *sanitary* conditions.

在巧克力生产厂家,我们在十分卫生的条件下工作。

sanitation ['sæniteiʃən] *n.* 公共卫生

sanitize ['sænitaiz] *v.* 消毒. sterilize

比较记忆:sanitizer(消毒剂)

sap [sæp] *n.* 树液;活力; *v.* 削弱. undermine

Maple sugar is made from the *sap* of some maple trees.

枫树糖浆是由枫树汁做的。

sapless ['sæplis] *a.* 没有元气的;枯萎的. feeble

sapient ['seipiənt] *a.* 智慧的. ↔ simple

The students enjoyed the professor's *sapient* digressions more than his formal lectures.

比起教授(严肃)的正式讲座来,学生们更喜欢他那些离题的充满智慧的小插曲。

sapling ['sæpliŋ] *n.* 小树;年轻人

They planted a *sapling* in the front yard in hopes that it would sprout leaves in the spring.

他们在院前种下棵小树,希望它春天会发芽。

sapphire ['sæfaiə] *n.* 蓝宝石; *a.* 天蓝色的. azure

参考:ruby(红宝石),amber(琥珀),emerald(绿宝石)

sarcasm ['sɑːkæzəm] *n*. 讥讽，嘲笑. ridicule

His feelings were hurt by the *sarcasm* of his supposed friends.

他的感情被他那些所谓的朋友们的讥笑刺伤了。

sarcophagus [sɑːˈkɔfəgəs] *n*. 石棺 (stone coffin)

The display of the *sarcophagus* in the art museum impresses me as a morbid exhibition.

艺术馆里展出的石棺使我感到这像个病态展览。

sardonic [sɑːˈdɔnik] *a*. 讽刺的，嘲笑的

The *sardonic* method is used to bar admission.

嘲讽的方法常被用在法律上的认可中。

sartorial [sɑːˈtɔːriəl] *a*. 缝制的

He was as famous for the *sartorial* splendor of his attire as he was for his acting.

他不仅表演出色，而且以他缝制华美的戏装而出名。

sash [sæʃ] *n*. 腰带，肩带；窗框

She wore a white dress with a blue *sash* around the waist.

她身着一条白裙子，腰间扎了条蓝色带子。

satanic [səˈtænik] *a*. 穷凶极恶的. sinister

来自：Satan（撒旦，与上帝作对的魔鬼）

satchel ['sætʃəl] *n*. 小背包. sack

She always takes her *satchel* whenever she goes out.

她只要出门总要拿上她的小背包。

sate [seit] *v*. 使充分满足. cloy

Its hunger *sated*, the lion dozed.

吃饱喝足，狮子睡了。

satellite ['sætəlait] *n*. 爪牙；马屁精. toady

satiate ['seiʃet] *v*. 使饱足，生腻. surfeit, cloy

The guests, having eaten until they were *satiated*, now

225

listened inattentively to the speakers.

客人们吃得酒足饭饱,现在正心不在蔫地听着演讲人(讲话)。

satiety [sə'taiəti] *n.* 饱足;满足

The *satiety* of the guests at the sumptuous feast became apparent when they refused the delicious dessert.

客人们拒绝美味的甜点,显然他们在华宴上已吃得酒足饭饱了。

satin ['sætin] *n.* 缎子

参考:nylon（尼龙）, linen（亚麻）

satiny ['sætini] *a.* 光滑的;柔软的. glossy

satire ['sætaiə] *n.* 讽刺作品

Gulliver's Travels, which is regarded by many as a tale for children, is actually a bitter *satire* attacking human folly.

许多人认为《格列佛游记》不过是写给小孩子们看的故事,而实际上它是抨击人类愚蠢的一部苦涩的讽刺(作品)。

satirical [sə'tirikl] *a.* 讽刺的. sarcastic

The humor of cartoonist Gray Trudeau often is *satirical*, through the comments of the Doonesbury characters, Trudeau ridicules political corruption and folly.

漫画家格雷·特鲁多的幽默常常是讽刺性的,他通过对人物的评议嘲弄了政治的腐败及愚蠢。

satrap ['sætrəp] *n.* 暴吏

The monarch and his *satraps* oppressed the citizens of the country.

君王及他的暴吏压制国民。

saturate ['sætʃəreit] *v.* 浸透;饱和. douse

Their clothes were *saturated* by the rain.

他们的衣服在雨中湿透了。

saturnalia [ˌsætə'neiliə] *n.* 纵情狂欢. orgy

来自罗马神话中的农神 Saturn

saturnine ['sætəːnain] *a.* 阴沉的,忧郁的. melancholy

Do not be misled by his **saturnine** countenance，he is not as gloomy as he looks.

别让他忧郁的脸色误导了你，他并不像看上去的那么阴郁。

satyric [sə'tirik] *a.* 色情狂的

来自性好欢娱淫乐的森林之神 satyr

The **satyric** often symbolizes carnal indulgence.

色情狂意味着肉体上的放纵。

saucy ['sɔːsi] *a.* 无礼的. sassy

We don't mean to be **saucy** when we refuse to follow the advice of our venerable leader.

在我们拒绝遵从我们那可敬的领导人的建议时，并不是想要有意无礼。

saunter ['sɔːntə] *v.* 漫步；闲逛

As we **sauntered** through the park we stopped frequently to admire the spring flowers.

我们在公园里信步，时不时停下欣赏春花。

savanna [sə'vænə] *n.* 热带大草原

Miles of **savanna** spread out before them.

在他们面前展现着(绵延)数英里的热带大草原(风光)。

savant ['sævənt] *n.* 博学之士

Our faculty includes many world-famous **savants**.

我们的教职员工中有几位在世界都很有名望的博学之士。

savoir faire [ˌsævwɑː'fɛə] *n.* 机敏处事的本领；才干

I envy his **savoir faire**，he always knows exactly what to do and say.

我真妒忌他的才干，他总知道该说什么，做什么。

savor ['seivə] *n.* 味道； *v.* 品尝，欣赏. relish

Relishing his triumph，Costner especially **savored** the chagrin of the critics who had predicted his failure.

享受着他成功的喜悦的同时，科斯特纳也在品味因预言他的失败的评论家们的恼羞成怒。

227

sawdust ['sɔ:dʌst] *n.* 锯屑

组合词：saw + dust → 锯屑

scab [skæb] *n.* 伤疤，痂. scar

Divorce has left him an indelible *scab*.

离婚在他心中留了下抹不去的伤痕。

scabbard ['skæbəd] *n.* (刀剑)鞘；枪套

The drill master told the recruit to wipe the blood from his sword before slipping it back into the *scabbard*.

教官告诉新兵在把剑插回剑鞘前，擦去剑上的血迹。

scabrous ['skeibrəs] *a.* 粗糙的；猥亵的. coarse；risque

The *scabrous* joke was currently making the rounds of the girls' dormitory.

女生宿舍里最近流传着个粗俗的玩笑。

scads [skædz] *n.* 大量，巨额. massive, gigantic

scaffold ['skæfəld] *n.* (建房搭的)脚手架；绞刑架

Before painting the house, the workers put up a *scaffold* to allow them to work on the second story.

油漆房子前，工人们搭起脚手架，这样他们可以在二楼上作业。

scalawag ['skæləwæg] *n.* 流氓，无赖. rogue

Her pet dog is such a lovable *scalawag*.

她的宠物狗真是个可爱的小调皮。

scald [skɔ:ld] *v.* 烫；烫伤

She *scalded* herself with hot grease.

她让热油给烫了。

scalding ['skɔ:ldiŋ] *a.* 滚烫的

scale [skeil] *n.* 鱼鳞；(音乐)音阶； *pl.* 天平

scale : fish = feathers : bird

scale [skeil] *v.* 攀登. mount

The erratic market *scaled* to new highs.

市场反复无常，而今又攀上新高。

scalp [skælp] *n.* 头皮；战利品； *v.* 击败

The pirate divided the *scalps* of a year's smuggling activities.

海盗分了分一年来走私获得的战利品。

scalpel ['skælpəl] *n.* 外科手术刀，解剖刀

scamp [skæmp] *n.* 流氓； *v.* 草率地做. rascal

She never dreamed that the *scamp* who cheated her going out would end up marrying her.

她做梦也不敢想像那个骗她出去的流氓最终会和她结婚。

比较记忆：swamp（沼泽），cramp（痉挛）

scamper ['skæmpə] *v.* 奔跑，快跑

The children *scampered* out of the house after the rain stopped.

雨一停，孩子们就跑出房去。

scandalize ['skændəlaiz] *v.* 恶意诽谤. slander

比较记忆：scandal（丑闻）

scandalous ['skændələs] *a.* 可耻的；诽谤的. defamatory

She had a series of *scandalous* affairs that shocked the community.

她那一连串的可耻事件令整个社区都震惊。

scant [skænt] *a.* 不足的，缺乏的. scarce

The new math gives *scant* attention to computation; process is considered more important.

这种新的数学方式不大注意结果，而是把过程看得更重要些。

scapegoat ['skeipgəut] *n.* 替罪羊

组合词：scape + goat → 替罪羊

scared [skɛəd] *a.* 害怕的，恐惧的

She was *scared* to walk in park at night since the woman was killed there.

因为那个妇女在公园里被害，她晚上不敢在那儿走。

scarp [skɑ:p] *n.* 悬崖；陡坡

比较记忆：scarf（围巾，披肩）

参考同类词：cliff, crag, bluff, escarpment, precipice

scathe [skeið] *v.* 损害；苛责

scathing ['skeðiŋ] *a.* 苛刻的，严厉的. harsh

His *scathing* remarks on free trade were rebuked by the critic.

他有关自由贸易的评论遭受到评论家们的非难。

scatological [ˌskætə'lɔdʒikəl] *a.* 色情的

Soldiers' language is larded with obscene and *scatological* references.

士兵的语言中常夹杂着关连猥亵色情的东西。

scavenge ['skævindʒ] *v.* 拣破烂；食腐肉

scavenger ['skævindʒə] *n.* 食腐动物；拣破烂者

The Oakland *Scavenger* Company is responsible for the collection and disposal of the community's garbage.

奥克兰废品公司负责收集处理该地区的垃圾。

scenario [si'nɑ:riəu] *n.* 剧情说明书；剧本

Scaramouche startled the other actors in the comedian troupe when he suddenly departed from their customary *scenario* and began to improvise.

当他突然抛开传统剧本于一边不顾而即兴发挥时,使他喜剧团里的其他演员大吃一惊。

scepter ['septə] *n.* 王权，君权

A *scepter* is a short rod carried by a ruler on ceremonial occasions as a sign of power.

权杖是统治者在仪式场合上执有的作为权力象征的短棒。

sceptic ['skeptik] *n.* 怀疑者；无神论者

Clearly refuting *sceptics*, researchers have demonstrated not only that gravitational radiation exists but that it also does exactly what theory.

研究人员已证明引力辐射不仅存在而且这一理论确实行得通，这明白无误地驳斥了持怀疑论者。

sceptical ['skeptikəl] *a.* 怀疑的；怀疑论的. skeptical

schematic [ski:'mætik] *a.* 扼要的；图解的

In working out the solution to an analytical logic question, you may find it helpful to construct a simple *schematic* diagram illustrating the relationships between the item of information given in the question.

想要做出一个逻辑分析问题的解答，建立一简单图表，表示出问题中给定条件的相互关系也许会有所帮助。

schematize ['ski:mətaiz] *v.* 用图式表示

来自：schema（图表，纲要）

scheme [ski:m] *n.* 阴谋；体制. conspiracy

The airport contains a *scheme* of crisscrossing runways.

飞机场有一十字交叉形状的跑道体系。

schism ['skizəm] *n.* 组织分裂

Let us not widen the *schism* by further backing.

我们不要通过得到进一步支持再扩大组织分裂了。

schismatic [siz'mætik] *a.* 分裂的

schizophrenia [ˌskitsəu'fri:niə] *n.* 精神分裂症

scholarly ['skɔləli] *a.* 博学的. erudite

schooner ['sku:nə] *n.* 大啤酒杯；大篷车

scintilla [sin'tilə] *n.* 一点；火花. ↔ blaze

You have not produced a *scintilla* of evidence to support your argument.

你可一点儿支持你论点的论据也拿不出来。

scintillate ['sintileit] *v.* 闪烁；流露智慧之光

I enjoy her dinner parties because the food is excellent and the conversation *scintillates*.

我很喜欢她的晚宴晚会，因为(晚会上)食物精美，谈话睿智。

scintillating [ˌsinti'leitiŋ] *a.* 才华横溢的. facile, ready

sciolism ['saiəlizəm] *n.* 一知半解的学问

His superficial scientific treatises were filled with *sciolism* and outmoded data.

他那肤浅的科学论文里满是一知半解的知识和行不通的数据。

scion ['saiən] *n.* 嫩芽；子孙. descendant

The farm boy felt out of place in the school attended by the *scions* of the wealthy and noble families.

在满是有钱人及贵族子弟来上学的这所学校里，那个农家男孩觉得自己像走错了地方似的。

scoff [skɔf] *v.* 嘲笑. jeer, flout

He *scoffed* at dentists until he had his first toothache.

他在第一次牙疼前，一直对牙医加以嘲笑。

scoff [skɔf] *v.* 狼吞虎咽. guttle

scold [skəuld] *n.* 泼妇. termagant

A man like him will never be able to tame a *scold* like her.

一个像他那样的男人永远也驯服不了她那样的泼妇。

scoop [skuːp] *n.* 铲子

scoop：concave = spatula：flat

scorch [skɔːtʃ] *v.* 烤焦，烧焦. char

A too-hot iron may *scorch* your clothes.

熨斗过热会烤焦你衣服的。

scorching ['skɔːtʃiŋ] *a.* 酷热的. fiery

score [skɔː] *n.* 乐谱；刻痕. groove

music：score = building：blueprint

scorpion ['skɔːpjən] *n.* 蝎子

参考：bug（臭虫），flea（跳蚤）

scotch [skɔtʃ] *v.* 镇压；伤害. crush

Heather tried to *scotch* the rumor that she had stolen

her best friends' finance.

海瑟企图压下有关她偷了她最好的朋友的钱财的流言。

scoundrel ['skaundrəl] *n.* 恶棍. cad, miscreant

His kindness to the *scoundrel* amazed all of us who had expected to hear severe punishment pronounced.

我们都还以为会听到严惩的宣判呢，而他对这个恶棍的善心却让我们大吃一惊。

scour ['skauə] *v.* 擦洗，擦亮

Use a *scouring* pad to scour the kitchen sink.

用擦洗布擦洗厨房的水槽。

scour ['skauə] *v.* 四处搜索

She *scoured* the closet for her old dress.

她乱翻了一通壁厨寻找她的旧裙子。

scourge [skə:dʒ] *v.* 鞭笞；磨难. lash; chasten

They feared the plague and regarded it as a deadly *scourge*.

他们很怕瘟疫，把它看成一种致命的磨难。

scowl [skaul] *v.* 怒目而视；愁眉苦脸

He *scowled* when I refused to lend him the money.

我拒绝借钱给他，他就对我怒目而视。

比较记忆：prowl（潜近），growl（咆哮）

scraggy ['skrægi] *a.* 皮包骨的；参差不齐的

scramble ['skræmbl] *v.* 攀登；争夺. scale; conflict

scrap [skræp] *n.* 碎屑；　*v.* 废弃. discord

They *scrapped* the jetfighter even before it was in full production, in favor of the faster interceptor.

为了便于生产速度更快的截击机，在大规模生产喷气战机前，就已废弃这种机型了。

比较记忆：scrape（擦掉）

scrappy ['skræpi] *a.* 片断的；好斗的. fragmentary; pugnacious

scrawl [skrɔ:l] *v.* 潦草地写. scratch

She *scrawled* the message on the first piece of paper she found so that she wouldn't forget it.

她找到一张纸就草草写下了这条信息，以防忘了。

比较记忆：scratchy（潦草的）

screed [skriːd] *n.* 冗长的演说，长篇大论

His letters were no more than *screeds* in which he listed his complaints.

他的信件不过是些长篇大论，罗列他那些抱怨而已。

screwdriver ['skruːˌdraivə] *n.* （螺丝）起子，旋凿

组合词：screw + driver → （螺丝）起子

scribble ['skribl] *v.* 乱写，乱涂

He *scribbled* down the idea on a paper napkin.

他在餐巾纸上涂抹写下他的想法。

scrimp [skrimp] *a.* 缩减的；不足的； *v.* 节省；吝啬

Until payday, we'll have to *scrimp* in groceries.

发薪日前，我们得在食品店里省着花钱。

script [skript] *n.* 脚本；手迹；手稿

script：play = score：symphony

scripture ['skriptʃə] *n.* 经文，圣典

scroll [skrəul] *n.* 卷轴；画卷

比较记忆：stroll（漫步）

scrooge [skruːdʒ] *n.* 吝啬鬼．skinflint

来自英国作家狄更斯小说人物 Scrooge，为一受人憎恨的老吝啬鬼

scrub [skrʌb] *n.* 矮树丛；身体矮小者

scrub [skrʌb] *v.* 擦洗，洗刷

The maid is responsible for *scrubbing* the kitchen and bathroom floors, vacuuming the carpet, and dusting the furniture.

这个女仆负责刷洗厨房和洗澡间地板，吸地毯，掸扫家具。

234

scrubby ['skrʌbi] *a.* 矮小的

scruffy ['skrʌfi] *a.* 可鄙的，无价值的. contemptible；shabby

Few criminals, even the most vicious, are so *scruffy* as those who traffic in drugs and prostitution.

即便是最邪恶的罪犯也没有人像做毒品和妓女生意的那些人这么可鄙。

scrumptious ['skrʌmpʃəs] *a.* 可口的；漂亮的. delicious；posh

She wore a *scrumptious* satin gown.

她穿了件漂亮的缎袍子。

scrunch ['skrʌntʃ] *v.* 压碎，挤碎；弄皱. crumple

I almost *scrunched* my shoulders to get through the door.

为过那扇门，我肩膀都快挤碎了。

scruple ['skru:pl] *v.* 顾忌，迟疑

He's a greedy person with no *scruples* when it comes to making a profit.

他是个贪婪的人，当有利可图时，他可毫无顾忌。

scrupulous ['skru:pjuləs] *a.* 谨慎小心的. meticulous

I can recommend him for a position of responsibility for I have found him a very *scrupulous* young man.

我可以给他推荐个重要的职位，因为我发现他是个很审慎的年轻人。

scrutable ['skru:teibl] *a.* 可辨认的；可被理解的

scrutinize ['skru:tinaiz] *v.* 细查，细读. ↔ dip

Searching for flaws, the sergeant *scrutinized* every detail of the private's uniform.

中士细细察看这个士兵的制服的每一细节，想找出点儿毛病来。

scrutiny ['skru:tini] *n.* 细看；细阅

Although the model looks good on the surface, it will not bear close *scrutiny*.

尽管这个模型表面上看来不错，细看就不行了。

235

scud [skʌd] *v.* 疾行，疾驶

> Just before the storm, the sailboats *scudded* like paper hats.
>
> 就在暴风雨（到来之前），帆船像纸帽一样（在水面上）疾行。

scuff [skʌf] *v.* 磨损. abrade

> A hard surface won't *scuff*.
>
> 硬表面不会磨损。
>
> 比较记忆：scoff（嘲弄，狼吞虎咽）

scuffle ['skʌfl] *v.* 混战；打斗. brawl

scullion ['skʌliən] *n.* 厨房仆人

> Lynette was angry because she thought she had been given a *scullion* to act as her defender.
>
> 莱内特很生气，因为（她们）给她派了个厨房里的仆人作（她的）保护人。

sculpt [skʌlpt] *v.* 雕刻. carve

scum [skʌm] *n.* 污垢；渣滓

scurrilous ['skʌriləs] *a.* 下流的；恶言诽谤的. obscene；opprobrious

> He should be dismissed for his *scurrilous* remarks about his immediate superiors.
>
> 他该为对顶头上司恶意诽谤的话语而被开除掉。

scurry ['skʌri] *v.* 急跑，疾行. scud

> The White Rabbit had to *scurry* to get to his appointment on time.
>
> 怀特·瑞贝特不得不飞跑以便按时赶赴他的约会。

scurvy ['skə:vi] *a.* 卑鄙的，可鄙的. base，vile

Unit Thirty-Two

scuttle [skʌtl] *v.* 疾走；逃避

The captain *scuttled* his ship rather than see it captured by the cnemy.

船长宁愿把船沉水也不愿看到敌人占有它。

scuttle [skʌtl] *n.* 舷窗，舱口盖

scythe [saið] *n.* 长柄大镰刀

The farmer cut a swathe through the high grass with his *scythe*.

农夫用大镰刀一行行地割向高高的草。

seafarer ['siːfɛərə] *n.* 水手，海员. seaman

seafaring [siːfɛəriŋ] *a.* 航海的

seam [siːm] *n.* 缝，接缝

seamstress ['semstris] *n.* 女裁缝

seamy ['siːmi] *a.* 讨嫌的；卑劣的. melancholy；sordid

In The Godfather, Corleone is unwilling to expose his wife and children to the *seamy* side of his life as the son of a Mafia don.

在《教父》中，科利昂不愿把其作为一个黑手党徒的儿子的生活的阴暗面暴露给妻子孩子。

sear [siə] *v.* 烧灼. cauterize

Before stewing the beef, the cook *seared* it over high heat to seal the juices in.

在炖牛肉前，厨师用高温烧烤它以便保留住里面的肉汁。

searing ['siəriŋ] *a.* 灼热的

seascape ['siːskeip] *n.* 海景

比较记忆: landscape (风景)

seasoned ['si:znd] *a.* 老练的. versed

Though pleased with her new batch of rookies, the basketball coach wished she had a few more *seasoned* players on the team.

尽管对新来的一批队员挺满意,这个篮球教练还是希望她的球队中能有几个更为老练的球员。

seasoning ['si:zniŋ] *n.* 调味品,作料. flavoring

sebaceous [si'beiʃəs] *a.* 油脂的

The *sebaceous* glands secrete oil to the hair follicles.

脂肪腺分泌油脂到毛囊里。

secede [si'si:d] *v.* 脱离. retract

se (without) + cede (go) → 脱离

secession [si'seʃən] *n.* 脱离,退出

The *secession* of the Southern states provided Lincoln with his first major problem after his inauguration.

南方诸州的退出给就职后的林肯提出了第一个重大问题。

seclude [si'klu:d] *v.* 隐退. sequester

se (apart) + clude (close) → 隐退

seclusion [si'klu:ʒən] *n.* 隐退

One moment she loved crowds; the next, she sought *seclusion*.

一会儿她喜欢人多聚堆;一会儿又独自隐遁一旁。

secretarial [ˌsekrə'tɛəriəl] *a.* 秘书的,文书的

来自: secretary (秘书)

secrete [si'kri:t] *v.* 分泌;藏匿

The pack rat *secretes* odds and ends in its nest.

北美鼠能分泌出一种难闻的气味而后逃回巢穴。

sect [sekt] *n.* 派系

The Mennonite *sect* was founded during the 16th century.

门诺教派于 16 世纪建立。

sectarian [sek'tɛəriən] *a.* 宗派的，派系的

As university chaplain, she sought to address universal religious issues and not limit herself to mere *sectarian* concerns.

作为大学里的牧师，她尽量宣讲世界范围内的宗教话题而不仅仅局限于对宗教派系的考虑。

sectile ['sektil] *a.* 可剖开的

secular ['sekjulə] *a.* 世俗的. ↔ clerical

The church leaders decided not to interfere in *secular* matters.

宗教领导人决定不干涉世俗事物。

secure [sɪ'kjuə] *v.* 使牢固，系. fasten

The ends of the hammock were *secured* to two well-spaced trees.

吊床两端固定在远近距离正好的两棵树上。

security [si'kjuəriti] *n.* 抵押品；　*pl.* 证券. gage; stock

sedan [si'dæn] *n.* 轿车；轿

sedate [si'deit] *a.* 安静的，镇静的. composed, staid

The parents were worried because they felt their son was too quiet and *sedate*.

父母有些担心，因为他们感到他们的儿子过于安静了。

sedative ['sedətiv] *a.* (药物)镇静的；　*n.* 镇静剂. tranquilizer

sedentary ['sentəri] *a.* 久坐的；固定不动的. ↔ migratory

sediment ['sedimənt] *n.* 沉积物；沉渣. deposit

sedition [si'diʃən] *n.* 煽动叛乱

His words, though not treasonous in themselves, were calculated to arouse thoughts of *sedition*.

他的话尽管本身没有什么叛乱色彩，却被当成是可以煽动起叛乱思想的言辞。

seditious [si'diʃəs] *a.* 煽动性的. mutinous

seduce [si'djuːs] *v.* 勾引；诱惑. lure

       se (apart) + duce (lead) → 勾引

seductive [si'dʌktiv] *a.* 诱人的；有魅力的. alluring

sedulous ['sedjuləs] *a.* 聚精会神的；勤勉的 diligent

       The young woman was so *sedulous* that she received a commendation for her hard work.

       这位年轻妇女勤勤恳恳,她因努力工作而获得了表扬。

seedling ['siːdliŋ] *n.* 幼苗，秧苗

       seed + ling (little) → 小苗

seedy ['siːdi] *a.* 破旧的；肮脏的. mangy

       I would rather stay in dormitory lodgings in a decent youth hostel than have a room of my own in a *seedy* downtown hotel.

       我宁愿住在一所体面的青年寄宿公寓的宿舍起居室里,也不去住闹市区里一座肮脏的宾馆里的单人房间。

seep [siːp] *v.* 渗漏. ooze

       During the rainstorm, water *seeped* through the crack in the basement wall and damaged the floor boards.

       在暴雨中,水渗透进地下室墙上的裂缝,泡坏了地板块。

seer [siə] *n.* 预言家

seethe ['siːð] *v.* 沸腾，汹涌

       The nation was *seething* with discontent as the noblemen continued their arrogant ways.

       贵族们还要坚持他们那傲慢的方式,这个国家(的人民)由于不满而沸腾了。

segregate ['segrigit] *v.* 隔离. ↔ aggregate

       se (apart) + greg (group) + ate (make) → 脱离

seine [sein] *n.* 拖拉大围网

       seine ∶ fish = snare ∶ bird

240

seismic ['saizmik] *a.* 地震的

比较记忆：seismograph（地震仪），seismology（地震学）

self-assertion ['selfə'səːʃən] *n.* 自作主张

self-deprecatory ['self'deprikətəri] *a.* 过分谦虚的，自我贬低的

self-effacing ['self-i'feisiŋ] *a.* 自我谦避的；自我轻视的

self-possession ['selfpə'zeʃən] *n.* 沉着，镇静

self-righteous ['self'raitʃəs] *a.* 自以为是的. priggish

self-seeker ['self'siːkə] *n.* 唯利是图者. snob

The *self-seeker* would have nothing to do with proletarians.

唯利是图者同无产阶级一点儿也不沾边儿。

semantics [si'mætiks] *n.* 语义学

semblance ['sembl.ans] *n.* 外貌；相似. air

Your lie does not have even the *semblance* of truth.

你的谎言没有丝毫真实性。

比较记忆：dissemble（掩饰）

seminal ['siːminl] *a.* 创新的. ↔ trite

比较记忆：disseminate（播种）

seminary ['seminəri] *n.* 神学院

比较记忆：seminar（研究小组）

senescence [si'nesəns] *n.* 衰老

He did not show any signs of *senescence* until he was well past seventy.

他 70 岁前，一点儿也不显老。

senescent [sə'nesnt] *a.* 衰老的，老化的

seneschal ['seniʃəl] *n.* 管家，总管

senile ['siːnail] *a.* 年老的

senility [si'niliti] *n.* 衰老

Most of the decisions are being made by the junior

members of the company because of the *senility* of the president.

由于这家公司总经理年迈,因此很多事是由资历较浅的成员决定的。

seniority ['si:ni'əriti] *n.* 年长;资深

sensation [sen'seiʃən] *n.* 知觉;轰动(的事)

比较记忆:sensible(明智的),sensitive(敏感的)

sensational [sen'seiʃənl] *a.* 耸人听闻的,轰动的

The boy was reading a *sensational* paperback novel.

这个男孩在读一本轰动一时的平装版的小说。

sensual ['senʃuəl] *a.* 肉欲的,淫荡的. lewd, voluptuous

I cannot understand what caused him to drop his *sensual* way of life and become so ascetic.

我无法理解是什么使他放弃了淫荡的生活,转而变成个苦行僧。

sensuous ['sensjuəs] *a.* 感觉上的;给人以美的享受的. luscious

The medieval church condemned man's partaking in *sensuous* pleasures.

中世纪教会诅咒人们享受感官快乐。

sententious [sen'tenʃəs] *a.* 好说教的;简要的. didactic;pithy

Being a man of maxims, he was *sententious* in what he said.

他是个好用箴言说教的人。

sentient ['senʃənt] *a.* 有知觉的,有感觉的

sentimental [ˌsenti'mentl] *a.* 多愁善感的. mushy, maudlin

No one could think it *sentimental* to weep at the death of a crony.

没人会把为亲密伙伴的去世而哭泣看成是多愁善感。

sentry ['sentri] *n.* 哨兵,步哨. sentinel

General Casey could not convince the *sentry* to allow him through the gate without proper identification.

凯西将军没有恰当的身份证明,因而无法说服哨兵放他过去。

sepsis ['sepsis] *n.* 败血

参考：anemia（贫血症），malaria（疟疾），polio（小儿麻痹症）

septic ['septik] *a.* 引起腐烂的，腐败性的. ↔ antiseptic

The hospital was in such a filthy state that we were afraid that many of the patients would suffer from *septic* poisoning.

医院处于这么一种肮脏状况，我们都怕病人会遭受感染中毒。

sepulcher ['sepəlkə] *n.* 坟墓. catacomb

Annabel Lee was buried in the *sepulcher* by the sea.

安娜贝尔·李被埋葬在海边坟墓里。

sepulchral [si'pʌkrəl] *a.* 坟墓的；阴森森的. gloomy

参考同类词：crypt（教堂地下室），cenotaph（纪念碑），mausoleum（陵墓），vault（墓穴）

sepulture ['sepəltʃə] *n.* 埋葬

sequacious [si'kweiʃəs] *a.* 前后连贯的；顺从的

The *sequacious* members of Parliament were only too willing to do the bidding of their leader.

顺从的议会成员是太过于愿意按其领导人的吩咐行事了。

sequester [si'kwestə] *v.* （使）隐退；使隔绝. withdraw

Although he had hoped for a long time to *sequester* himself in a small community, he never was able to drop his busy round of activities in the city.

尽管他一直希望可以到个小地方去隐居，却一直不能抛下他在市内那繁忙的商务活动。

sequestrate [si'kwestreit] *v.* 扣押，没收. confiscate

Customs officials have the right to *sequestrate* goods being smuggled into their country.

海关官员有权没收走私进来的货物。

seraglio [se'rɑːliəu] *n.* 闺房；宫殿

seraph ['serəf] *n.* 六翼天使

In his eternal sleep, he was greeted by the *seraphs* at the Pearly Gates.

他长眠了,受到在天国之门的六翼天使的迎接。

seraphic [sə'ræfik] *a.* 天使般的;美丽的. comely, elegant

sere [siə] *a.* 干枯的;枯萎的. faded, wilted

After the unseasonably dry winter, the Berkeley hills looked dusty and *sere*.

不合时宜的干燥冬季过后,伯克利山看上去干枯凋萎且灰蒙蒙的。

serenade [seri'neid] *n.* 小夜曲

比较记忆:serene(宁静的)

serendipity [ˌserən'dipiti] *n.* 偶然发现珍宝的运气

Many scientific discoveries are a matter of *serendipity*.

许多科学发现不过是偶然发现的巧合而已。

sermonize ['sə:mənaiz] *v.* 说教;讲道. mission

参考:homiletics(布道学), pilgrim(朝圣客)

serpentine ['sə:pənti:n] *a.* 蜿蜒的. sinuous

比较记忆:serpent(蛇)

serrated ['seritid] *a.* 呈锯齿状的

The beech tree is one of many plants that have *serrated* leaves.

山毛榉树是长有锯齿形树叶的树木中的一种。

serration [se'reiʃən] *n.* 锯齿;锯齿状

servile ['sə:vail] *a.* 百依百顺的. slavish

Constantly fawning on his employer, humble Uriah Heap was a *servile* creature.

总是对老板一脸的奉承、谦卑的尤赖亚·希普真是个温顺的动物。

servitude ['sə:vitju:d] *n.* 苦役

244

Born a slave, Douglass resented his life of *servitude* and plotted to escape to the Noon.

生为奴隶，道格拉斯憎恨他的苦役生涯，密谋要逃到月亮上去。

setback ['setbæk] *n.* 挫折

Although there are weeds of negotiations ahead and perhaps *setbacks* and new surprises, leaders of both parties are optimistic that their differences can be resolved.

尽管谈判的路上有荆棘，也许还有新的意外及挫折，两党领导都很乐观，认为他们之间的分歧可以解决。

sever ['sevə] *v.* 切断；脱离. incise; dissociate

Unless agreement is reached by the end of the week, the two countries will *sever* diplomatic relations.

除非本周末达成协议，否则这两个国家要断绝外交关系了。

比较记忆：severe（严重的）

severance ['sevərəns] *n.* 切断；分离

The *severance* of church and state is a basic principle of our government.

我们政府的一项基本准则是政教分离。

sewer ['sjuːə] *n.* 排水沟，下水道

sextant ['sekstənt] *n.* 六分仪

sextant : navigate = abacus : tally

shack [ʃæk] *n.* 简陋小屋. hut

shackle ['ʃækl] *n.* & *v.* 脚镣，枷锁

The criminal's ankles were *shackled* to prevent his escape.

罪犯脚踝上套着脚镣，以防他逃跑。

shade [ʃeid] *n.* 细微差别；色度

shaft [ʃɑːft] *n.* 矛柄；电梯通道

shaft : elevator = cylinder : piston

shaggy [ˈʃægi] *a.* 头发零乱的

比较记忆：shabby（褴褛的）

shale [ʃeil] *n.* （可发现石油的）页岩

参考：granite（花岗岩），gneiss（片麻岩），porphyry（斑岩）

shallop [ˈʃæləp] *n.* 轻舟，小舟

sham [ʃæm] *n.* 假货； *v.* 假装. assume

He *shammed* sickness to get out of going to school.

他装病不去上学。

shambles [ˈʃæmblz] *n.* 混乱

You must keep calm when you face the *shambles*.

当你面临混乱时，一定要保持镇定。

比较记忆：shamble（蹒跚）

shanty [ˈʃænti] *n.* 简陋小屋. shack

shard [ʃɑːd] *n.* （陶器等）碎片

shard : pottery = fragment : bone

shareholder [ˈʃɛəˌhəuldə] *n.* 股东

组合词：share ＋ holder → 股东

shark [ʃɑːk] *n.* 骗子；敲诈勒索者；鲨鱼

参考：carp（鲤鱼），crocodile（鳄鱼）

shavings [ˈʃeiviŋz] *n.* 刨花

shavings : wood = filings : metal

shawl [ʃɔːl] *n.* （妇女用）披肩，围巾. poncho

Take your *shawl* with you because it will probably be chilly when you come back.

拿上围巾吧，回来时可能会很冷的。

sheaf [ʃiːf] *n.* 捆，束

The lawyer picked up a *sheaf* of papers as he rose to question the witness.

律师站起来提问证人时，拿起一迭纸来。

246

shear [ʃiə] *n.* 剪刀； *v.* 剪发

sheath [ʃiːθ] *n.* (刀、剑)鞘，套

Store the knife in its **sheath** after each time use so that it will stay in good condition.

每次用完刀都要把它放回刀鞘里，这样刀才会保持完好。

shed [ʃed] *v.* 流出(眼泪)；脱落(叶子、衣服)

Snakes **shed** their skins periodically.

蛇要定期蜕皮的。

sheen [ʃiːn] *n.* 光辉，光泽

He polished the fire engine to such a **sheen** that it looked new.

他把救火车擦拭得光亮如新。

sheepish ['ʃiːpiʃ] *a.* 局促不安的. abashed

I wonder what is concealed behind that **sheepish** grin of hers.

我在想她局促不安的笑后面隐藏了什么。

sheer [ʃiə] *v.* 偏航；避开. yaw；dodge

The boat came close to the rocks and then **sheered** away.

船驶近礁岩而后又避开了。

shell [ʃel] *n.* 炮弹

参考：cartridge (子弹)，cannon (大炮)

shelve [ʃelv] *v.* 搁置. ↔ examine

来自：shelf (架子)

sheriff ['ʃerif] *n.* 行政司法长官

sheriff：deputy = star：understudy

shibboleth ['ʃibəleθ] *n.* 陈词滥调；习俗. cliche

We are often misled by **shibboleths**.

我们常被习俗给误导。

shiftless ['ʃiftlis] *a.* 无能的；偷懒的. idle

247

This office has no place for a *shiftless* worker.

办公室里没有给偷懒的人准备地方。

shifty ['ʃifti] *a*. 善于应变的；诡诈的

shimmer ['ʃimə] *v*. 闪烁，微亮

The moonlight *shimmered* on the water as the moon broke through the cloud for a moment.

一会儿月亮穿破云层，月光洒在水面上，波光麟麟。

shindy ['ʃindi] *n*. 吵闹；盛大舞会

shingle ['ʃiŋgl] *n*. 木瓦，屋顶板

shipshape ['ʃipʃeip] *a*. 整洁的，井然有序的. trim

The room was *shipshape* as she had left it, although dust had settled over everything.

尽管一切物品上落满灰尘，房间仍保持着她走时的整洁。

shipwright ['ʃiprait] *n*. 造船者，船木工

ship + wright (workman) → 造船者

参考：cartwrinht（造车匠）

shirk [ʃəːk] *v*. 逃避，规避. evade, dodge

Brian had a strong sense of duty; he would never *shirk* any responsibility.

布赖恩怀有强烈的责任感，他从不会规避任何责任。

shoddy ['ʃɔdi] *a*. 劣质的. ↔ superior

You will never get the public to buy such *shoddy* material.

你永远也没法子让公众买这种劣质材料。

shoplifter ['ʃɔpˌliftə] *n*. (超级市场)顺手牵羊者，扒手

shoplifter：goods = spy：information

shopsoiled ['ʃɔpˌsɔild] *a*. 残破的；陈旧的. dilapidated

shore [ʃɔː] *n*. (房屋等的)斜撑柱； *v*. 支持

shortfall ['ʃɔːtfɔːl] *n*. 不足额. deficit

shove [ʃʌv] *v*. 推. propel

比较记忆：shovel（铁锨）

showpiece [ˈʃəupiːs] *n*. 陈列品；样品

       组合词：show ＋ piece → 陈列品

showy [ˈʃəui] *a*. 鲜艳的，显眼的. flamboyant

       Her dress is a little too ***showy***.

       她的裙子有点儿过于鲜艳了。

shred [ʃred] *n*. 碎片；   *v*. 撕碎. fragmentary

       The machine tore the paper into ***shreds***.

       机器把纸撕成碎片。

shrew [ʃruː] *n*. 泼妇. virago

       No one wanted to marry Shakespeare's Kate because

       she was a ***shrew***.

       没人愿意娶莎士比亚笔下的凯特，因为她是个泼妇。

shrine [ʃrain] *n*. 神龛；圣地

       比较记忆：enshrine（奉……为神）

       shrine : pilgrim ＝ peak : climber

shrivel [ˈʃrivl] *v*. 枯萎；皱缩. flag

       The peach is ***shriveled*** in the sun.

       桃子在阳光下枯萎了。

shroud [ʃraud] *n*. 寿衣；遮蔽物；   *v*. 覆盖. veil

shrug [ʃrʌg] *v*. 耸肩（表示怀疑）

       shrug : deny ＝ frown : abhor

shuck [ʃʌk] *n*. 壳，荚；无用之物. shell；doit

shuffle [ˈʃʌfl] *v*. 拖着脚走；支吾

       比较记忆：reshuffle（改组）

shunt [ʃʌnt] *v*. （火车）调轨；转移方向

       If the switchman failed to ***shunt*** the Silver Streak onto a

       side track, the train would plow right into Union Sta-

       tion.

       要是扳道工没把银光列车转入岔道，火车会直穿进联合车站的。

sibilant ['sibilənt] *a.* 发咝咝声的

sibling ['sibliŋ] *n.* 兄弟或姐妹

We may not enjoy being *siblings*, but we cannot forget that we still belong to the same family.

我们也许不能做愉快相处的兄弟姐妹,但我们不能忘记我们仍同属同一家庭。

sibyl ['sibil] *n.* 女预言家,女先知

sibyl : seer = hind : hart

sibylline ['sibilain] *a.* 预言的

Until their destruction by fire in 83 B.C., the *sibylline* books were often consulted by the Romans.

罗马人常参照预言书,直到它毁于公元前 83 年的大火中。

sickle ['sikl] *n.* 镰刀

sidereal [sai'diəriəl] *a.* 恒星的

The study of *sidereal* bodies has been greatly advanced by new telescope.

新型望远镜大大推进了恒星天体的研究。

sideshow ['saidʃəu] *n.* 穿插表演

sidesplitting ['said,splitiŋ] *a.* 令人捧腹大笑的

sidestep ['saidstep] *v.* 避开. bypass, skirt

He drove home over the bridge to *sidestep* the traffic congestion at the tunnel.

他开车过桥回家以避开隧道那里的交通阻塞。

sidle ['saidl] *v.* (偷偷地)侧身而行

siege [si:dʒ] *n.* 包围,围攻

The *siege* of the castle lasted for six months.

城堡被围困了六个月。

siesta [si'estə] *n.* 午休

If you are planning to be out late tonight, take a *siesta* this afternoon.

要是你打算今晚外出,今天下午该午休一会儿。

sieve [siv] *n.* 筛; *v.* 筛出,滤出

Remove all the water from the pasta by draining it in the *sieve*.

用筛子把面条上的水都沥干。

sift [sift] *v.* 筛;过滤

sifter ['siftə] *n.* 筛子. sieve

sigh [sai] *v.* 叹气

比较记忆:sign(签字)

signatory ['signətəri] *n.* 签约国,签署者

signify ['signifai] *v.* 意味;表明. evince

He *signified* his agreement (that he agreed) by nodding.

他点点头以示他同意。

silhouette [ˌsilu(:)'et] *n.* (投射)黑影;轮廓

He had the artist draw a *silhouette* of his daughter to give to his wife for her birthday.

他让画家画了幅他女儿的素描,送给他妻子作生日礼物。

silicon ['silikən] *n.* 硅

比较记忆:salmon(鲑鱼)

sill [sil] *n.* 基石;门槛;窗台

silt [silt] *n.* 淤泥. 淤沙. slime

The harbor channel must be dredged annually to remove the *silt*.

港口的河道必须年年挖掘以清除淤泥。

simian ['simiən] *a.* 类人猿的;猴的

His *simian* features remind me of the missing link.

他的返祖现象使我想起那缺少的一环。

simile ['simili] *n.* 直喻,明喻. ↔ metaphor

"I am as strong as a lion" is an example of *simile*.

"我像雄狮一样强壮"是个明喻的例子。

simmer ['simə] *v.* 慢慢煮

He was *simmering* with anger and could hardly speak politely.

他被愤怒煎熬着,几乎没法子礼貌地讲话。

simper ['simpə] *v.* 傻笑;假笑. giggle

simper : smile = babble : talk

simplistic [sim'plistik] *a.* 极其简单的

Though Jack's solution dealt adequately with one aspect of the problem, it was *simplistic* in failing to consider various complicating factors that might arise.

尽管杰克的解决方案充分解决了这一问题的一个方面,要是考虑到可能出现的各种各样的复杂化因素,(这一方案就显得)过于简单,不够全面了。

simultaneous [ˌsiməl'teinjəs] *a.* 同时发生的. concurrent

sinecure ['sainikjuə] *n.* 挂名职务;闲职

My job is no *sinecure*, I work long hours and have much responsibility.

我的工作可不是闲差,我有许多职责,工作时间也很长。

sinew ['sinju:] *n.* 腱;力量;精力. thew

sinewy ['sinju(:)i] *a.* 强壮有力的. sturdy, mighty

The steak was too *sinewy* to chew.

牛排太硬了,嚼不动。

singe ['sindʒ] *v.* (轻微)烧焦,烤焦

She *singed* her neck when the curling iron came too close to her skin.

当铁卷发条挨皮肤过近时,烫伤了她的脖子。

single ['sigl] *v.* 选出,选拔

singularity [ˌsiŋgju'læriti] *n.* 异常;奇特

sinister ['sinistə] *a.* 不吉祥的;凶恶的. ominous

We must defeat the *sinister* forces that seek our downfall.

我们必须打败要让我们垮掉的邪恶势力。

比较记忆：minister（管理）

sink [siŋk] *n.* 下水道，污水井

sinuous ['sinjuəs] *a.* 蜿蜒的，迂回的. crooked

The snake moved in a *sinuous* manner.

蛇蜿蜒地前进。

比较记忆：insinuate（暗指）

sip [sip] *v.* 啜饮. sup

比较记忆：insipid（乏味的）

siren ['saiərin] *n.* 汽笛；警报器

ambulance：siren ＝ train：whistle

sirocco [si'rɔkəu] *n.* 热风

We can understand the popularity of the siesta in south-ern Spain; when the *sirocco* blows, the afternoon heat is unbearable.

我们可以理解在西班牙南部为什么盛行午睡,因为热带风吹起时,下午的炎热是无法忍受的。

site ['sait] *n.* 遗址

The successful reconstruction of an archaeological *site* requires scientific knowledge as well as cultural sensi-tivity.

成功重修一考古遗址既要有科学知识,也不可缺少文化感悟力。

size [saiz] *n.* 浆糊；　　*v.* 糊住

sizzler ['sizlə] *n.* 炎热的一天

sizzling ['sizliŋ] *a.* 极热的

Sunbathers are lying on the *sizzling* sand.

日光浴者躺在炎热的沙滩上。

skein [skein] *n.* （一束）线或纱.

A university training enables a man to see things as

they are, to go right to the point, to disentangle a *skein* of thought.

接受大学教育可以使一个人看清事物的本来面目，一下子就抓住要点，理清一团纷乱的思绪。

skeptic ['skeptik] *n.* 无神论者；怀疑论者. agnostic

skeptical ['skeptikəl] *a.* 怀疑的；怀疑宗教的

Although ordinarily *skeptical* about the purity of Robinson's motives, in this instance Jenkins did not consider Robinson's generosity to be alloyed with consideration of personal gain.

尽管一般地都对鲁宾逊的动机的纯洁性抱有怀疑，在这个例子里，詹金斯却不认为鲁宾逊的动机中含有任何个人所图利益的想法成分。

skepticism ['skeptisizəm] *n.* 怀疑态度

To be gullible is to be without *skepticism*.

容易上当受骗就是说没有怀疑的态度。

sketchy ['sketʃi] *a.* 概略的. ↔ perfect

来自：sketch（素描）

sketch：painting = outline：essay

skew [skju:] *a.* 不正的，歪斜的. slanting

skewer [skjuə] *n.* （烤肉用的）串肉扦； *v.* （用扦）串

skiff [skif] *n.* 轻舟；小快艇. shallop

Tom dreamed of owning an ocean-going yacht but had to settle for a *skiff* he could sail in the bay.

汤姆曾梦想能拥有一艘在海上行驶的游艇，但却不得不安于一只能在海湾里行驶的小船。

skillet ['skilit] *n.* 煎锅（frying pan）

I have all the kitchen utensils I need expect a *skillet* large enough to fry potatoes.

除了一个足够大能用来煎土豆的煎锅外，所有厨房用具我都有了。

skim [skim] *v.* 擦掉；浏览. dip

If you don't have time to read the entire article, at least *skim* it.

你要是没时间把整篇文章都读了，至少得浏览一下吧!

skimp [skimp] *v.* 吝啬. scrimp

They were forced to *skimp* on necessities in order to make their limited supplies last the winter.

他们不得不省着用(他们的生活)必需品，以便可以用有限的供给品维持过冬。

skimpy ['skimpi] *a.* 吝啬的；贫乏的. meager

You'll need to wear more than that *skimpy* outfit in this cold weather.

这么冷的天，你就穿这么点衣服可不行，得多穿些。

skinflint ['skinflint] *n.* 吝啬鬼. niggard

The old *skinflint* refused to give her a raise.

这个老吝啬鬼拒绝给她长工资。

skinny ['skini] *a.* 瘦削的. lean, emaciated

She holds a *skinny* and hungry look.

她瘦削的脸上一副饥饿的神态。

skirmish ['skə:miʃ] *n.* 小冲突，小争吵. miff

Custer's troops expected they might run into a *skirmish* or two on maneuvers, they did not expect to face a major battle.

卡斯特的队伍还以为会调遣他们去参加一两场小战役呢，没成想他们要面对这么一场(大规模的)主要战役。

skirt [skə:t] *v.* 位于……边缘；沿边缘而行

Unit Thirty-Three

skit [skit] *n.* 滑稽短剧

When we graduated, the school newspaper had *skits* about each one of us.

在我们毕业的时候，校报给我们每个人登了一小段介绍。

skittish ['skitiʃ] *a.* (人)害羞的；(马)易受惊的

She is as *skittish* as a kitten playing with a piece or string.

她像只玩线球的小猫一样敏感害羞。

skull [skʌl] *n.* 头盖骨，脑壳

The human *skull* may conveniently be divided into three principal portions：the cranium or cranial vault, the face, and the lower jaw or mandible.

人类的颅骨可简单地大致分成三个主要部分：脑颅骨，面颅骨和下颌骨。

skullduggery [skʌl'dʌgəri] *n.* 舞弊，作假；阴谋诡计，欺骗.

The investigation into municipal corruption turned up new instance of *skullduggery* daily.

有关市政腐败的调查又提供了一个日常舞弊现象的新证。

skunk [skʌŋk] *n.* 臭鼬，黄鼠狼. weasel

参考：hyena（鬣狗），chipmunk（金花鼠）

skyrocket ['skaiˌrɔkit] *v.* 陡升，猛涨

The incidence of cheating among students *skyrocketed* before the honor system went into effect.

在荣誉体系生效前，学生中的舞弊事件猛增。

slab [slæb] *n.* 厚板；厚片

比较记忆：stab（刺，戳）

slacken ['slækən] *v.* (使)松弛，放松. relax

As they passed the finish line, the runners *slackened* their pace.

当他们冲过终点线后,运动员们放慢了步伐。

slacker ['slækə] *n.* 逃避责任的人；偷懒的人

The captain ordered the sergeant to punish all *slackers*.

上尉命令中士惩罚所有偷懒的人。

slag [slæg] *n.* 炉渣，矿渣. clinker

The blast furnace had a special opening at the bottom to allow the workers to remove the worthless *slag*.

高炉底部有一特殊开口,以便使工人可以清除无用的矿渣。

slake [sleik] *v.* 消除；平息；使缓和

When we reached the oasis, we were able to *slake* our thirst.

当我们抵达沙漠中的绿洲时,终于可以一解我们的干渴了。

slanderous ['slɑːndərəs] *a.* 诽谤的，中伤的

slant [slɑːnt] *n.* 斜面；看法；　*v.* 倾斜

The writer *slanted* the story in favor of the candidate.

作者把这个故事向利于那个候选人的一面歪曲了。

slanting ['slɑːntiŋ] *a.* 倾斜的；歪的. oblique

slapdash ['slæpdæʃ] *a.* 草率的，马虎的

From the number of types and misspellings, I've found in it, it's clear that Mario proofread the report in a remarkably *slapdash*.

从我找出的这么多拼读和打字错误看来,很明显马里奥校对这个报告时是极为草率马虎的。

slash [slæʃ] *v.* 鞭笞；削减. lash；abridge

The shop plans to *slush* fur prices after Christmas.

商店打算圣诞节后削减皮革(商品的)价格。

比较记忆：slosh（泼，溅）

slate [sleit] *n.* 石板；候选人名单；

    v. 提名……为候选人（古希腊选举时在石板上刻上候选人名单）

slattern ['slætə(ː)n] *n.* 邋遢女人. sloven

    If you persist in wearing such sloppy clothes, people will call you *slattern*.

    你要总坚持这么马马虎虎地穿衣服，别人就会叫你邋遢女人了。

slatternly ['slætə(ː)nli] *a.* 邋遢的. frowzy

slaver ['sleivə] *n.* 口水； *v.* 渴望；淌口水. slobber, drool

    She *slavered* to be as attractive as the most popular girl in her class.

    她渴望成为她班上最有魅力，最受欢迎的女孩儿。

slay [slei] *v.* 杀，残杀

    When he went hunting with his older brothers, he did not want them to *slay* the deer.

    当他和哥哥们去打猎的时候，他不想让哥哥们杀死那只鹿。

sleazy ['sliːzi] *a.* 低劣的. ↔ sturdy

    This is a *sleazy* fabric, it will not wear well.

    这种织品质量低劣，穿不住的。

sledgehammer ['sledʒˌhæmə] *n.* 长柄大锤

    分割记忆：sledge（雪橇）＋ hammer（锤子）

sleek [sliːk] *a.* 光滑的； *v.* （使）光滑. ↔ coarse

sleeper ['sliːpə] *n.* 暂时未受赏识的商品

    Unnoticed by the critics at its publication, the eventual Pulitzer Prize winner was a classic *sleeper*.

    他的作品的出版没有受到批评家们的关注，而作为一个暂时未受到赏识的一流作家他最终赢得了普利策奖。

sleight [slait] *n.* 巧妙手法，巧计. legerdemain

    The magician amazed the audience with his *sleight* of hand.

258

魔术师手上奇妙的手法使观众大为惊异。

sleuth [slu:θ] *n.* 侦探. detective

They hired a *sleuth* to uncover the reason for her action.

他们雇了个侦探去揭露她这种行动的原因。

slew [slu:] *n.* 大量; *v.* (使)旋转. rotate

She *slewed* around in her seat, craning backward.

她坐在转椅上旋转着,脖子向后仰着。

slick [slik] *a.* 光滑的; 机智的; 圆滑的. glib

She is a *slick* customer, all right.

不错吧,她是个机智的顾客。

slide [slaid] *n.* 幻灯片

slimy ['slaimi] *a.* 泥泞的; 谄媚的. flattery

sling [sliŋ] *n.* 吊索; *v.* 投掷. fling, pitch

The bandits *slinged* stones and curses at their helpless victim.

土匪扔石头,还咒骂他们那个孤助无依的受害人。

slink [sliŋk] *v.* 偷偷走动

The beggar, refused a meal, *slunk* away into the shadows.

乞丐拒绝了(人家施舍的)一顿饭,偷偷走开,走进了阴影中去。

slip [slip] *n.* & *v.* 犯大错. blunder

Offering to negotiate with the enemy at that time was an inexcusable *slip*.

在那种时候提出和敌人谈判是不可饶恕的大错。

slipshod ['slipʃɔd] *a.* 邋遢的; 马虎的. disheveled; slapdash

She cleaned her room in such a *slipshod* manner that it wasn't any neater after she finished.

她这么马虎地打扫房间,以致房间打扫后也不比打扫前整洁多少。

slit [slit] *n.* 裂缝; *v.* 撕裂. cleft

The stretches of snow trembled and broke open in *slits* at every step he took.

他每踏出一步，延伸的雪原就在他脚下颤抖、裂开。

比较记忆：split（分裂），slice（切开）

slither ['sliðə] *v.* (蛇)扭动前进；蜿蜒地滑行

snake：slither = duck：waddle

sliver ['slivə] *n.* 长条，小片； *v.* 裂成小片

She *slivered* the meat into several slices.

她把肉撕成几条细片。

slobber ['slɔbə] *n.* 口水； *v.* 流口水. drivel

slogan ['sləugən] *n.* 标语；口号

Slogans are probably the kind of advertisement with which we are almost all familiar because constant repetition is the technique used to fix a slogan in the memory.

标语可是我们几乎都熟知的一种广告形式，因为不断地重复就是把一条标语在人们的记忆中打上烙印的技巧。

sloop [slu:p] *n.* 小帆船

A *sloop* is a fore-and-aft-rigged sailboat with a single mast, a mainsail, and a jib.

小帆船是一种有一根桅杆，一个主帆和一个三角帆的纵向装帆的帆船。

slop [slɔp] *v.* 溢出，溅出. overflow

sloppy ['slɔpi] *a.* 邋遢的，不整洁的. unkempt

The boss castigated the secretaries for their *sloppy* job of filing.

老板严厉申斥了秘书们档案整理工作中的拖遢。

slosh [slɔʃ] *v.* 溅，泼. splash

slot [slɔt] *n.* 缝，孔. orifice

Put a penny in the *slot* to get a stick of gum from this

machine.

往小孔里塞进一便士，这架机器就送出一片口香糖。

sloth [sləuθ] *n.* 树懒（一种动物）；懒惰. ↔ industry

Such *sloth* in a young person is deplorable go to work.

年轻人的这种懒惰真是可悲可叹。

slouch [slautʃ] *n.* 笨拙的人； *v.* 垂头丧气地走. bungler

slough [slau] *n.* 沼泽地；绝望境地； *v.* 使陷入困境

slough [slʌf] *v.* （蛇等）蜕皮，蜕壳

Each spring the snake *sloughs* off its skin.

每年春天蛇都蜕皮。

snake : slough = bird : molt

sloven ['slʌvən] *n.* 不修边幅的人

slovenly ['slʌvənli] *a.* 不整洁的

Such *slovenly* work habits will never produce good products.

这种不整洁的工作习惯永远也造不出好产品来。

slue [sluː] *v.* （使）旋转. slew

sluggard ['slʌgəd] *n.* 懒汉. laggard

"You are a *sluggard*, a drone, a parasite," the angry father shouted at his lazy son.

一位父亲生气地冲他那懒儿子喊道："你这个懒鬼，寄生虫，寄生虫!"

sluggish ['slʌgiʃ] *a.* 行动迟钝的；懒散的. languid

After two nights without sleep, she felt *sluggish* and incapable of exertion.

两宿没睡觉了,她感觉（浑身上下像散了架子似地）懒散,什么也干不动了。

sluice [sluːs] *n.* 水闸； *v.* 冲洗；奔流

This *sluice* gate is opened only in times of drought to provide water for irrigation.

这个水闸只在干旱的时候才开,放水作灌溉用。

slumber ['slʌmbə] *v.* & *n.* 睡眠；微睡

How long did the volcano *slumber*?

火山会休眠多长时间呢?

slump [slʌmp] *v.* 猛然落下；暴跌

Tired from his walk, he *slumped* into a chair.

他走得累了,一屁股跌坐在椅子里。

slur [slə:] *n.* 毁谤；   *v.* 含糊不清地讲

Polls revealed that the front-runner's standing had been damaged by the *slurs* and innuendoes circulated by his opponent's staff.

民意调查表明领先的竞选人的名望被他对物的手下人传播的诽谤中伤给毁了。

slurp [slə:p] *n.* 吃喝时不雅声

slurp : eat = snore : sleep

slut [slʌt] *n.* 邋遢女人. sloven

smack [smæk] *n.* 滋味,味道

smarmy ['smɑ:mi] *a.* 一味讨好的

smashing ['smæʃiŋ] *a.* 极佳的

smattering ['smætəriŋ] *n.* 略知,少数

I don't know whether it is better to be ignorant of a subject or to have a mere *smattering* of information about it.

我不知道对一个话题是一点不懂为好,还是略知一二为妙。

smear [smiə] *n.* 污迹,污点；   *v.* 玷污. daub

Anything written with a soft pencil *smears* easily.

任何用软铅笔写的东西都容易模糊不清。

smelt [smelt] *v.* 熔炼. melt ↔ liquefy

Please list the different temperatures at which various metals *smelt*.

请列出不同金属熔融时的不同温度。

smirch [sməːtʃ] *n.* 污点； *v.* 玷污. soil

smirk [sməːk] *v.* 假笑. ↔ smile

Wipe that *smirk* off your face!

快放下你那一脸的皮笑肉不笑吧!

smithereens [ˌsmiðəˈriːnz] *n.* 碎片

smolder [ˈsməuldə] *v.* 用文火闷烧；压抑

The rags *smoldered* for hours before they burst into flame.

烂布闷烧了几小时,而后猛地燃成一团大火。

smother [ˈsmʌðə] *v.* 覆盖；(使)闷死

The killer *smothered* the victim with a pillow.

杀手用枕头闷住他的受害人(使他窒息而死)。

smudge [smʌdʒ] *n.* 污点,渍痕； *v.* 弄脏. blot

Her reputation is *smudged* by her promiscuous behavior.

她那些乱七八糟的行为弄坏了她的名声。

smug [smʌg] *a.* 自命不凡的. priggish

She *smugly* chooses to stay at American hotel throughout Europe in order to avoid unscrupulous foreigners.

整个呆在欧洲的期间,她都自命不凡地选择住在美国宾馆里,以避开肆无忌惮的外国人。

比较记忆：smuggle（走私）

smutty [ˈsmʌti] *a.* 淫秽的. pornographic

It was incredible that a *smutty* film was shown at stage party openly.

在戏剧晚会上公开放映色情片,真不可思议。

snag [snæg] *n.* 暗礁；障碍. reef；encumbrance

Their plans for going into business sound ideal, but there is sure to be a *snag* somewhere.

他们经商的计划听上去挺理想,但肯定在什么环节上存在障碍。

snaky [ˈsneiki] *a.* 弯曲的；阴险的. sinuous；wily

snappish ['snæpiʃ] *a.* 脾气暴燥的. pettish

snappy ['snæpi] *a.* 精力充沛的；明快的. thewy

snare [snɛə] *n.* 罗网；陷阱. trap

> 比较记忆：ensnare（使入圈套）

snarl [snɑːl] *v.* 纠缠. importune

> Rover *snarled* when I took away the bone.
>
> 我把骨头拿开，罗弗纠缠住不放。

snazzy ['snæzi] *a.* 时髦的. smart

sneak [sniːk] *v.* 鬼鬼祟祟；偷窃. skulk；filch

> Bill *sneaked* out the back door so that no one would see him leave.
>
> 比尔从后门悄悄溜走，这样就没人看见他离开了。

sneaking ['sniːkiŋ] *a.* 秘密的. furtive

snicker ['snikə] *v.* & *n.* 窃笑

> A *snicker* escaped her lips even while her mother was scolding her.
>
> 甚至在她妈妈责备她时，她嘴角还挂着情不自禁的窃笑。

snide [snaid] *a.* 含沙射影的；劣等的. nasty；mean

snigger ['snigə] *v.* 暗笑，窃笑

> The boys *sniggered* as the poor dog ran about with a tin can tied to its tail.
>
> 男孩子们看着那只尾巴上拴了个铁皮罐，四处乱窜的狗，暗自好笑。

snip [snip] *v.* 剪；剪断

snipe [snaip] *v.* 狙击；伏击. ambush

> The bandits waited to *snipe* him from the seclusion of the shadowed alley.
>
> 强盗们躲在街道的阴影里，等着要伏击他。

snips [snips] *n.* 铁丝剪

snitch [snitʃ] *v.* 偷窃；泄密. pilfer；tattle

264

比较记忆：snatch（攫取）

snoop [snu:p] *n.* 窥探者；　*v.* 窥探

The detective **snooped** the felon's comings and goings with a camera planted in a building across the street from his home.

侦探在案犯家街对面的一座大楼里装了架照像机，窥探他的进进出出，来来去去。

snooty ['snu:ti] *a.* 自大的，傲慢的

The general is **snooty** in seizure of the powers of state at the end of the civil war.

将军在内战行将结束的时候，自大地攫取州的权力。

snowdrift ['snəudrift] *n.* 雪堆

组合词：snow ＋ drift（漂流物，吹积物）

snub [snʌb] *v.* 冷落

She deliberately **snubbed** him by turning and walking away in the middle of his sentence.

她有意冷落他，在他话讲到一半的时候，转身就走了。

比较记忆：snob（势利小人）

snuff [snʌf] *v.* 熄灭；嗅. quench

His life was finally **snuffed** by the onset of pneumonia.

由于突发肺炎，他的生命之火最终熄灭了。

snug [snʌg] *a.* 温暖的；舒适的. cozy

The hunters found a **snug** cabin in the woods.

猎人们在林中找到一个温暖舒适的小木屋。

snuggle ['snʌgl] *v.* 挨近，依偎. nestle

比较记忆：smuggle（走私）

soak [səuk] *v.* 浸泡；渗透. drench

Water **soaked** into the soil.

水渗进土壤里去。

soaked ['səukid] *a.* 湿透的

soar [sɔː] *v.* 升高；飞翔. tower

Jets designed for commercial use in the 1980s will *soar* at 760 miles an hour.

20 世纪 80 年代设计的商用喷气飞机一小时可飞行 700 英里。

sober ['səubə] *a.* 清醒的，庄重的

Authorities state that a person whose blood contains less than 0.05 percent of alcohol is *sober*.

权威人士宣布当一个人血液中酒精浓度含量低于 0.05％时，这个人是清醒的。

sobriety [səu'braiəti] *n.* 节制；清醒

Neither drunkards nor comics are noted for *sobriety*.

没有一个醉鬼或喜剧演员以头脑清醒而闻名。

sobriquet ['səubrikei] *n.* 浑名，绰号

Despite all his protests, his classmates continued to call him by that unflattering *sobriquet*.

尽管他竭力反抗，他的同学们仍叫他那个不太雅观的绰号。

socialite ['səuʃəlait] *n.* 社会名流，名士. elite

sociopath ['səusiəpæθ] *n.* 反社会者；不爱社交者

sock [sɔk] *n.* & *v.* 重击，痛打. punch

The fighter fell his opponent with a mighty *sock*.

斗士一记重击打倒了对手。

socket ['sɔkit] *n.* 插孔

socket : bulb = setting（镶座）: gem

sodden ['sɔdn] *a.* 浸透了的. steeped, drenched

He set his *sodden* overcoat near the radiator to dry.

他把湿透了的外套大衣挂在暖气近旁烘烤着。

sodium ['səudjəm] *n.* 钠

参考：aluminum（铝），copper（铜），zinc（锌）

soft-spoken ['sɔft'spəukən] *a.* 说话温柔的

soggy ['sɔgi] *a.* 湿透的

266

Although the air was warm, the grass was still too *soggy* to walk across.

尽管空气温暖，草地仍旧潮湿，不能从那里走过。

soil [sɔil] *v.* 弄脏，污损. defile

He *soiled* the towel by not thoroughly washing his hands.

他不好好洗净手，结果把毛巾弄脏了。

sojourn ['sɔdʒəːn] *v.* & *n.* 逗留；旅居

After his *sojourn* in Florida, he began to long for the colder climate of his native New England home.

在佛罗里达住了一段时间之后，他开始渴望他家乡新英格兰那凉爽的气候了。

solace ['sɔləs] *v.* & *n.* 安慰，慰藉. console

I hope you will find *solace* in the thought that all of us share your loss.

我们都在分担你的损失，我希望你能从精神上得到些许安慰。

solatium [səu'leiʃiəm] *n.* 赔偿金. compensation

solder ['sɔldə] *v.* 焊接，焊合

The plumber fixed the leak in the pipes by *soldering* a couple of joints from which water had been oozing.

水管工焊上几处渗水的接头，修好了漏水的水管。

solecism ['sɔlisizəm] *n.* 语法错误；举止失礼

I must give this paper a failing mark because it contains many *solecisms*.

我不得不给这篇文章打不及格，因为文中有许多文法错误。

solemnity [sə'lemniti] *n.* 庄严；肃穆

The minister was concerned that nothing should disturb the *solemnity* of the marriage service.

牧师考虑到什么也不该干扰婚礼仪式的庄严肃穆。

solicit [sə'lisit] *v.* 恳求；教唆. ↔ veto

Knowing she needed to have a solid majority for the

budget to pass, the mayor telephoned all the members of the city council to *solicit* their votes.

当了解到她需要多数票才能使财政预算得以通过,市长给市议会的每位成员打电话拉他们的选票。

solicitous [sə'lisitəs] *a.* 热切的;挂念的. desirous

The employer was very *solicitous* about the health of her employees as replacements were difficult to get.

老板十分挂念她雇员们的健康,因为不好找到能够顶替(生病的雇员)的人。

solidarity [ˌsɔli'dæriti] *n.* 团结(一致). cohesion

比较记忆:solidify (使凝固,巩固)

soliloquy [sə'liləkwi] *n.* 自言自语;独白

soli (alone) + loquy (speak) → 独白

solipsism ['səulipsizəm] *n.* 唯我论

Those avant-garde writers are in such *solipsism* that they don't even attempt to communicate with their audiences.

那些先锋派作家们抱定唯我论的观念,甚至不试着同他们的读者群沟通沟通。

solitary ['sɔlitəri] *a.* 孤独的; *n.* 隐居者. hermit

There are no *solitary*, free-living creatures, every form of life is dependent on other forms.

不存在孤独的、自由生存的生命体,因为每种生命形式都要依赖其他的生命形式。

solitude ['sɔlitjuːd] *n.* 孤独. ↔ resort

solo ['səuləu] *a.* 单独的; *n.* 独唱

参考:trio (三重奏), duet (二重奏), quartet (四重奏)

solvency ['sɔlvənsi] *n.* 溶解;清偿能力

solvent ['sɔlvənt] *a.* 有偿付能力的; *n.* 溶剂

By dint of very frugal living, he was finally able to become *solvent* and avoid bankruptcy proceedings.

在歌剧里女低音一般不如女高音有那么多的领衔角色。

sorcery ['sɔːsəri] *n.* 巫术；魔法. witchcraft

参考：exorcise（驱邪），sorcerer（巫师）

sordid ['sɔːdid] *a.* 卑鄙的；肮脏的. vile；squalid

The social worker was angered by the *sordid* housing provided for the homeless.

社会工作者对提供给无家可归者的那肮脏的住房感到气愤。

sorority [sə'rɔriti] *n.* 妇女社团

sound [saund] *v.* 测量（水深）. fathom

sound [saund] *n.* 海峡；　*a.* 健康的；全面的

soundness ['saundnis] *n.* 健康

Overindulgence debilitates character as well as physical *soundness*.

过分放任不仅有损身体健康，也磨蚀性情。

soupcon ['suːpsɜːŋ] *n.* 微量，一点点

There was a *soupcon* of boredom in her tone.

她声音中有一点点厌烦的味道。

sourpuss ['sauəpus] *n.* 牢骚满腹的人

souse [saus] *v.* 浸入水中；使湿透. plunge

He was wet blanket, *sousing* everyone's spirits.

他真是个扫兴的人，把大家的情绪全搞坏了。

souvenir ['suːvəniə] *n.* 纪念物，纪念品. keepsake

She kept the pinecone as a *souvenir* of that weekend in the country.

她保留着那个松塔，作为在乡村度过的那个周末的留念。

sovereign ['sɔvrin] *n.* 最高统治者，君主. potentate；　*a.* 最高的.

No one questions the queen's *sovereign* authority.

没人对皇后的绝对权威提出质疑。

sovereignty ['sɔvrənti] *n.* 主权；统治权

271

sow [sau] *n.* 母猪； *v.* 播种；散步. disseminate；foment

参考：hog（公猪），pork（猪肉）

spacious ['speiʃəs] *a.* 广阔的；宽敞的. commodious, capacious

比较记忆：specious（似是而非的）

spangle ['spæŋgl] *n.* （缝在衣服上的）金属亮片； *v.* 闪光

The thousands of *spangles* on her dress sparkled in the glare of the stage lights.

在舞台灯光的照射下，她裙子上成千上万的金属亮片闪着光泽。

spank [spæŋk] *v.* 拍打（在屁股上）

Mother *spanked* her for running into the street.

母亲因为她跑上街而打了她的屁股。

spanking ['spæŋkiŋ] *a.* 快的，敏捷的. brisk

He passed us in a *spanking* walk.

他从我们眼前轻快地走过。

sparing ['spεəriŋ] *a.* 节俭的，节约的. frugal

注意区别：sparing（拳击）

spark [spɑ:k] *n.* 火花，火星

比较记忆：sparkle（闪耀）

sparse [spɑ:s] *a.* 稀少的，贫乏的. meager，scarce

A *sparse* crowd scattered thinly through the auditorium.

演讲厅里稀稀落落地散坐着不多的几个人。

Spartan ['spɑ:tən] *a.* 简朴的；艰苦的. austere

He led a *Spartan* life in his one-room apartment with few items of comfort.

他住在只有一间房间的公寓里，房间里几乎没有什么奢侈品。

spasm ['spæzəm] *n.* 痉挛，抽搐. convulsion

spasmodic [spæz'mɔdik] *a.* 痉挛的；间歇的

The *spasmodic* coughing is in the glare of the stage lights.

272

舞台灯光射向那个时不时咳嗽的人。

spat [spæt] *n.* 口角，小争吵. skirmish

What had started out as a mere *spat* escalated into a full-blown argument.

本来开始时只是小争论，最后却升级为一场大论战。

spatchcock ['spætʃkɔk] *v.* 把（文字）插入

spate [speit] *n.* 大批；洪水泛滥. freshet

I am worried about the possibility of a *spate* if the rains do not diminish soon.

要是雨水还是这么大，不很快减少的话，我真担忧会发洪水。

spatula ['spætjulə] *n.* （调拌等用的）抹刀，刮铲

The manufacturers of this frying pan recommend the use of a rubber *spatula* to avoid scratching the specially treated surface.

这种煎锅的制造商建议使用橡胶铲刀，以免划伤经过特殊处理的表面。

spawn [spɔːn] *n.* （鱼等）卵，子； *v.* 产卵；大量生产

Fish ladders had to be built in the dams to assist the salmon returning to *spawn* in their native streams.

大坝上要建些鱼梯，帮助回游的马哈鱼游回它们的出生地的小溪流中去产卵。

spear [spiə] *n.* 幼苗；（草）叶片 *v.* 刺，戳. lance

specifics [spi'sifiks] *n.* 详细说明书

比较记忆：specimen（标本），species（种类）

speciosity [ˌspiːʃi'ɔsiti] *n.* 似是而非

specious ['spiːʃəs] *a.* 似是而非的；华而不实的. ostensible

The reasoning in this editorial is so *specious* that we cannot see how anyone can be deceived by it.

这篇社论中的推理这么似是而非，我们认为没有任何人会上它的当，受它的骗。

speck [spek] *n.* 斑点；少量. fleck；iota

Is that a *speck* of dust on the page or a period?

页面上那是个灰尘点还是个句号?

specter ['spektə] *n.* 幽灵;恐惧. phantom

The *specter* of her father did not scare her.

他父亲的幽灵没有吓着她。

spectral ['spektrəl] *a.* 幽灵的,鬼魂的. otherworldly

We were frightened by the *spectral* glow that filled the room.

我们可让那满屋幽灵般的闪光给吓坏了。

speleology [ˌspiːliˈɔlədʒi] *n.* 洞穴学

spell [spel] *n.* 连续一段时间;咒语; *v.* 使入谜. charm

spellbind ['spelbaind] *v.* 迷住,魅惑. enthrall

Looking at the New York City's skyscrapers *spellbinds* tourists.

看着纽约市内的摩天大厦,游客们都迷住了。

spelunker [spiˈlʌŋkə] *n.* 爱好探察洞穴者

spelunker : cavern = philatelist : stamp

spendthrift ['spendθrift] *a.* & *n.* 挥金如土的(人). profligate

Easy access to credit encourages people to turn into *spendthrifts* who shop till they drop.

很容易就可得到贷款促使一些人变成了挥金如土之士,他们大肆购物直到破产。

sphinx [sfiŋks] *n.* 狮身人面像,谜一样的人

来自埃及金字塔附近的狮身人面像

参考:unicorn(独角兽),mermaid(美人鱼),centaur(半人半马怪物)

spiel [spiːl] *n.* 滔滔不绝的话

spike [spaik] *n.* 长钉,大钉

spindle ['spindl] *n.* 锭子,纺锤

A *spindle* is a round pointed pin used for twisting the

thread in spinning.

纺锤是一个中间圆圆两头尖尖的钉，用来旋转捻线。

spindly ['spindli] *a.* 细长的；纤弱的. lanky, rangy

The child is unable to stand on his *spindly* little legs.

孩子还不能用他细弱的小脚站起来。

spineless ['spainlis] *a.* 没骨气的. timid

比较记忆：spine（脊椎，刺）

spinster ['spinstə] *n.* 老处女

参考：bachelor（单身汉）

spiny ['spaini] *a.* 多刺的；困难重重的

spiral ['spaiərəl] *n.* 螺旋(形)；螺线

spire ['spaiə] *n.* (教堂)尖顶；塔尖

spirited ['spiritid] *a.* 活泼的；勇敢的. vivacious; bold

The *spirited* firemen rescued people from a burning
building.

勇敢的消防队员从燃烧着的大楼里往外救人。

spite [spait] *n.* 怨恨；恶意. malice

spiteful ['spaitful] *a.* 恶意的；怀恨的

The *spiteful* girl deliberately broke the doll when she
was told she couldn't keep it.

当小女孩听说她不能留下那个娃娃时，心怀怨恨地摔碎了娃娃。

splashy ['splæʃi] *a.* 引人注目的. striking

来自：splash（溅水，显著地展示）

spleen [spli:n] *n.* 脾脏；怒气. petulance

spleenish ['spli:niʃ] *a.* 易怒的；怨恨的. touchy; malicious

That very beautiful woman is tiresome because of her
spleenish temper.

那相貌极美的女人却很令人厌烦，因为她性情好怨恨。

Unit Thirty-Four

splendor ['splendə] *n.* 壮丽，辉煌. grandeur
比较记忆：splendid（壮观的）

splenetic [spli'netik] *a.* 脾气暴的，易怒的. testy
People shunned him because of his *splenetic*.
人们因他脾气暴躁而避着他。

splice [splais] *v.* 接合，衔接
splice：rope = weld：metal

splint [splint] *n.* (固定断骨的)夹板，托板
splint：mobility = lubricant：friction

splinter ['splintə] *n.* 裂片； *v.* 裂成碎片. sliver
Pull the *splinter* out with a tweezers.
用小镊子把裂片夹出来。

splurge [splə:dʒ] *v.* 炫耀，夸示. flaunt
He openly *splurges* his vices with no regard for the conventions of society.
他一点儿也不考虑社会习俗,公开炫耀他的恶行。

spoil [spɔil] *v.* 损坏；宠坏； *n. pl .* 战利品. pine；coddle
His grandparents would *spoil* him if we let them.
要是我们允许的话,他祖父母会宠坏他的。

spoke [spəuk] *n.* (车轮上)辐条

spontaneity [ˌspɔntə'ni:iti] *n.* 自发性
The President's State of the Union Address, as it has evolved through successive Administrations and Congresses, has become a very formal ceremony, governed by a specific protocol, that leaves little room for *spon-*

taneity.

总统的国情演讲历经在一系列的行政及国会会议上的磨砺,已演变成了一种非常正式的仪式性讲话,受其特定礼仪的约束,这种讲话没有多少可即兴自由发挥的余地。

spontaneous [spɔn'teinjəs] *a.* 自发的;自然的

spoof [spu:f] *v.* 揶揄,嘲讽. hoax

spook [spu:k] *n.* 鬼怪. wraith

She claimed she had seen a *spook* in the haunted house.

她声称她看到这所鬼魂萦绕的房子里有一个鬼。

spool [spu:l] *n.* (缠录音带等的)卷轴

spoonerism ['spu:nərizəm] *n.* 首音互换

When the radio announcer introduced the President as Hoopert Herver, he was guilty of a *spoonerism*.

当电台播音员介绍总统时,把赫伯特·胡佛说成胡伯特·赫佛了,他犯了个首音互换的错误。

spoor [spuə] *n.* (野兽的)足迹

sporadic [spə'rædik] *a.* 零星的. scattered.

Although there are *sporadic* outbursts of gunfire, we can report that the major rebellion has been suppressed.

尽管还是有零星枪声响起,我们可以报告说主要的叛乱(分子)都已镇压下去了。

spore [spɔ:] *n.* 孢子;事物的根源

sport [spɔ:t] *v.* 炫耀,卖弄. vaunt

She *sported* her new miniskirt in the party.

她在晚会上炫耀她的新迷你裙。

sporty ['spɔ:ti] *a.* 供娱乐的;时髦漂亮的. stylish

spout ['spaut] *v.* 喷出;滔滔不绝地讲. gush

Wounded to the quick, the whale began to *spout* blood.

鲸鱼一直伤到皮下,开始汩汩冒出血来。

sprain [sprein] *v.* 扭伤

sprawl [sprɔ:l] *v.* 懒散地躺

The people ***sprawled*** on the beach in their bathing suits.

人们穿着浴衣懒散地躺在海滩上。

spree [spri:] *n.* 狂欢；狂饮. revel

He was hung over for days after his ***spree***.

狂欢后几天他都没醒过酒来。

sprig [sprig] *n.* 嫩枝，小枝

sprightly ['spraitli] *a.* 活泼的. frisky，brisk

The taciturn man became ***sprightly*** and talkative after drinking one cocktail.

喝了杯鸡尾酒后，这个沉默寡言的人变得活泼，话也多起来。

sprinkling ['spriŋkliŋ] *n.* 略知；少数. smattering

sprint [sprint] *v.* 全速奔跑

The players ***sprinted*** across the football field.

橄榄球手全速跑过球场。

sprinter ['sprintə] *n.* 短跑选手

sprinter：gun = fighter：bell（以示开始）

sprout [spraut] *n.* 嫩芽；　*v.* 萌芽. germinate

比较记忆：spout（喷出）

spruce [spru:s] *n.* 云杉；　*a.* 整洁的；潇洒的. trim；chic

Every button buttoned, tie firmly in place, young Alex Keaton looked ***spruce*** and tidy for his job interview at the bank.

每个扣子都扣好了，领带扎得紧紧乎乎的，年轻的亚历克斯·基顿到银行去接受求职面试时看上去整洁潇洒。

spry [sprai] *a.* 活泼的；敏捷的. agile

She was eighty years old yet still ***spry*** and alert.

她都 80 岁了，还那么敏捷机警。

spume [spju:m] *n.* 泡沫. scum

The ***spume*** at the base of the waterfall extended for a

278

quarter of a mile down river.

瀑布下边激起的泡沫一直顺河水铺出四分之一英里去。

spunk [spʌŋk] *n.* 勇气，胆量. mettle

spur [spə:] *v.* 刺激；疾驰. goad; trot

The encouragement was a helpful *spur* to his ego.

鼓励有助于刺激他的自尊。

spurious ['spjuəriəs] *a.* 假的；伪造的. phony

She tried to pay the check with a *spurious* ten-dollar bill.

她想用张 10 美元的伪钞付账。

spurn [spə:n] *v.* 拒绝，摈弃. denounce

The heroine *spurned* the villain's advances.

女主人公拒绝了那个恶棍的求爱。

spurt [spə:t] *v.* 喷出；迸发. gush; spout

He squeezed the plunger of the hypodermic until the needle *spurted* out a few drops.

他往上推了一下注射器的活塞直到针尖喷出几滴药水。

sputum ['spju:təm] *n.* 唾液，口涎

What was the result of the analysis of his *sputum*?

他的唾液分析结果怎样?

squabble ['skwɔbl] *n.* (为琐事)争吵. miff

Children invariably get involved in petty *squabbles*, wise parents know when to interfere and when to let the children work things out on their own.

孩子们无一例外地会卷入些无关紧要的争吵,明智的父母知道什么时候该加以干涉,什么时候该由着他们自己解决。

squad [skwɔd] *n.* 小队;(军队)班

squalid ['skwɔlid] *a.* 污秽的, 肮脏的. filthy

It is easy to see how crime can breed in such a *squalid* neighborhood.

不难看出,在这样污秽的生活环境里,罪行是多么容易繁衍开来。

squall [skwɔːl] *n.* 狂风； *v.* 尖叫. yell；gust

A *squall* hit the resort town and ruined the weekend for the tourists.

狂风袭击了那个度假胜地的小镇,也破坏了游客们的周末。

squalor ['skwɔlə] *n.* 不洁，污秽. foulness

The *squalor* of the apartment was unbelievable；it was difficult to realize that men could live in such filth.

公寓污浊得令人难以置信；很难相信那些人能生活在这样的肮脏中。

squander ['skwɔndə] *v.* 浪费，挥霍. dissipate，lavish

The prodigal son *squanderd* the family estate.

这个败家子把祖传的房地产都败光了。

squash [skwɔʃ] *n.* 南瓜属植物； *v.* 压碎，挤压. quash

The check-out girl always puts the bread on top of the other groceries so that it does not get *squashed*.

收款处的女孩总把面包放在其他东西上面,这样就不会把面包压碎了。

squat [skwɔt] *a.* 矮胖的； *v.* 蹲下

squeak [skwiːk] *v.* (鼠)吱吱叫

squeamish ['skwiːmiʃ] *a.* 易呕吐的. queasy

She would get *squeamish* at the sight of blood.

她一看见血就会恶心作呕。

squelch [skweltʃ] *v.* 压制；压碎. quench

The trash compactor *squelched* the leftovers into tiny piles.

垃圾压缩机把剩下的东西压成小摞。

squib [skwib] *n.* 爆竹；讽刺性短文(讲话)

squirm [skwəːm] *v.* 蠕动. wriggle

The little girl tried desperately to *squirm* free from the tangled bedclothes.

小女孩绝望地挣扎蠕动着,想从床上(卷成一团)的铺盖里拱出来。

squirt [skwəːt] *v.* 喷出. snuff

Water *squirted* from the fire hose.

水从消防水管里喷涌而出。

stab [stæb] *v.* 刺伤. thrust

The killer *stabbed* his victim with a carving knife.

杀手用切肉刀刺他的受害人。

staccato [stəˈkɑːtəu] *a.* （音乐）断奏的；不连贯的

His *staccato* speech reminded one of the sound of a machine gun.

他那爆豆似的话语使人想起机枪的声音。

staddle [ˈstædl] *n.* 基础

stagger [ˈstægə] *v.* 蹒跚；摇晃. totter

The news of his death *staggered* the country.

他的死讯令全国为之震惊。

staggering [ˈstægəriŋ] *a.* 令人吃惊的

stagnant [ˈstægnənt] *a.* 不流动的；不新鲜的. static

The *stagnant* water was a breeding ground for disease.

不流动的死水是疾病的孕育之地。

stagy [ˈsteidʒi] *a.* 不自然的，演戏般的. theatrical

staid [steid] *a.* 稳重的；固定的. ↔ flighty

Her conduct during the funeral ceremony was *staid* and solemn.

她在葬礼仪式上的举止庄严稳重。

stain [stein] *v.* 玷污；染色. blot；tint

He *stained* his military record by going AWOL.

（AWOL = absent without leave）

他的军旅记录中由于有未准假离职而染上污点。

stake [steik] *n.* 柱子；赌注

gamble：stake = invest：capital

stalactite [ˈstæləktait] *n.* 钟乳石

stalagmite ['stæləgmait] *n.* 石笋

stale [steil] *a.* 不新鲜的；疲惫的. banal

> The *stale* Victorianisms are mercifully disappearing from the language.
>
> 早已不再新鲜的维多利亚女王时代的风尚在语言中正在渐渐地消失。

stalemate ['steil'meit] *n.* 僵局. deadlock

> Negotiations between the union and the employers have reached a *stalemate*; neither side is willing to budge from previously stated positions.
>
> 雇主与工会间的谈判陷入了僵局，双方谁也不愿从先前阐明的立场上稍作让步。

stalk [stɔ:k] *n.* 茎，杆；   *v.* 潜近猎物. skulk

> The lion *stalked* the zebra for hours before attacking.
>
> 狮子在伏击斑马前，跟踪了斑马好几个小时。

stall [stɔ:l] *n.* 诈术；托辞 (ruse to deceive or delay)

> stall : delay = bluff : deceive（目的）

stallion ['stæljən] *n.* 公马

> Your *stallions* are very spirited animals.
>
> 你那些公马是十分有活力的动物。
>
> 参考：mare（母马）

stalwart ['stɔ:lwət] *a.* 健壮的；坚定的. robust; formidable

> His consistent support of the party has proved that he is a *stalwart* and loyal member.
>
> 他始终如一地支持他的党派证明他是个忠诚坚定的成员。

stamen ['steimən] *n.* 雄蕊

> 参考：pistil（雌蕊）

stamina ['stæminə] *n.* 精力；耐力

> I doubt that she has the *stamina* to run the full distance of the marathon race.
>
> 我怀疑她有没有跑完马拉松比赛全程的耐力。

stammer ['stæmə] *v.* 口吃，结巴. falter

He *stammered* most when he was nervous.

他多在紧张时才会结巴。

stampede [stæm'pi:d] *v.* & *n.* 蜂拥；惊跑

The loud, unexpected noise sent the flock into a *stampede*.

那出人意料的巨大响声吓得人们四下蜂拥而逃。

stance [stæns] *n.* 站姿；姿态

stanch ['sta:ntʃ] *v.* 止(血)；止住

It is imperative that we *stanch* the gushing wound before we attend to the other injuries.

要紧的是我们应该先止住伤口的流血，而后再处理其他伤处。

stand [stænd] *v.* 忍受. abide

The society woman will *stand* the eccentric guests so long as they are artists.

那位社交界女士总能忍受得了她那些怪异的客人，只要他们是艺术家。

stand [stænd] *n.* 林分，个体植物群丛

stand : tree = swarm : bee

stand-in ['stænd'in] *n.* 替身

standoffish ['sænd'ɔfiʃ] *a.* 不友好的，冷淡的. aloof

She always seems so *standoffish* about everything; you just can't approach him at all.

他看上去总是对一切都冷冷的，你根本就没法接近他。

stanza ['stænzə] *n.* (诗)节

stanza : poem = act : opera

staple ['steipl] *n.* 订书钉

staple ['steipl] *n.* 主要产品；主题

The weather forms still the *staple* of their conversation.

天气还是他们交谈的主要话题。

stapler ['steiplə] *n.* 订书机

starchy ['stɑːtʃi] *a.* 古板的. prim

比较记忆：starch（淀粉）

star-crossed ['stɑːkrɔst] *a.* 时运不济的，倒霉的

stark [stɑːk] *a.* （外表）僵硬的；完全的. rigid

We have to face the *stark* reality of the schedule's deadline.

我们得面对计划最终期限这一铁定的现实。

starry ['stɑːri] *a.* 星光灿烂的

stash [stæʃ] *v.* 藏匿，隐藏. hoard

The miser *stashed* all his money in the secret compartment of the wall.

守财奴把他所有的钱都藏在墙中一个秘密小间里。

stately ['steitli] *a.* 高贵的；雄伟的. regal

The dining room in the castle was grand and *stately*.

城堡的餐厅雄伟辉煌。

static ['stætik] *a.* 静态的；呆板的. inert

Nothing had changed at home things were *static* there.

家里什么也没有变，那里事物是静止不变的。

stationary ['steiʃənəri] *a.* 静止的，不动的

stationery ['steiʃənəri] *n.* 文具

statuary ['stætjuəri] *n.* 雕像；雕塑艺术

来自；statue（雕像）

statuette [ˌstætju'et] *n.* 小雕像

statue + ette (little) → 小雕像

stature ['stætʃə] *n.* 身高，身材

status ['steitəs] *n.* 身份，地位

He strived constantly for *status* in the middle class.

他不断努力，想在中产阶级中争得一席之地。

statute ['stætjuːt] *n.* 法规，法令

We have many *statutes* in our law books which should be repealed.

我们法律书中的许多法规都该撤消了。

statutory ['stætjutəri] *a.* 法定的

The judicial courts review and try *statutory* crimes.

法庭复审并再宣判法定罪行。

staunch [stɔ:ntʃ] *a.* 密封的；坚定的. watertight；resolute

He delivered a *staunch* defense of the government.

他发表了一坚定维护政府(尊严的讲话)。

steadfast ['stedfə:st] *a.* 坚定的. loyal

I am sure you will remain *steadfast* in your support of the cause.

我确信你会一直坚定地支持这一奋斗目标。

stealth [stelθ] *n.* 秘密行动

Fearing detection by the sentries on duty, the scout inched his way toward the enemy camp with great *stealth*.

担心被值勤哨兵发现,侦察员极为隐蔽地一寸一寸挪向敌营。

steep [sti:p] *v.* 浸. soak

Be sure to *steep* the fabric in the dye bath for the full time prescribed.

一定得按规定,把织物在染色池里浸泡足够长的时间。

steeple ['sti:pl] *n.* 尖塔；尖顶

steer [stiə] *n.* 小公牛；菜牛

steer [stiə] *v.* 掌舵,驾驶

He turned the car run and *steered* for home.

他调转车头往家行驶。

steer : cart = bow : boat

stellar ['stelə] *a.* 星的；显著的. noteworthy

He has the *stellar* attraction of the entire performance.

他在整个演出中有着显著的吸引力。

stem [stem] *n.* 茎； *v.* 遏制（水流等）

The paramedic used tourniquet to *stem* the bleeding from the slashed artery.

救护人员用止血带止住从破裂的血管中流出的血。

stench [stentʃ] *n.* 臭气，恶臭. ↔ fragrance

The air was permeated with *stench* in the battlefield after a slaughter.

一场血腥杀戮后,战场上空的空气中浸透着一种恶臭味。

比较记忆：stanch（止住）

stencil ['stensil] *n.* 模板； *v.* 用模板刻写

stencil：lettering = pattern：sewing

stenography [ste'nɔgrəfi] *n.* 速记；速记法

stentorian [sten'tɔːriən] *a.*（声音）极响亮的

来自希腊神话中的特洛伊战争中的传令官 Stentor，其声音极其洪亮

The *stentorian* voice rang through the valley.

响亮的声音在整个山谷中回荡。

steppe [step] *n.*（无森林）大平原

The *steppes* of Russia have always fascinated writers all over the world.

俄罗斯大平原一直吸引着世界各地的作家。

stereotype ['stiəriətaip] *n.* 固定形式，老套

sterile ['steril] *a.* 不孕的；无菌的. barren

The debate was *sterile* of results.

这场辩论产生不了什么结果。

sterilize ['sterilaiz] *v.* 使不育；杀菌. geld

stern [stəːn] *n.* 船尾. ↔ bow

sternum ['stəːnəm] *n.* 胸骨

The human *sternum* has seven pairs of ribs attached to it.

人类胸骨有七对肋骨与其相连。

stethoscope ['steθəskəup] *n.* 听诊器

　　sterho (bosom) + scope (observance) → 听诊器

stickler ['stiklə] *n.* 坚持细节之人，为琐事争执的人

　　stickler：approximation ＝ perfectionist：defect

sticky ['stiki] *a.* 黏的. viscous

stifle ['staifl] *v.* 使窒息. choke，suffocate

　　She *stifled* her desire to show the child the way since
　　she knew it was better if he tried it alone.

　　她知道最好让孩子自己去努力,因而她扼杀了自己想给孩子指出
　　出路的欲望。

stigmatize ['stigmətaiz] *v.* 玷污. besmirch

　　I do not want to *stigmatize* this young offender for life
　　by sending her to prison.

　　我不想把这个年轻的犯人送进监狱,让她一生为此而玷污。

　　比较记忆：stigma（耻辱）

stiletto [sti'letəu] *n.* 短剑，匕首. dagger

　　参考同类词：dagger，dirk，poniard

stilted ['stiltid] *a.* 夸张做作的；不自然的. pompous；artificial

　　His *stilted* rhetoric did not impress the college audi-
　　ence；they were immune to bombastic utterances.

　　他自负的修辞打动不了大学里的听众们,他们对夸夸其谈的言
　　词可不买账。

stimulant ['stimjulənt] *n.* 兴奋剂

stimulus ['stimjuləs] *n.* 刺激，激励；　*pl.* stimuli

　　There are more *stimulus* on suggestive film advertise-
　　ments than the films they are used to publicize.

　　引人联想的电影广告比实际的影片更加富有刺激性。

stingy ['stindʒi] *a.* 吝啬的. parsimonious

　　Their *stingy* piling up of wealth had not made up for

their inability to have children.

他们吝啬地积聚起来的财富也弥补不了没有孩子的缺憾。

stink [stiŋk] v. 发臭；   n. 臭味. stench

There was an odor of fear in the air; he made quite a *stink* about it.

空气中有种恐惧的味道,是他制造的。

stint [stink] n. 定额工作；限额

The soldier had just finished his two-hour *stint* on guard duty.

士兵刚刚执行完他两个小时的站哨任务。

stint [stint] v. 吝惜，节省

The old man could not have been accused of *stinting* his affection; his conduct toward the child betrayed his adoration of her.

这位老人不可能受到冷酷的指责,他对孩子们的行为暴露了他对她的爱慕。

stipend ['staipend] n. 薪金；养老金

There is a nominal *stipend* for this position.

这一职位只有很少一点象征性的薪水。

stipple [stipl] n. 点画；点刻.

stipple : dot = striate : band

stipulate ['stipjuleit] v. 约定

Before agreeing to reduce American military forces in Europe the president *stipulated* that NATO teams be allowed to inspect Soviet bases.

在同意削减美国在欧洲的驻军时,总统约定北约组织要视察前苏联的(军事)基地。

stitch [stitʃ] n. 一针；   v. 缝合

stitch : sampler = tile : mosaic

stock [stɔk] a. 普通的；惯用的. corny

stock : bond = owner : lender

stockade [stɔ'keid] *n.* 栅栏；围栏(防御用)

stocky ['stɔki] *a.* 矮胖的，粗壮的. chunky

The *stocky*, lumbering stevedore possesses the bullneck and barrel-shaped chest.

粗壮的木材装卸工长了个像牛一样短粗的脖子。

比较记忆：stock（树桩）

stodge [stɔdʒ] *n.* 乏味的食物；乏味的作品

stodgy ['stɔdʒi] *a.* 乏味的. stuffy

The month I spent confined to a hospital bed was so *stodgy* that I couldn't wait to get back to work.

我被困在医院病床过的那个月太乏味了，我都几乎等不及要回去工作了。

stoic ['stəuik] *n.* 坚忍克己之人，禁欲主义者

来自希腊哲学流派 Stoic（斯多葛派），主张坚忍克己

The doctor called her patient a *stoic* because he had borne the pain of the examination without whimpering.

医生称她的病人真是坚忍克己，他忍着检查的疼痛一声不吭。

stoke [stəuk] *v.* 添加燃料；司炉

As a Scout, Marisa learned how to light a fire, how to *stoke* it if it started to die down and how to extinguish it completely.

作为一个童子军，马里沙学会了怎么生堆火，火要不旺了怎么添柴，以及怎么把火彻底熄掉。

stolid ['stɔlid] *a.* 感情麻木的. indifferent

stolidity [stɔ'liditi] *n.* 不易激动；感觉迟钝

Voters responded to the levy of a new tax with *stolidity* because they have become inured to the fickle nature of government policies.

选民们对政府政策的变幻无常早已习以为常，因而对一项强行征税的新举措反应木然。

stomach ['stʌmək] *v.* 吃得下；容忍. stand

stonewall ['stəunwɔːl] *v.* 阻碍议事；妨碍. hamper

stoop [stuːp] *v.* 俯身，降低身份.

storehouse ['stɔːhaus] *n.* 宝库；见识广博者

stout [staut] *a.* 坚定的；肥胖的；强壮的. plump；hardy

His *stout* self-confidence makes you feel you can depend on him.

他坚定的自信使你感到可以依靠他。

stouthearted ['staut'hɑːtid] *a.* 勇敢的. intrepid

stowaway ['stəuəwei] *n.* (藏于轮船、飞机中的)偷乘者

比较记忆：bestow（遗赠）

stowaway：fare = smuggler：tariff

strafe [strɑːf] *v.* 扫射. rake

参考：rifle（步枪）

straggle ['strægl] *v.* 迷路；离群，掉队. stray

The chickens *straggled* across the yard after she left the hen house open.

她没有关上鸡房门，小鸡们跑了出来，跳到院子那边去了。

strain [strein] *n.* 世系；气质；旋律

The *strain* of meeting a daily deadline made the columnist very nervous.

必须赶上每日期限的气氛弄得专栏作家十分紧张。

strained [streind] *a.* 不自然的；不友好的. far-fetched

strait [streit] *n.* 海峡； *a.* 狭窄的

参考：isthmus（地峡）

straitened ['streitnd] *a.* 贫困的

straits [streits] *n.* 困难；窘境

He always seems to be in financial *straits* since he cannot manage his monetary matters.

他处理不好他金钱方面的事物，因此看上去他总处在一种经济困境中。

strand [strænd] *n.* 海滩；一缕. littoral

There are many sea pools along the ***strand*** where many sea creatures live between high tides.

沿海滩有许多海水池溏，在那里许多海洋生物靠海潮生活。

stranded ['strændid] *a.* 搁浅的. grounded

strangle [ˌstræŋgl] *v.* 扼杀；抑制. smother

strangulation ['stræŋgjuˈleiʃən] *n.* 扼杀，勒死

stratagem [ˌstrætidʒəm] *n.* 谋略，策略

The general's clever ***stratagem*** was successful against the enemy.

将军聪明的策略对付敌人很成功。

stratify ['strætifai] *v.* 使分层；使形成阶层

As the economic gap between the rich and the poor increased, Roman society grew increasingly ***stratified***.

随着罗马穷人与富人间的差异增大，罗马社会愈发贫富不均。

stratum ['streitəm] *n.* 地层；阶层

Unless we alleviate conditions in the lowest ***stratum*** of our society we may expect grumbling and revolt.

除非我们缓和我们社会最底层人民的生存条件，否则我们可预见他们会抱怨甚至反叛。

stray [strei] *a.* 漂泊的； *v.* 漂泊. rove

The kitten must have ***strayed*** from its mother.

小猫一定从它妈妈那走离了。

streak [striːk] *n.* 线条； *v.* 加线条

You have a ***streak*** of paint on your forehead.

你额头上有条油漆道子。

streamlined ['striːmlaind] *a.* 简单化的；现代化的

strenuous ['strenjuəs] *a.* 费力的；精力允沛的. arduous；energetic

The young foxes held the ***strenuous*** job of digging new

foxholes overnight.

年轻的狐狸担当了那项费力的活儿，一夜就挖好了新的狐狸洞。

strew [stru:] *v.* 撒，播. scatter

There were papers *strewn* all over the floor.

地上撒满纸屑。

比较记忆：screw（螺钉）

striated ['strai'eitid] *a.* 有条纹的

striated : groove = braided : strand

stricture ['striktʃə] *n.* 苛评；严厉. animadversion

His *strictures* on the author's style are prejudiced and unwarranted.

他对作者风格的苛评含有偏见而且并不可信。

stride [straid] *v.* 大步行走

The tall man *strides* rapidly down the street.

那个子高高的人大步沿街走去。

strident ['straidənt] *a.* 尖声的，刺耳的. shrill, grating

She scolded him in a *strident* voice.

她用刺耳的声音责备他。

stridulate ['stridjuleit] *v.* （昆虫）唧唧鸣叫

strife [straif] *v.* 纷争，倾轧. conflict

Their *strife* was over the use the equipment.

他们为设备的使用发生纷争。

比较记忆：strafe（扫射）

striking ['straikiŋ] *a.* 引人注目的. conspicuous

stringent ['strindʒənt] *a.* 严苛的；缺钱的. severe

比较记忆：astringent（收缩的）

strip [strip] *n.* 狭长的一片；   *v.* 剥去. divest

He was *stripped* of all his rights pending his appeal to the higher court.

他被剥夺了所有向上一级法院申诉的权利。

292

比较记忆：stripe（条纹）

stripling ['stripliŋ] *n.* 年轻男子

strolling ['strəuliŋ] *a.* 巡回演出的

stronghold ['strɔŋhəuld] *n.* 堡垒，要塞. fort

strum [strʌm] *v.* 乱奏

strut [strʌt] *v.* 昂首阔步地走； *n.* 高视阔步

His *strut* as he marched about the parade ground revealed him for what he was a pompous buffoon.

当他在游行场地里昂首阔步地四下走动时，暴露出他那华而不实的小丑的真面目。

stub [stʌb] *n.* 树桩； *v.* 连根拔起

He bruised himself by *stubbing* his toe in the dark.

黑夜里他绊了一跤，摔伤了。

比较记忆：stubborn（顽固不化的）

studied ['stʌdid] *a.* 精心筹划的. calculated

Given Jill's previous sights, Jack felt that the omission of his name from the guest list was a *studied* insult.

回想吉尔先前的预见，杰克感到客人名单上没有他的名字是一精心策划的对他的侮辱。

stuffy ['stʌfi] *a.* 空气沉闷的

It became *stuffy* in the crowded lecture hall.

拥挤的演讲厅里空气变得污浊不堪。

参考：muggy（潮闷的）

stultify ['stʌltifai] *v.* 使无效. invalidate

His long hours in the blacking factory left young Dickens numb and incurious as if the menial labor had *stultified* his mind.

长时间在生产黑鞋油的工厂里工作使得年轻的狄更斯麻木，对什么也不好奇，就好像这奴役劳动使他的头脑也不好使了。

stump [stʌmp] *n.* 树桩；残干

比较记忆：stumpy（短胖的）

stun [stʌn] *v.* 使昏迷；使发愣. confound

The blow to his head ***stunned*** him for a few moments.

头上受到的一击使他昏迷过去一会儿。

stunning ['stʌniŋ] *a.* 极好的；极富魅力的. gorgeous

stunt [stʌnt] *n.* 绝技； *v.* 阻碍(成长)

It used to be said that smoking would ***stunt*** one's growth.

过去有人讲吸烟阻碍身体生长。

stuntman ['stʌntmæn] *n.* 特技替身演员

stupefy ['stju:pifai] *v.* (使)茫然，吓呆

Disapproving of drugs in general, Laura refused to take sleeping pills or any other medicine that might ***stupefy*** her.

劳拉一般说来不赞成用药,她拒绝吃安眠药或其他任何可能使她发呆的药。

stupendous [stju(:)'pendəs] *a.* 巨大的. prodigious

The ***stupendous*** size of the building prevented them from seeing around it.

这所建筑如此巨大,他们都不能四下转转看看。

stupor ['stju:pə] *n.* 昏迷，不醒人事

In his ***stupor***, the addict was unaware of the events taking place around him.

瘾君子在昏迷时不知道他周围发生了些什么事。

sturdy ['stə:di] *a.* 强健的，结实的. robust

This chair is not ***sturdy*** enough to stand on.

这把椅子不太结实,不能站在上面。

stutter ['stʌtə] *v.* 口吃，结巴. stumble, stammer

He was finally able to ***stutter*** out how much he loved her.

他最终结结巴巴地说出了他有多么地爱她。

stylet ['stailit] *n.* 匕首. dirk

294

stylish ['staili∫] *a.* 时髦的. chic，classy

The dandy always discarded all garments which were no longer *stylish*.

那个花花公子总把过时的衣服扔了。

stymie ['staimi] *v.* 妨碍，阻挠. obstacle

The detective was *stymied* by the contradictory evidence in the robbery investigation.

侦探被抢劫案调查中取得的相互矛盾的证据给难住了。

styptic ['stiptik] *a.* 止血的； *n.* 止血剂. astringent

Unit Thirty-Five

subaltern ['sʌbltən] *n.* 副官

The captain treated his *subalterns* as though they were children rather than commissioned officers.

上尉对待他的副官们像对待小孩子似的，而不像在对待受委任的军官。

subcelestial ['sʌbsi'lestjəl] *a.* 世俗的. secular

sub (under) + celestial → 天底下的

subcutaneous ['sʌbkjuː'teiniəs] *n.* 皮下的

subdue [səb'djuː] *v.* 征服；减轻. conquer; mollify

The police used tear gas to *subdue* the rioters.

警方用催泪弹制服了暴乱分子。

subfusc ['sʌbfʌsk] *a.* 暗淡的；单调的. drab

sub (less) + fuse → 暗淡的

subjection [səb'dʒekʃən] *n.* 征服

subjoin [ˌsʌb'dʒɔin] *v.* 增补

subjugate ['sʌbdʒugeit] *v.* 征服；制服. ↔ foment

It is not our aim to *subjugate* our foe; we are interested only in establishing peaceful relations.

我们的目的不是征服敌人，而只是对建立起一种和平友好的关系感兴趣。

sublate [sʌb'leit] *v.* 否定；消除. veto

She *sublated* his suggestion to go away for the weekend.

她否决了他离开(这里)去海滨度周末的建议。

sublimate ['sʌblimeit] *v.* (使)升华；纯化

We must strive to *sublimate* these desires and emotions into worthwhile activities.

我们必须努力把这些情感和欲望净化升华为更有价值的行动。

sublime [sə'blaim] *a.* 崇高的. peerless

Mother Tersa has been honored for her *sublime* deeds.

泰尔萨妈妈因她崇高的事迹而获得荣誉。

subliminal [sʌb'liminəl] *a.* 潜意识的

submission [səb'miʃən] *n.* 服从，恭顺. compliance

The losing animal in a struggle saves itself from destruction by an act of *submission*, an act usually recognized and accepted by the winner.

在一场打斗中动物失败的一方可以用一种恭顺的行动保住性命，胜利的一方通常会认可并接受这一行动的。

submissive [səb'misiv] *a.* 恭顺的

Crushed by his authoritarian father, Will had no defiance left in him; he was totally *submissive* in the face of authority.

威尔被他那权力主义的父亲给制服了，他再也没有一点点的公然反抗，在权威面前，他是绝对恭顺的。

subordinate [sə'bɔːdineit] *a.* 下级的，附属的；*n.* 部属. underling

sub (under) | ordinate → 下属

suborn [sə'bɔːn] *v.* 贿赂；诱使作伪证. bribe

In *The Godfather*, the mobsters used bribery and threats to *suborn* the witnesses against Don Michael Corleone.

在《教父》中，黑手党徒用贿赂和恐吓来诱使证人作不利于唐·迈克尔·科利昂的伪证。

subpoena [səb'piːnə] *n.* （法律）传票； *v.* 传唤

They issued a *subpoena* to the man who saw the accident.

他们给看见那起事故的人发了张传票。

subrogate ['sʌbrəgeit] *v.* 代替，取代. supersede，substitute

She ***subrogated*** the amber necklace with a string of pearls to see which she liked better.

她把琥珀项链换成一串珍珠链，看看她更喜欢哪串项链。

sub rosa [ˌsʌb'rəuzə] *a.* 极端秘密的

I heard of this ***sub rosa*** and I cannot tell you about it.

我听说了这个极端秘密的事，但我不能告诉你。

subscribe [səb'skraib] *v.* 同意；捐助；订购. donate

I don't ***subscribe*** to the idea that money brings happiness.

我不认同钱能带来快乐这种观点。

subservient [səb'səːviənt] *a.* 屈从的. servile

He was proud and dignified, he refused to be ***subservient*** to anyone.

他既骄傲又高贵，拒绝屈从任何人。

subsidiary [səb'sidiəri] *a.* 辅助的；次要的. tributary

This information may be used as ***subsidiary*** evidence but is not sufficient by itself to prove your argument.

这条信息可以作为辅助性证据，但要单独用来证明你的论点还不充足。

subsidy ['sʌbsidi] *n.* 补助金

Without this ***subsidy***, American ship operators would not be able to compete in world markets.

没有补助金，美国船业经营者在世界市场上就没竞争力。

substantiate [səb'stænʃieit] *v.* 证实，确证. corroborate

I intend to ***substantiate*** my statement by producing witnesses.

我打算提供证人以证明我的说法。

substratum [ˌsʌb'strʌtəm] *n.* 基础，根基. staddle

sub (under) + stratum → 基础

subsume [səb'sjuːm] *v.* 包含，包容

Does the general theory of relativity contradict Newto-
nian physics, or is Newton's law of gravity **subsumed**
into Einstein's larger scheme?

广义相对论是同牛顿的物理学理论相矛盾，还是牛顿的引力定律
包括在爱因斯坦更大的体系中？

subterfuge ['sʌbtəfjuːdʒ] *n.* 诡计，托辞. ploy

subter (underearth) + fuge (flee) → 诡计，借口

The professor was beguiled by his **subterfuge** and com-
muted his punishment to a lesser one.

教授被他的托辞给哄骗了，把惩罚减轻了些。

subterranean [ˌsʌbtə'reiniən] *a.* 地下的. ↔ superterrene

sub (under) + terr (earth) + anean → 地下的

比较记忆：terrain（地形），terrace（梯田）

subtlety ['sʌtlti] *n.* 狡猾；微妙（的感情）

The **subtlety** of his remarks was unnoticed by most of
his audience.

大多数听众没有注意到他话中那微妙的感情。

suburban [sə'bəːbən] *a.* 孤陋寡闻的. ↔ informed

subvention [səb'venʃən] *n.* 补助金；津贴. allowance

subversive [sʌb'vəːsiv] *a.* 颠覆性的

We must destroy such **subversive** publications.

我们必须毁掉这些颠覆性出版物。

subvert [sʌb'vəːt] *v.* 颠覆，推翻. overthrow

sub (below) + vert (turn) → 往下面转 → 推翻

succinct [sək'siŋkt] *a.* 简明的；简洁的. concise

You should delete this paragraph in order to make the
essay more **succinct**.

你应删去这一段，使全文更加简洁。

succor ['sʌkə] *v.* 救济；援助

We shall be ever grateful for the **succor** your country

gave us when we were in need.

我们会永远感激你们国家在我们需要的时候所给予我们的援助。

succubus [ˈsʌkjubəs] *n.* 妖精. demon

succulent [ˈsʌkjulənt] *a.* 多汁的. juicy

The citrus foods from Florida are more *succulent* to some people than those from California.

佛罗里达产的柑橘属水果对于有些人来说比加州产的要多汁些。

succumb [səˈkʌm] *v.* 屈从；因……死亡. yield

I *succumb* to temptation whenever it comes my way.

当诱惑来到面前时,我总是抵御不住。

suckle [ˈsʌkl] *v.* 喂奶；养育. nurture

sudorific [ˌsjuːdəˈrifik] *a.* 发汗的

Manufacturers of deodorants have made the public conscious often need to avoid offending people with *sudorific*.

除臭剂制造商们使公众意识到,常常要去避免由于出汗而冒犯了旁人。

sue [sjuː] *v.* 控告. litigate

If he does not pay me by the first of the month, I will have to *sue* him.

他要是一号还不付我钱,我就不得不起诉他了。

suede [sweid] *n.* 粗糙的软皮革,绒面革, 起毛革

suffice [səˈfais] *v.* 足够；(食物)满足

比较记忆：sufficient（充足的）

suffocate [ˈsʌfəkeit] *v.* (使)窒息而死. strangle

suffrage [ˈsʌfridʒ] *n.* 选举权,投票权

When was the *suffrage* extended to women in Great Britain?

在英国,妇女什么时候取得投票权的?

suffuse [səˈfjuːz] *v.* (色彩等)弥漫,染遍

A blush *suffused* her cheeks when we teased her about her love affair.

我们拿她的艳遇开玩笑时,她两颊染满了红晕。

suggestible [sə'dʒestəbl] *a.* 易受暗示影响的

suggestive [sə'dʒestiv] *a.* 暗示的;挑动色情的

That sort of parental lecture on the facts of life that is, in its embarrassed delivery, bewildering and *suggestive* rather than dispassionate and informative.

那种父母(讲给孩子的)有关性知识的讲座,(总是)难以启齿,(常常是)充满暗示,令人迷惑,(看上去)一点儿也不冷静而又具有知识性。

suicide ['sjuisaid] *n.* & *v.* 自杀. ↔ murder

suite [swi:t] *n.* 一群随员;套房

suitor ['sju:tə] *n.* 求婚者;原告. plaintiff

比较记忆:suit(恳求,求婚)

sulk [sʌlk] *v.* 生气

She *sulked* in her room after her father told her that she could not buy that coat.

她父亲告诉她不能买那件衣服后,她就在自己房间呕气。

sulky ['sʌlki] *a.* 生气的. churlish

sullen ['sʌlən] *n.* 忧郁的,不高兴的. overcast

She couldn't appease the *sullen* child.

她没法安抚那个不开心的小孩。

sully ['sʌli] *v.* 玷污;污染. taint

He felt that it was beneath his dignity to *sully* his hands in such menial labor.

他感到去做这种仆人才做的事脏了他的手,不是他这种高贵的人(该做的事,有损他的尊严)。

sultry ['sʌltri] *a.* 闷热的;(人)风骚的. torrid

He could not adjust himself to the *sultry* climate of the tropics.

他适应不了热带地区闷热的气候。

summary ['sʌməri] *a.* 概括的；草率的. curt

His *summary* of the case omitted the most important facts.

他仓促地概括了一下这个案例,却漏掉了最重要的事实。

summon ['sʌmən] *v.* 振奋

She had to *summon* all her strength to face them again.

她得振作全部力量再次面对他们。

sumptuary ['sʌmptʃuəri] *a.* 禁止奢侈浪费的

While no *sumptuary* law has been enacted, the public will never tolerate the expenditure of so large a sum.

尽管没有什么限制奢侈浪费的法律,公众也永远不会容忍这么大一笔数目的开销。

sumptuous ['sʌmptʃuəs] *a.* 奢侈的；豪华的. luxurious

I cannot recall when I have had such a *sumptuous* Thanksgiving feast.

我记不起我什么时候有过这么奢华的感恩节盛宴。

sunder ['sʌndə] *v.* 碎裂；分离. sever

The civil war *sundered* father from son and brother from brother.

内战使父子、兄弟分离。

比较记忆：asunder（分开的）

sundry ['sʌndri] *a.* 各式各样的

My suspicious were aroused when I read *sundry* items in the newspapers about your behavior.

我在报上读到的有关你行为的各式各样的报导文章引起了我的怀疑。

superannuated [ˌsjuːpəˈrænjueit] *a.* 年迈的；老式的. antique

The *superannuated* man was indignant because he felt that he could still perform a good day's work.

那位老先生很愤怒,因为他感到他仍旧有能力做好一天的工作。

superb [sju(ː)'pəːb] *a.* 华丽的；出色的

They put up for sale a *superb* Persian rug.

他们在一条华丽的波斯地毯上挂上出售标志。

supercilious [ˌsjuːpə'siliəs] *a.* 目中无人的. haughty

I prefer Jill's modesty to Jack's *supercilious* and arrogant attitude.

比起杰克那傲慢的态度和目中无人来，我更喜欢吉尔的谦虚。

supererogatory [ˌsjuːpəre'rɔgətəri] *a.* 多余的；累赘的. redundant

We have more than enough witnesses to corroborate your statement; to present any more would be *supererogatory*.

我们已有足够的证人证实你所说的，再提供更多的证人是多余的了。

superficial [ˌsjuːpə'fiʃəl] *a.* 表面的；肤浅的. perfunctory

super (above) + fic (face) + ial → 在上面做表面的

superfluous [sju(ː)'pəːfluəs] *a.* 多余的，累赘的. surplus

super (more) + flu (flow) + ous → 多余的

superimpose [ˌsjuːpərim'pəuz] *v.* 附加

super (upon) + impose → 加在上面

superimpose : over = splice : between

superintend [ˌsjuːprin'tend] *v.* 监督

super (above) + intend → 监督

superlative [sju:'pəːlətiv] *a.* 最佳的

super + lative (suppletive) → 最佳的

supernal [sju(ː)'pəːnl] *a.* 天堂的，天上的

His tale of *supernal* beings was skeptically received.

人们怀有疑惑地接受了他关于天堂景物的故事。

supernumerary [ˌsjuːpə'njuːmərəri] *n.* 多余的人或物

His first appearance on the stage was as a *supernumer-*

ary in a Shakespearean tragedy.

他第一次出现在舞台上是在莎士比亚的悲剧中扮演个（无足轻重的）小角色。

supersede [ˌsjuːpəˈsiːd] *v.* 淘汰；取代. restitute

This regulation will *supersede* all previous rules.

这项规定将取代所有从前的条例。

supervene [sjuːˌpəˈviːn] *v.* 意外发生

super (beyond) + vene (come) → 意外发生

supine [sjuːˈpain] *a.* 仰卧的；懒散的. ↔ vigilant

The defeated pugilist lay *supine* on the canvas.

被打败的拳击手懒懒躺在地板上。

supplant [səˈplɑːnt] *v.* 排挤；取代

Industrialists seized economic power only after industry had *supplanted* agriculture as the preeminent form of production; previously such power had resided in land ownership.

在工业取代农业成为首要的生产形式后，工业家们攫取了经济权力；而在这之前，这种权力掌握在土地主手中。

supple [ˈsʌpl] *a.* 柔软的；伸屈自如的，灵活的. resilient

The angler found a *supple* limb and used it as a fishing rod too.

钓鱼人找到根细长柔韧的树枝，把它也用来钓鱼。

比较记忆：supplement（增补）

supplicant [ˈsʌplikənt] *n.* 乞求者

比较记忆：suppliant（恳求的）

supplicate [ˈsʌplikeit] *v.* 恳求，祈求. implore

We *supplicate* Your Majesty to grant him amnesty.

我们恳请陛下赦免他。

supposition [ˌsʌpəˈziʃən] *n.* 猜想；推测

I based my decision to confide in him on the *supposition* that he would be discreet.

我信任他的决定是以他是谨慎的这一推测作依据基础的。

来自：suppose（假定，料想）

supposititious [səˌpɔziˈtiʃəs] *a.* 假设的

I find no similarity between your *supposititious* illustration and the problem we are facing.

我发现你那假设的例证同我们面临的问题之间似乎没有什么相似性。

suppurate [ˈsʌpjuəreit] *v.* 化脓. fester

The surgeon refused to lance the abscess until it *suppurated*.

直到它化了脓，外科医生才同意刺破了脓肿。

supremacy [sjuˈpreməsi] *n.* 霸权；最高权力. sovereignty

surcharge [səˈtʃɑːdʒ] *v.* 额外索价. ↔ discount

sur (addition) + charge → 额外索价

surefire [ˈʃuəfaiə] *a.* 可靠的；一定会成功的

surf [səːf] *n.* 浪花

The *surf* is high just after a storm.

风暴过后，浪花高涨。

surfeit [ˈsəːfit] *v.* （食物）过量；超载. ↔ famish

sur (over) + feit (do) → 过量

surly [ˈsəːli] *a.* 脾气暴躁的；阴沉的

Because of his *surly* attitude many people avoided his company.

因为他阴沉的态度，许多人避免同他在一起。

surmise [ˈsəːmaiz] *v.* 推测，猜测

I *surmise* that he will be late for this meeting.

我猜他可能会开会迟到。

surmount [səːmaunt] *v.* 战胜；越过

He had to *surmount* many obstacles in order to succeed.

他要想成功得战胜许多的障碍。

surpass [səˈpɑːs] *v.* 超越

Her SAT scores *surpassed* our expectations.

她的学业成绩考试超过我们预期的分数。

surreptitious [ˌsʌrəpˈtiʃəs] *a.* 保密的

    smuggler : surreptitious = teachers : explanatory

surrogate [ˈsʌrəgit] *n.* 代用品；代理人

    For a fatherless child, a male teacher may become a father *surrogate.*

    对于一个没有父亲的孩子来说，一位男性教师可能成为父亲角色的代理人。

surveillance [səːˈveiləns] *n.* 监视

    The FBI kept the house under constant *surveillance* in the hope of capturing all the criminals at one time.

    联邦调查局一直监视着那所房子，希望可以一网打尽所有的罪犯。

susceptibilities [səˌseptəˈbilitiz] *n.* 脆弱的感情

susceptible [səˈseptəbl] *a.* 易受影响的，多情的

    He was a very *susceptible* young man, and so his parents worried that he might fall into bad company.

    他是个极易受影响的年轻人，因此他的父母担心他结交坏朋友。

sustained [səsˈteind] *a.* 持久的，经久的. abiding

sustenance [ˈsʌstinəns] *n.* 粮食；生计. foodstuff

    In the tropics the native find *sustenance* easy to obtain due to all the fruit trees.

    在热带地区，因为有各种果树，土著人发现维持生计不是件难事。

suture [ˈsuːtʃə] *v.* 缝合. seam

    We will remove the *sutures* as soon as the wound heals.

    伤口一愈合，我们就拿掉缝合线。

svelte [svelt] *a.* （女人）体态苗条的

    The models for that fashion magazine are all tall, *svelte* and beautiful.

    那家时装杂志的模特儿都是个子高挑、身材苗条、容貌美丽。

swagger ['swægə] *v.* 大摇大摆地走

The candidate who *swaggered* about the room like a latter-day Napoleon.

在房间里大摇大摆地走动的候选人,真像个现代拿破仑。

参考:waddle(摇摇摆摆地走)

swamp [swɔmp] *n.* 沼泽; *v.* 压倒. overwhelm

The farmer will drain the *swamp* so that he can plant crops there.

农夫要淘干沼泽地,好在那里种庄稼。

参考同类词:bog, everglade, fen, morass, marsh, slough, quagmire, mire

swan [swɔn] *n.* 天鹅; *v.* 闲逛. loiter

He *swanned* out for the whole afternoon.

他一下午都在闲逛。

swank [swæŋk] *a.* 时髦的; *v.* 炫耀. smart; sport

That *swank* girl is wearing a plaited translucent skirt.

那个时髦姑娘穿了条半透明的褶裙。

swap [swɔp] *v.* 交换;交易. barter, exchange

I'll *swap* my roller-skater for your football boots.

我用我的旱冰鞋换你的足球鞋。

swarf [swɔːf] *n.* 铁屑. filings

swarm [swɔːm] *n.* (蜜蜂、人)一群; *v.* 攀爬

When the baseball landed in their hive, a *swarm* of bees flew onto the field.

当棒球落在蜂窝上时,一群蜜蜂飞到棒球场上。

swart [swɔːt] *a.* 恶毒的,有害的. malicious

swarthy ['swɔːði] *a.* (皮肤等)黝黑的

Despite the stereotypes, not all Italians are *swarthy*; many are fair and blond.

尽管典型的意大利人肤色黝黑,但并不是所有意大利人都这样,许多人是金发碧眼的。

swathe [sweið] *v.* 绑扎

When I visited him in the hospital, I found him *swathed* in bandages.

我去医院看他时,发现他(浑身上下)缠满绷带。

swell [swel] *n.* (人)丰满; *v.* 肿胀

His eye *swelled* painfully after the blow.

他的眼睛挨了一下后开始痛苦地肿胀了起来。

sweltering ['sweltəriŋ] *a.* 酷热的

swerve [swəːv] *v.* 转向;突然改变方向

The vehicles swerved to the right to avoid the obstacle in the road.

汽车猛向右转以避开路中央的障碍物。

fall : plummet = turn : swerve

swill [swil] *n.* 泔脚饲料; *v.* 狼吞虎咽. offal; guzzle

Singing "Yo, ho, ho, and a bottle of rum", Long John Silver and his fellow pirates *swilled* their grog.

唱着"哟嗬嗬,来瓶朗姆酒",大个子约翰·西尔弗和他的海盗同伴们开始喝酒。

swim [swim] *v.* 眩晕. swoon

She *swam* under the rain of his kisses.

他雨点儿般(落在她脸上)的吻令她晕眩。

swindle ['swindl] *v.* 诈骗,骗取. con, cozen

The avaricious stockbroker had *swindled* his own parents out of the title to their land.

那个贪婪的证券经纪人骗取了他自己父母对属于他们的土地的拥有权。

swine [swain] *n.* 猪

A large drove of *swine* filled the roadway.

一大群猪塞满了街道。

swipe [swaip] *v.* 猛击;偷. punch; purloin

They *swiped* some newspapers from the stand and disappeared in the crowd.

他们从报亭偷了些报纸就消失在人群中了。

参考同类词：pilfer, pinch, sneak, purloin, filch

swirl [swəːl] *n.* 漩涡； *v.* 旋转；弯曲. whirl, twirl

The drum major *swirled* his baton at the head of a parade.

鼓乐队指挥转动着指挥棒走在游行队伍的最前列。

swish [swiʃ] *a.* 时髦的. stylish

swivel ['swivl] *v.* 旋转. pivot

swoon [swuːn] *v.* 晕厥. faint

He frightened her so much that he *swooned*.

他把她吓坏了，她都晕过去了。

swoop [swuːp] *v.* 猛扑

An airplane *swooped* down on the fish.

一架飞机猛向下俯冲向鱼雷。

sybarite ['sibərait] *n.* 骄奢淫逸的人. voluptuary

Rich people are not always *sybarites*, some of them have little taste for a life of luxury.

有钱人也不总是骄奢淫逸的，有些人对奢华的生活索然无味。

sycophant ['sikəfənt] *n.* 马屁精. toady. ↔ critic

The king enjoyed his servile compliments and attentions of the *sycophants* in his retinue.

国王受用着他随从中那些马屁精的奴颜卑膝的恭维奉承。

sycophantic [ˌsikə'fæntik] *a.* 谄媚的. ↔ frank

Some have been chosen rather for their *sycophantic* talents than for their intellectual acumen.

一些人被选中不是因为他们有聪明才智，而是由于他们谄媚的天才。

syllabus ['siləbəs] *n.* 教学大纲

The head of department arrogated the right of deciding how each person of his staff should teach his *syllabus*.

系领导擅取了决定他的教员们每个人该怎么教授他的教学大纲的权利。

syllogism [ˈsilədʒizəm] *n.* 演绎推理

There must be a fallacy in this *syllogism*, I cannot accept its conclusion.

这一演绎中一定存在什么谬误,我无法接受它的结论。

sylvan [ˈsilvən] *a.* 森林的

His paintings of nymphs in *sylvan* backgrounds were criticized as over-sentimental.

他以森林为背景画的仙女受到过于情绪化的批评。

symbiosis [ˌsimbaiˈəusis] *n.* 共生,共栖

sym (same) + bio (life) + sis → 共生

symposium [simˈpəuzjəm] *n.* 专题研讨会

There will be a *symposium* this afternoon on modern Chinese literature.

今天下午有个关于现代中国文学的专题研讨会。

synapse [siˈnæps] *n.* 突触

synchronize [ˈsiŋkrənaiz] *v.* 使同步

syn (same) + chron (time) + ize → 同步

synchronous [ˈsiŋkrənəs] *a.* 同时发生的;同步的

We have many examples of scientists in different parts of the world who have made *synchronous* discoveries.

我们可以举出许多世界上不同地方的科学家同时作出某一(科学)发现的事例。

syncopate [ˈsiŋkəpeit] *v.* 词中省略;缩写

syndrome [ˈsindrəum] *n.* 综合征

syn (same) + drome (run) → 综合征

比较记忆:dromometer(速度计)

synergetic [ˈsinəːˈdʒetik] *a.* (药)配合的;(功能)协同的

synonymous [siˈnɔniməs] *a.* 同义的

syno（same）＋ nym（name）＋ ous → 同义的

synopsis [si'nɔpsis] *n.* 摘要. excerpt

Although I have not seen the entire script，I have read a *synopsis* of the plot.

尽管我没有看到全部手稿，我已读了情节的摘要。

synoptic [si'nɔptik] *a.* 摘要的；高瞻远瞩的

The sheer bulk of data from the mass media seems to overpower us and drive us to *synoptic* accounts for an easily and readily digestible portion of news.

来源于大众媒介那大量的信息，看起来远非我们能够应付，也就促使我们摘要出易读易理解消化的那些部分。

syntax ['sintæks] *n.* 句法

Your vocabulary is excellent，but your *syntax* is confused.

你的词汇（用得）好极了，但句法混乱不堪。

synthetic [sin'θetik] *a.* 综合的；人造的

The introduction of fabrics made from rayonylon and other *synthetic* materials has made many changes in our civilization.

人造丝，尼龙及其他人造材料制作的织品的引入带来了我们文明中的许多变化。

syringe [si'rindʒ] *n.* 注射器

syrup ['sirəp] *n.* 糖浆

The maple *syrup* is obtained from the sap that exudes from the trees in early spring.

枫树糖浆是从早春枫树渗出的树汁中得来的。

tab [tæb] *n.* 账单；监督. check

table ['teibl] *v.* 搁置，不加考虑. shelve. ↔ consider

tableau ['tæbləu] *n.* 画面；舞台造型（活人扮的静态画面）

tableau：movement ＝ pantomime：dialogue

tableland ['teibllænd] *n.* 高原，台地. plateau

比较记忆：tablet（药片）

tablespoon ['teiblspu:n] *n.* 大汤匙

比较记忆：teaspoon（茶匙）

taboo [tə'bu:] *a.* 忌讳的； *n.* 禁忌. interdiction

You villain, why do you infringe the *taboo* to seduce your girlfriend to intercourse before espousing her?

你这个流氓，为什么要违反禁忌，引诱你的女友在你娶她之前同你发生关系？

tabulate ['tæbjuleit] *a.* 平面的； *v.* 使成平面；制表

Tabulate the contributions into separate categories according to quality.

根据它们的性质（不同），可将投稿划分成几类。

tachometer [tæ'kɔmitə] *n.* 转速计；流速计

tacit ['tæsit] *a.* 心照不宣的. ↔ express

The trainees were given copies of a finished manual to see whether they could themselves begin to derive the inflexible, though *tacit* rules for composing more of such instructional materials.

受训人员得到一份已做好的手册，让他们看他们自己能不能开始找出一些用来创作更多的类似的指导性材料的固定的却又心照不宣的规则。

taciturn ['tæsitə:n] *a.* 沉默寡言的. reserved

New Englanders are reputedly *taciturn* people.

新英格兰人是出了名地沉默寡言。

tack [tæk] *v.* 钉住

比较记忆：sack（掠夺），rack（使痛苦），spike（大钉，道钉）

tackle ['tækl] *v.* 处理；擒抱； *n.* 器具

比较记忆：tickle（使愉悦；棘手的）

312

tacky ['tæki] *a.* 粘的；破烂的. sticky；dowdy

tact [tækt] *n.* 机智；圆滑. diplomacy

比较记忆：tack（平头钉）

tactful ['tæktful] *a.* 圆滑的，机敏的. judicious

Good look and a ***tactful*** press agent were the principal instruments of her success.

新闻广告员的漂亮长相以及她的机敏圆滑是她成功的主要法宝。

比较记忆：tactless（笨拙的，不圆滑的）

tactic ['tæktik] *n.* 策略；战术

Tactics are subordinate to strategy.

战术从属于战略。

tactile ['tæktail] *a.* 有触觉的

Her callused hands had lost their ***tactile*** sensitivity.

她结满茧子的手已失去了触觉敏感性。

tadpole ['tædpəul] *n.* 蝌蚪

tad（toad）+ pole（head）→ 蝌蚪

taffy ['tæfi] *n.* 谄媚（insincere flattery）

tailwind ['teilwind] *n.* 顺风

taint [teint] *v.* 玷污，败坏. stain；contaminate

Health authorities are always trying to prevent the sale and use of ***tainted*** food.

保健专家们总是努力去阻止变质食品的出售和食用。

比较记忆：attaint（玷污，染色）

taking ['teikiŋ] *a.* 楚楚动人的； *n. pl.* 收入. captivating

比较记忆：token（纪念品）

talebearer ['teil,bɛərə] *n.* 散布谣言者

Industrial mediators lost their effectiveness as soon as either side suspects them of being ***talebearers***.

只要任何一方怀疑他们散步摇言，工业调停人就失去了他们的效力。

313

参考：informer（告密者）

talisman ['tælizmən] *n*. 避邪物，护身符. charm

She wore the *talisman* to ward off evil.

她戴护身符以避邪。

tally ['tæli] *v*. 符合；计算. match；reckon

The calculations of two scientists working on the same problem *tallied* exactly.

两位科学家对同一问题的计算完全吻合。

比较记忆：dally（嬉戏），sally（突围；远足）

talon ['tælən] *n*. 猛禽的爪

The falconer wore a leather gauntlet to avoid being clawed by the hawk's *talons*.

猎鹰人戴了只长手套以免被鹰爪抓伤。

talon：eagle ＝ claw：panther

tambourine [,tæmbə'ri:n] *n*. 铃鼓，手鼓

tambourine：drum ＝ trumpet：horn

tamp [tæmp] *v*. 捣实，砸实

He *tamped* down the earth at the dam site.

他把水坝那儿的土砸实。

tamper ['tæmpə] *v*. 窜改；玩弄. color；toy

The man who *tampered* the history would be punished sternly by history.

窜改历史的人会受到历史的严惩。

比较记忆：temper（锻造，减轻）

tan [tæn] *v*. 鞣（革）

比较记忆：tannery（制革工厂）

tang [tæŋ] *n*. 气息；味道. odor

tangent ['tændʒənt] *n*. 切线

tangential [tæn'dʒenʃəl] *a*. 切线的；离题的. digressive

Despite Clark's attempts to distract her with *tangential*

remarks, Lois kept on coming back to her main question: why couldn't he come out to dinner with Superman and her?

尽管克拉克总企图用些离题的话分散她的注意力,路易斯却总是回复到她的主要问题上:他为什么不能出来同她和超人共进晚餐?

tangible ['tændʒəbl] *a.* 可触摸的. palpable

Her remarkable speed eventually earned for her some *tangible* rewards, including a full athletic scholarship and several first place trophies.

她惊人的速度最终为她赢得一些看得见摸得着的实用的奖励,这包括一份全额体育奖学金及几个第一名的奖品。

tango ['tæŋgəu] *n.* 探戈舞

参考:waltz(华尔兹舞,圆舞曲)

tankard ['tæŋkəd] *n.* 单柄大酒杯

比较记忆:tanker(油船)

tanner ['tænə] *n.* 制革工人

miller : grain = tanner : hide

tantamount ['tæntəmaunt] *a.* 等于的,相当于的. equivalent

tanta (equal) + amount → 相等的

tantrum ['tæntrəm] *n.* 勃然大怒,发脾气

The minx learned that he could have almost anything if she went into *tantrum*.

这个顽皮的姑娘知道,只要她大发脾气,想要什么就能够得到什么。

tap [tæp] *n.* 水龙头; *v.* 窃听(电话等)

All conversations having to do with the planned merger of the two companies were *tapped* by a competitor.

所有有关那两家公司计划中的合并事宜的谈话都被竞争对手窃听去了。

taper ['teipə] *v.* 逐渐变细;逐渐减少

As defense demands *tapered*, prices started down.

由于防务需求越来越少,价格开始下降。

tapestry ['tæpistri] *n.* 挂毯;织锦

tarantula [tə'ræntjulə] *n.* 鸟蛛;狼蛛

We need an antitoxin to counteract the bite of the *tarantula*.

我需要一种可以对抗毒蜘蛛叮咬的(毒液的)抗毒剂。

tardy ['tɑ:di] *a.* 缓慢的,迟缓的. dilatory

比较记忆:retard (阻碍)

tare [tɛə] *n.* 稗子

tariff ['tærif] *n.* 关税;价目表

Seven nations made a compact to regulate *tariffs*.

七国间制定一份调整关税的契约。

tariff : importation = fare : transportation

tarn [tɑ:n] *n.* 山中小湖

比较记忆:darn (补缀)

tarpaulin [tɑ:'pɔ:lin] *n.* 防水布,油布

tar + paulin (palling) → 油布

tarry ['tæri] *v.* 迟延,逗留. linger

We can't *tarry* it when want to get to the airport on time.

我们想按时赶到机场,不能逗留。

比较记忆:tar (柏油)

tart [tɑ:t] *a.* 酸的;尖酸的. pungent

These girls are just common *tart*, nothing more.

这些女孩子没怎么,只是通常的(女孩子的)尖酸。

tassel ['tæsəl] *n.* 流苏;穗

参考:glean (拾落穗)

tat [tæt] *v.* 梭织

参考:darn (补缀),crochet (用钩针编织)

316

tatter ['tætə] *n.* 破布条； *v.* 撕碎. rag；mangle

比较记忆：totter（步履艰难）

tatterdemalion [ˌtætədə'meiljən] *n.* 衣衫褴褛者. ragamuffin

Do you expect an army of ***tatterdemalions*** and beggars to put up a real fight?

你认为这么个由乞丐、衣衫褴褛的人们组成的军队可以打一场真正的战斗吗？

tattered ['tætəd] *a.* 衣衫褴褛的；破旧的. ragged，dilapidated

比较记忆：tatters（破衣服），totter（摇摇欲坠的）

tattle ['tætl] *v.* 闲聊；泄密. blab

tattler ['tætlə] *n.* 爱说长道短的人；闲谈者

The professional ***tattlers*** purport to reveal the private lives of Hollywood stars.

那些专以饶舌为业的人声言他们能揭露好莱坞明星们的私生活。

taunt [tɔːnt] *v.* 嘲笑，讥笑. jibe

taunt：challenge ＝ flout：disregard

比较记忆：gaunt（憔悴的）

317

Unit Thirty-Six

taut [tɔːt] *a.* 拉紧的，绷紧的. tensile

tautological [ˌtɔːtə'lɔdʒikəl] *a.* 冗赘的. ↔ pithy

> tauto (same) + log (say) + ical → 相同话语 → 冗赘的
>
> 比较记忆：tautochronous（等时的），tautomerism（互变）

tavern ['tævə(ː)n] *n.* 客栈；酒馆

> Hotels have taken the place of the old *taverns*.
>
> 宾馆已取代了古老的客栈。

tawdry ['tɔːdri] *a.* 俗丽的，花哨而不值钱的. gaudy

> He won a few *tawdry* trinket in gambling.
>
> 他赌钱赢了些花哨却不值钱的小玩意儿。

taxonomy [tæk'sɔnəmi] *n.* （动植物的）分类学

> taxo (arrange) + nomy (name) → 按名称排列 → 分类学

tearing ['tɛəriŋ] *a.* 极痛苦的；猛烈的. vehement

tease [tiːz] *v.* 梳理；取笑

> You must never *tease* a child because it stutters.
>
> 别因为小孩子说话结巴就取笑他。

teat [tiːt] *n.* 奶嘴；奶头. nipple, tit

technocracy [tek'nɔkrəsi] *n.* 技术统治

> techno (technology) + cracy (state) → 技术统治

tedium ['tiːdjəm] *n.* 单调，乏味. doldrums

> We hope this radio will help overcome the *tedium* of your stay in the hospital.

318

我希望这个收音机能帮你排遣住院时的单调乏味。

参考：tedious（冗长的，沉闷的），odium（讨厌）

teem [ti:m] *v.* 充满；(雨、水)倾注. swarm；monsoon

The novel *teems* with memorable characters and incidents.

小说里满是令人难以忘怀的人物和事件。

比较记忆：deem（相信，认为）

teeming ['ti:miŋ] *a.* 丰富的. luxuriant

teeter ['ti:tə] *v.* 蹒跚；摇摆. totter，rock

The plate *teetered* on the edge of the table before crashing to the floor.

碟子摔到地上前，在桌子边上摇晃了(几下)。

teetotal [ti:'təutl] *a.* 滴酒不沾的

来自英国戒酒运动拥护者 Teetotaler

teetotaler : alcohol = ascetic : luxury

tegument ['tegjumənt] *n.* 皮，壳. integument

teleology [ˌteli'ɔlədʒi] *n.* 目的论(一种唯心主义哲学理论)

tele (end) + ology (theory) → 目的论

telepathy [ti'lepəθi] *n.* 心灵感应

tele (distant) + pathy (feeling) → 从远方传递感情 → 精神感应

temerity [ti'meriti] *n.* 鲁莽；冒失. ↔ timidity

If you have the *temerity* to argue with him and conquer him，you are a qualified zero.

要是你有胆量同他争辩而且还能胜了他的话，那你真是前所未有的首创者了。

temper ['tempə] *v.* 锻炼；缓和(脾气). moderate

Not even her supervisor's grumpiness could *temper* Nancy's enthusiasm for her new job.

就是她上司的坏脾气也(丝毫)减损不了南希对她那份新工作的

热情。

temperamental [ˌtempərəˈmentl] a. 喜怒无常的

来自：temperament（气质，性情）

temperance [ˈtempərəns] n. 节制；禁酒. moderation

temperate [ˈtempərit] a. 有节制的

Noted for her *temperate* appetite, she seldom gained weight; she is slim.

因为她那出名的节食，她很少长胖，很苗条。

tempest [ˈtempist] n. 暴风雨；骚动. squall; turmoil

参考：blizzard（暴风雪），cyclone（旋风）

tempestuous [temˈpestjuəs] a. 狂暴的. tumultuous

tempo [ˈtempəu] n. 步调；速度；节奏

I found the conductor's *tempo* too slow for such a brilliant piece of music.

我发现演奏这么一段辉煌的曲子，指挥定的速度太慢了。

temporal [ˈtempərəl] a. 时间的；世俗的. secular

At one time in our history, *temporal* rulers assumed that they had been given their thrones by divine right.

我们历史上有一段时候，世俗的统治者认为他们的王位得自于天赐的权利。

比较记忆：temporary（短暂的，暂时的）

temporize [ˈtempəraiz] v. 拖延. linger, protract

I can not permit you to *temporize* any longer, I must have a definite answer today.

我再也不能允许你再拖延了，我今天必须得到确切的答案。

tenable [ˈtenəbl] a. 站得住脚的，无懈可击的. ↔ untenable

tenacious [tiˈneiʃəs] a. 坚韧不拔的，固执的. obstinate

tenacity [tiˈnæsiti] n. 顽强；坚持

It is extremely difficult to overcome the *tenacity* of a habit such as smoking, lechery, wager.

要克服像吸烟、赌博、纵欲这些顽固的恶习是极难的事。

tendentious [ten'denʃəs] *a.* 有偏见的，有倾向的. biased

> The editorials in this periodical are ***tendentious*** rather than truth-seeking
>
> 这本期刊中的社论不是以探求真理（为目的），而是含有倾向性的。
>
> 来自：tendency（倾向，爱好）

tender ['tendə] *v.* 提出（present for acceptance proffer）

> Although no formal charges had been made against him, in the wake of the recent scandal, the mayor felt he should ***tender*** his resignation.
>
> 尽管没对他正式进行指控，由于最近揭穿的那桩丑闻，市长觉得他该提出辞职。

tender ['tendə] *a.* 温柔的；娇嫩的. delicate

tenderfoot ['tendəfut] *n.* 生手，新手

tenebrous ['tenibrəs] *a.* 黑暗的；晦涩难懂的. murky；obscure

> At times he seemed purposely to ***tenebrous*** his meaning, preferring mystery to clarity.
>
> 他有时看起来故意把他要表达的意义弄得晦涩难懂，不喜欢清晰明了，而愿意神秘莫测。

tenement ['tenimənt] *n.* 住宅；保有物

tenet ['tenit] *n.* 宗旨；信条. credo

> The agnostic did not accept the ***tenets*** of their faith.
>
> 不可知论者拒绝接受他们信仰的信条。
>
> 参考同类词：dogma（教条），doctrine（学说），creed（教义）

tenon ['tenən] *n.* 凸榫，榫舌

> 参考：mortise（榫眼）

tenor ['tenə] *n.* 男高音；要旨，pith

> 参考：soprano（女高音），contralto（女低音），bass（男低音）

321

tentacle [ˈtentəkl] *n.* 触角；触须

tentative [ˈtentətiv] *a.* 尝试性的；暂时的

> In scientific inquiry, it becomes a matter of duty to expose a ***tentative*** hypothesis to every possible kind of examination.
>
> 把一暂时性假设付诸各种可能性的检验，这在科学探索中已成为一个惯例了。

tenterhook [ˈtentəhuk] *v.* 拉幅钩

> 参考：on tenterhooks（如坐针毡）

tenuous [ˈtenjuəs] *a.* 单薄的；稀薄的

> 比较记忆：attenuate（使变稀薄），extenuate（减轻，掩饰）

tenure [ˈtenjuə] *n.* 任期；终身职位

> He is a permanent ***tenure*** in position of president and can't be fired.
>
> 他是终身董事长，而且不能被解雇。

tepid [ˈtepid] *a.* 微温的. lukewarm

> Considering how long she had yearned to see Italy, her first reaction was curiously ***tepid***.
>
> 想想长久以来，她就一直渴望能到意大利去看看，有趣地是，她最初的反应不够热烈。
>
> 比较记忆：tepidarium（温水浴室）

tergal [ˈtəːgəl] *a.* 背的；背甲的

> 参考：guttural（喉的），ventral（腹部的）

tergiversate [ˈtəːdʒivəːseit] *v.* 变节；支吾. equivocate

> tergi（back）＋ vers（turn）＋ ate → 变节

termagant [ˈtəːməgənt] *n.* 泼妇. vixen, shrew

> If you are to succeed in preventing other from calling you ***termagant***, you must first be liberal.
>
> 要想成功阻止别人叫你泼妇，你自己首先得心胸宽广。

terminable ['tə:minəbl] *a.* 可终止的. ↔ interminable

来自：terminate（终止，结束）

terminology [ˌtə:mi'nɔlədʒi] *n.* 术语；术语学. jargon

termin（term）+ ology（science）→ 术语(学)

terminus ['tə:minəs] *n.* 终点站

After we reached the railroad *terminus*, we continued our journey into the wilderness on saddle horses.

我们乘火车到终点站后,换乘马匹在旷野上继续我们的旅程。

termite ['tə:mait] *n.* 白蚁

terpsichorean [ˌtə:psikə'ri:ən] *a.* 舞蹈的

来自希腊神话中的九位缪斯之一 Tersichore，掌管舞蹈

terpsichorean : dance = sartorial : tailor

terrace ['terəs] *n.* 一层梯田；阳台. balcony

比较记忆：subterranean（地下室）

terrain ['terein] *n.* 地势，地形

As we moved on to Melford shortly after noon on Saturday, the clear air and the rolling *terrain* made one wonder whether this festival would lead all others, at least in altitude.

在周六午后不久,我们继续向前爬上了梅尔弗山,那清新的空气,起伏的地势使我们情不自禁地想到这一节日。是否会把其他人也都吸引来,至少吸引到这么高的地方来。

terrapin ['terəpin] *n.* 泥龟，水龟

The flesh of the diamondback *terrapin* is considered by many epicures to be a delicacy.

许多美食家认为菱纹背泥龟的肉实在是美味。

terrestrial [ti'restriəl] *a.* 地球的；陆地的；世俗的. ↔ celestial

We have been able to explore the *terrestrial* regions much more thoroughly than the aquatic or celestial regions.

我们对陆地区域的探索比对水域、空域的探索彻底得多。

比较记忆：territory（领土，领域）

terse [təːs] *a.* 简洁的，简明的. concise

I admire his *terse* style of writing; he comes directly to the point.

我很羡慕他简洁的写作风格，他总能开门见山，直切要点。

tertiary ['təːʃəri] *a.* 第三位的

He is so thorough that he analyzes *tertiary* causes where other writers are content with primary and secondary reasons.

他很彻底，其他作家只满足于(分析)首要的和次要的原因，而他还分析了第三位的原因。

tessellated ['tesileitid] *a.* 镶嵌图案的. inlaid

I recall seeing a table with a *tessellated* top of bits of stone and glass in a very interesting pattern.

我记得见过一张桌面有用石子、玻璃片镶嵌出有趣图案的桌子。

testament ['testəmənt] *n.* 遗嘱；证明

比较记忆：testify（证实），testimony（证言，证明）

testate ['testeit] *v.* 立遗嘱

testator [tes'teitə] *n.* 立有遗嘱者

The attorney called in his secretary and his partner to witness the signature of the *testator*.

律师叫来他的秘书和搭档来作为遗嘱签署的见证人。

testimonial [ˌtesti'məunjəl] *n.* 证明书；奖状. certificate

The monument at the entrance to the library is a *testimonial* to the mayor's great service to the city.

图书馆入口处的纪念碑是市长为这座城市所作出的巨大的贡献的证明。

testimony ['testiməni] *n.* 证言；证明. deposition

The lawyer tried to correlate the *testimony* of the two witnesses.

324

律师试图把两个证人的证言联系起来。

testy ['testi] *a.* 性急的，暴躁的. tetchy

My advice is to avoid discussing this problem with him today as he is rather ***testy*** and may shout at you.

我建议今天避免同他讨论这一问题，因为他今天性情急躁，可能会对你大喊大叫的。

tether ['teðə] *v.* 系，拴. batten

Before we went to sleep, we ***tethered*** the horses to prevent their wandering off during the night.

我们睡觉前，要把马拴好，以防它们夜里跑开。

tetragon ['tetrəgən] *n.* 四边形

tetra (four) + gon → 四边形

texture ['tekstʃə] *n.* 质地，结构

比较记忆：textile (纺织品)

thatch [θætʃ] *n.* 茅草屋顶；浓密的头发

参考：hirsute (多发的)

thaumaturgy ['θɔːmətəːdʒi] *n.* 魔术. witchcraft

thaw [θɔː] *n.* & *v.* 解冻，融化. liquefy. ↔ congeal

Melting snow redounds the flow of water in many streams during spring ***thaws***.

在春天雪融化的时候，融化的雪水注入许多小溪，加大了它们的水流。

theatrical [θiˈætrikəl] *a.* 戏剧的，矫揉造作的. thespian

Her success in the school plays convinced her she was destined for a ***theatrical*** career.

她在学校剧目演出中的成功使她相信她注定该去从事戏剧事业。

theism ['θiːizəm] *n.* 一神论；有神论. ↔ atheism

the (god) + ism → 有神论

theocracy [θiˈɔkrəsi] *n.* 神权政治

theo (god) + cracy (state) → 神权政治

theology [θi'ɔlədʒi] *n.* 神学

    theo (god) ＋ ology (theory) → 神学

theosophy [θi'ɔsəfi] *n.* 神智学

    Theosophy seeks to embrace the essential truth in all religions.

    神智学要探索的是抓住所有宗教的本质真理。

therapeutic [ˌθerə'pjuːtik] *a.* 治疗的. curative

    These springs are famous for their *therapeutic* and healing qualities.

    这些泉水以能治病、愈合伤口的特性著称。

therapy ['θerəpi] *n.* 疗法. massage

thermos ['θəːmɔs] *n.* 热水瓶

    比较记忆：thermal（热的）

theroid ['θiərɔid] *a.* 兽性的，残忍的. atrocious

    The Japanese, sons of bitch, has exerted *theroid* actions on us in eight year's incursion; all that must be answered for in multiplies.

    可恶的日本人在八年侵略中,对我们犯下了多少残忍的兽行,这一切都必须加倍偿还。

thesaurus [θi(ː)'θɔːrəs] *n.* 词典，分类词汇汇编

thespian ['θespiən] *a.* 戏剧的；悲剧的； *n.* 演员. trouper

    来自古希腊悲剧创始者 Thespis

thewy ['θjuːi] *a.* 强健的. sinewy

    With your *thewy* stature, you can beat that rogue easily.

    以你健壮的身材,可以轻松打败那个无赖。

thicket ['θikit] *n.* 植丛，灌木丛. copse, brush

    Crossing this extensive lawn, there are the tract of *thicket*.

    在那辽阔的草坪那边,是一片灌木丛。

thorax ['θɔːræks] *n.* 胸部. bosom

The *thorax* contains both the heart and the lungs.

胸腔内有心脏和肺。

thorn [θɔːn] *n.* 荆棘；刺. prickle

The jibes of other children were the *thorn* of his existence.

其他孩子们的嘲弄令他有如芒刺在背。

thoughtful ['θɔːtful] *a.* 沉思的；体贴的. pensive；considerate

Even those who disagreed with Carmen's views rarely faulted her for expressing them, for the positions she took were as *thoughtful* as they were controversial.

即使那些不同意卡门见解的人，也极少有人挑剔她不该这样表达了出来（她的观点），因为她所持的立场虽有争议，却也是经过了深思熟虑的。

thrall [θrɔːl] *n.* 奴隶；农奴. bondage

The captured soldier was held in *thrall* by the conquering army.

获胜军队把俘获的士兵当奴隶一样看待。

比较记忆：enthrall（迷住，吸引住），thralldom（奴役）

threadbare ['θredbɛə] *a.* 磨破的；老一套的. shabby；hackneyed

The story was *threadbare* and unoriginal.

这个故事已广为传颂，没什么新鲜的了。

threnody ['θrenədi] *n.* 挽歌，哀歌. requiem, dirge

When he died, many poets wrote *threnodies* about his passing.

他去世时，许多诗人为此写了挽歌。

threshold ['θreʃhəuld] *n.* 门槛

They request that we leave our boots at the *threshold* before entering the room.

他们请求我们进门前，把靴子脱在门槛外边。

thrifty ['θrifti] *a.* 繁荣的；节俭的. frugal, thriving

A *thrifty* shopper compares prices before making major purchase.

节俭的购物者在买大件商品前要比较一下（各家店不同的）价格。

thrill [θril] *v.* 极度兴奋；振动. enthuse；tingle

throaty ['θrəuti] *a.* 嗓子沙哑的. hoarse

throb [θrɔb] *v.* 悸动. palpitate

The dog's tail *throbbed* excitedly when he saw that she was bringing his meal.

狗一见她拿来了狗食,尾巴就兴奋地摇动起来。

throes [θrəuz] *n.* 剧痛. pang, torment

The *throes* of despair can be as devastating as the spasms accompanying physical pain.

绝望的剧痛像伴随身体疼痛而来的痉挛一样极具破坏性。

thrombosis [θrɔm'bəusis] *n.* 血栓形成；交通阻塞

throng [θrɔŋ] *n.* 一大群； *v.* 拥挤. horde, swarm

Throngs of shoppers jammed the aisles.

一大群购物者拥在货柜间的过廊里。

throttle ['θrɔtl] *n.* 节流阀； *v.* 掐脖子, 扼制. strangle

The criminal tried to *throttle* the old man with his bare hand.

罪犯企图徒手掐住老人的脖子。

thrum [θrʌm] *v.* (漫不经心地)弹弹

Under the tree, he *thrummed* his guitar slowly in the summer night.

在夏日的夜晚,他(坐)在树下,缓缓拨弄着他的吉他。

thug [θʌg] *n.* 恶棍；凶手. ruffian

The *thugs* ran a protection racket in the center of the city.

这个恶棍在市中心经营一非法的(收)保护(费的买卖)。

参考同类词：desperado（暴徒），racketeer（诈骗者），

hood（强盗）, scoundrel（恶棍）, cad（无赖）, knave（流氓）, rogue（流氓）, scalawag（无赖）, scamp（流氓）, rascal（流氓）, heel（小偷）, miscreant（歹徒）, ruffian（流氓）, hooligan（小流氓）, blackguard（恶棍）

thump [θʌmp] v. 重击. cudgel

He *thumped* into bed and went to sleep.

他重重倒在床上睡着了。

thwack [θwæk] n. & v. 重击. pound, wallop

I am going to give you a *thwack* in the nose.

我要对准你鼻子狠狠打一下。

thwart [θwɔ:t] v. 阻挠. baffle, foil

He felt that everyone was trying to *thwart* his plans and prevent his success.

他觉得每个人都在竭力阻挠他的计划,不想让他成功。

thyroid ['θairɔid] n. 甲状腺

thyroxin [θai'rɔksin] n. 甲状腺素

thyroxin : thyroid = insulin : pancreas

tiara [ti'ɑ:rə] n. 妇女冕状头饰

She looked like a queen when the *tiara* was placed on her head.

当那个头冕戴在她头上时,她看上去(简直)像个女王。

tickler ['tiklə] n. 棘手的问题,难题

tidbit ['tidbit] n. 少量的食品；珍闻（morsel of food）

She will get sick if she continues to consume only *tidbits*.

她要还吃这么点儿东西,该生病了。

tidings ['taidiŋz] n. 消息

tidings : harbinger = day : dawn

tiff [tif] v. & n. 吵嘴, 呕气（slight quarrel）. miff

They seldom fight, but sometimes they have *tiff*.

他们极少打架，但有时也呕呕气。

tightwad ['taitwɔd] *n.* 吝啬鬼. skinflint

They called Jack a *tightwad* because he never picked up the check.

他们管杰克叫吝啬鬼，因为他从来也不付账单。

tiller ['tilə] *n.* 舵柄

Fearing the wind might shift suddenly and capsize the skiff, Tom kept one hand on the *tiller* at all times.

因为怕风突然改变方向，弄翻小船，汤姆的一只手一直把在舵柄上。

tilt [tilt] *n.* 斜坡；　*v.* (使)倾斜. incline

When the restaurant was closed, the chairs were *tilted* forward against the tables.

餐馆关门时，椅子往上斜靠在桌子上。

比较记忆：stilt（高跷）

timber ['timbə] *n.* 木材，(人)品质，素质. caliber

The professor was impressed by the high *timber* of his students,

教师对他学生素质很高印象深刻。

timbre ['timbə] *n.* (音乐)音色，音质

We identify the instrument producing a musical sound by its *timbre*.

我们通过其产生的声音音色来鉴别乐器。

timorous ['timərəs] *a.* 胆小的；胆怯的. timid

His *timorous* manner betrayed the fear he felt at the moment.

他胆怯的行为暴露出他在那一刻感到了害怕。

参考：timid（胆小的），intimidate（恐吓）

tincture ['tiŋktʃə] *n.* 色泽

tinder ['tində] *n.* 火绒，火种

tined [taind] *a.* 尖端的；有齿的

330

tinge [tindʒ] *n.* 色彩；味道； *v.* 染色. stain

She *tinged* a white dress red by soaking it for several hours in a dyeing solution.

她把白裙子在一染色液中浸了几小时染成了红色。

tingle ['tiŋgl] *v.* 兴奋；作叮当响

tinkle ['tiŋkl] *v.* 发叮当声(以引起注意)

tint [tint] *n.* 色泽； *v.* 染色. hue；tinge

tipple ['tipl] *n.* 烈酒；致醉的饮料； *v.* 酗酒. booze

He found that his most enjoyable evenings occurred when he *tippled* with his friends at the local pub.

他发现他最愉快的夜晚是同他的朋友们在当地小酒店里喝酒的时候(才会有的)。

tipsy ['tipsi] *a.* 微醉的

Even a little wine can make some people *tipsy*.

就是喝上一点点的葡萄酒也会使一些人微醉的。

tirade [tai'reid] *n.* 长篇攻击性演说

Long before he had finished his *tirade*, we were sufficiently aware of the seriousness of our misconduct.

远在他讲完那攻击性的长篇大论前,我们就意识到我们处置不当的严重性了。

tit [tit] *n.* 乳头；乳房. teat；bosom

titanic [tai'tænik] *a.* 巨大的,力大无比的. gigantic

来自希腊神话中的巨神 Tita

tithe [taið] *n.* (教会)什一税

Because he was an agnostic, he refused to pay his *tithes* to the clergy.

因为他是个不可认知者,所以拒绝交给牧师(教会)十分之一税。

tithe：church ＝ tuition：school

titillate ['titileit] *v.* 刺激；使愉快. tickle

I am here not to *titillate* my audience but to enlighten

331

it.

我来这里不是要来取悦我的听众，而是要来启发他们。

titivate ['titiveit] *v.* 打扮 (deck out)

She *titivated* her old gown with a new belt.

她穿了一件旧袍子，但扎了条新腰带。

titter ['titə] *n.* 神经质的笑

Her aunt's constant *titter* nearly drove her mad.

她姑妈那不停的神经质的笑都快把她弄发疯了。

参考同类词：chortle（哈哈大笑），chuckle（暗自笑），guffaw（狂笑），snigger（窃笑），simper（假笑），smirk（傻笑），giggle（咯咯笑），grin（露齿而笑）

titular ['titjulə] *a.* 有名无实的，名义上的. nominal

As *titular* head of the organization, he attended social functions and civic meetings but had no voice in the formulation of company policy.

作为这一组织有名无实的首脑，他出席社会会议和市民会议，但在公司政策的制定中他没有发言权。

toadstool ['təudstu:l] *n.* 毒菌

参考：fungus（真菌），bacterium（细菌）

toady ['təudi] *n.* 谄媚者； *v.* 谄媚 (yes man)

Never tell the boss anything he doesn't wish to hear; he doesn't want an independent adviser, he just wants a *toady*.

从不要对老板讲任何他不想听到的话，他只想要个溜须拍马的人，并不需要能独立思考的顾问。

tocsin ['tɔksin] *n.* 报警信号；警报

Awakened by the sound of the *tocsin*, we rushed to our positions to await the attack.

我们被警报声惊醒，冲向我们的（躲避空袭的）地点，等待袭击。

toddler ['tɔdlə] *n.* 学步的儿童

He tried to explain the meaning of death to the *toddler*.

他试图给这小孩解释死亡的意义。

toga ['təugə] *n.* 官服；（宽松）托加袍

Marc Antony pointed to the slashes in Caesar's *toga*.

马克·安东尼指着恺撒外袍上的衣叉。

toil [tɔil] *n.* 劳累； *v.* 艰苦劳作. moil

The mothers' *toiling* to better their children often goes unrewarded.

母亲为给孩子提供更好的条件的艰苦劳作常常并不能够得到回报。

比较记忆：foil（阻挠，金属箔）

token ['təukən] *n.* 纪念品；象征

We give the Queen flowers as a *token* of their grief.

我们送给王后鲜花,作为他们的悲哀的象征。

toll [təul] *n.* 通行费

tome [təum] *n.* 大册书（large volume）

He spent much time in the libraries poring over ancient *tomes*.

他在图书馆里花费大量时间钻研古籍。

tonality [təu'næliti] *n.* 声调，音调. timbre

tongs [tɔŋz] *n.* 夹子，钳子

Sugar *tongs* are used for picking up lumps of sugar.

糖夹子用来夹起糖块。

tonic ['tɔnik] *n.* 补品

tonsure ['tɔnʃə] *v.* 剃光头； *n.* 光顶

His *tonsure*, even more than his monastic garb, indicated that he was a member of the religious order.

他的光头比他那修道士的装束更能表明他是一宗教团体的成员。

topography [tə'pɔgrəfi] *n.* 地形学；地形

topo (place) ＋ graphy (write) → 地形学

比较记忆：toponym（地名）

topple ['tɔpl] *v.* 倾覆，推倒. invert

top + ple (make) → 倾覆

参考：muddle（使混乱）

topsoil ['tɔpsɔil] *n.* 表土层

topsoil : erode = paint : peel

toque [təuk] *n.* 无边女帽

toreador ['tɔ(:)riədɔ:] *n.* 斗牛士. picador, matador

One of the tourist attraction in Spain is to watch the *toreador*.

西班牙吸引游客的魅力之一是去看斗牛。

tornado [tɔː'neidəu] *n.* 旋风；龙卷风. hurricane

A *tornado* destroyed the towns on the coast.

龙卷风摧毁了海滨小镇。

torpid ['tɔːpid] *a.* 懒散的，死气沉沉的. sluggish

The *torpid* bear had just come out of his cave after his long hibernation.

懒洋洋的大熊刚冬眠了好长一段时间,从洞里爬了出来。

torpor ['tɔːpə] *n.* 麻痹；麻木；迟钝；蛰伏. lethargy

Nothing seemed to arouse him from his *torpor*, he had wholly surrendered himself to sluggishness.

什么也不能刺激他摆脱有气无力的情形,他彻底被懒惰征服了。

torque [tɔːk] *n.* 转矩；金属项圈

torque : rotate = tension : elongate

torrid ['tɔrid] *a.* 酷热的

She burned her hands when she submerged them in the *torrid* water.

她把手伸进滚热的水里时烫伤了。

参考：torrefy（焙烧）

参考同类词：sultry（闷热的）, sizzling（极热的）, scorching（灼热的）

torso ['tɔːsəu] *n.* (人体的)躯干；躯干像

This ***torso***, found in the ruins of Pompeii, is now in exhibition in the museum.

在庞贝发现的干尸现在博物馆展出。

tortuous ['tɔ:tjuəs] *a.* 弯弯曲曲的，蜿蜒的. winding

Because this road is so ***tortuous***, it is unwise to go faster
than twenty miles an hour on it.

这条路这么曲曲弯弯的，(行进)时速要是超过 20 英里可不太明
智。

torture ['tɔ:tʃə] *n.* 酷刑，折磨；　*v.* 拷打；折磨

After sentencing the man, the judge was ***tortured*** by
doubts.

给这个人判刑后，法官也遭受了怀疑的折磨。

totalitarian [ˌtəutæli'tɛəriən] *a.* 极权主义的

The Puritans of the New World who, out of self-de-
fense, constructed what amounted to a ***totalitarian***
state.

出于自卫，新世界的清教徒们建立起了极权主义。

totem ['təutəm] *n.* 图腾，崇拜物

totter ['tɔtə] *v.* 摇摇欲坠，步伐蹒跚. stagger

The ***tottering*** object tottered on flimsy stand.

那个摇摇晃晃的物体在一个不大稳固的支架上晃荡着。

touchstone ['tʌtʃstəun] *n.* 试金石，基准. criterion

What ***touchstone*** can be used to measure Democracy?

可以用什么基准来衡量民主？

比较记忆：milestone（里程碑）

touchy ['tʌtʃi] *a.* 敏感的；易怒的. acute; irascible

Do not discuss this phase of the problem as he is very
touchy about it.

别去讨论这个问题的这一阶段，他对此很敏感。

toupee ['tu:pei] *n.* 男用假发

tournament ['tuənəmənt] *n.* 比赛，(旧时)骑士马上比武大会

tourniquet [ˈtuənikei] *n.* 止血带

　　　　tourniquet : blood = dam : water

tousle [ˈtauzl] *v.* 弄乱（头发）

　　　　来自：touse（吵闹，弄乱）

tout [taut] *v.* 招徕顾客；极力赞扬

　　　　The current penchant for *touting* a product by denigrat-
　　　　ing a rival, named in the advertisement by brand name,
　　　　seems somewhat foolhardy. Suppose the consumer re-
　　　　members only the rival's name?

　　　　最近一项招徕顾客的倾向是，在广告中打出品牌名称，称赞自己
　　　　的产品，贬低对手。这看上去有些蛮干。要是顾客光记住对手的名
　　　　称了怎么办呢?

towering [ˈtauəriŋ] *a.* 高耸的；激烈的. lofty

　　　　The *towering* giant of a man was walking towards us.
　　　　一个高耸的巨人向我们走来。

toxic [ˈtɔksik] *a.* 有毒的；中毒的. noxious

　　　　To prevent a repetition of this dreadful occurrence, we
　　　　must discover the *toxic* element in the food that was
　　　　served.

　　　　为防止这种可怕的事件再次发生，我们必须找出所吃食物中的有
　　　　毒因素。

toxin [ˈtɔksin] *n.* 毒素，毒质

　　　　比较记忆：detoxify（解毒），toxication（中毒）

toy [tɔi] *v.* 玩弄. philander

　　　　The coy young girl *toyed* with the boys.
　　　　那个忸怩作态的姑娘玩弄男性。

trachea [trəˈki(ː)ə] *n.* 气管

　　　　Some food was caught in his *trachea*.
　　　　食物堵住了他的气管。

tract [trækt] *n.* 广大的一片；小册子. pamphlet

　　　　Were this *tract* of land more level and the access to the

main road more direct, the builder would be more hope-
ful of making a profit struction.

要是这一大片土地更平坦些,通向大道的通路更近便些的话,建
筑商就有指望可以建所带来一大笔利润的建筑物了。

tractable ['træktəbl] *a.* 易于驾御的;温顺的. meek

tract (draw) + able → (易牵引的,温顺的)

traction ['trækʃən] *n.* 拖拉;牵引力

traduce [trə'djuːs] *v.* 中伤,诽谤. revile, defame

His opponents tried to **traduce** the candidate's reputation by spreading rumors about his past.

他的对手通过四处传播有关他的过去的谣言来毁那个候选人的
名誉。

tragedienne [trəˌʒiːdi'en] *n.* 悲剧女演员

tragedy + enne (actress) → 悲剧女演员

trait [treit] *n.* 性格,天性

Some biologists argue that each specifically human **trait**
must have arisen gradually and erratically, and that it
is therefore difficult to isolate definite milestones in the
evolution of the species.

一些生物学家持有这样的观点:每一独特的人类特征都是渐进
地、反复经常地出现的,因而要在种类进化(进程)中划分出孤立
的(标志性)里程碑是很困难的。

比较记忆:traitor(叛徒),traitress(女叛徒)

trajectory ['trædʒiktəri] *n.* (射体)轨道,弹道

The police tried to locate the spot from which the assas-
sin had fired the fatal shot by tracing the **trajectory** of
the bullet.

警察试图通过追寻子弹弹道,确定刺客在什么地点开了那致命的
一枪。

trammel ['træməl] *n.* (鱼)网; *v.* 束缚. fetter

The current generation is **trammeled** to its lust for

speed and rapid changes of pace.

新一代人被其对速度及快速变化的节奏的渴求所束缚。

tramontane [trə'mɔntein] *a.* 异国的. extraneous

trample ['træmpl] *v.* 蹂躏；践踏. tread

You couldn't ***trample*** that girl's feeling so atrociously.

你不能如此凶残地践踏那女孩的感情。

比较记忆：tramp（跋涉；流浪）

tranquilizer ['træŋkwilaizə] *n.* 镇静剂. sedative

tranquillity [træŋ'kwiliti] *n.* 宁静，安静. quietude

After the commotion and excitement of the city, I appreciate the ***tranquillity*** of these fields and forests.

（经历了）城市的混乱和骚动后，我喜爱这种土地和森林中的宁静。

transcendence [træn'sendəns] *n.* 超越，卓越. singularity

transcendental [ˌtrænsen'dentl] *a.* 超越经验的；先验的.

Generally, Babylonian mythology lacks the ***transcendental*** quality of the myth of Osiris; it is more earthbound and more materialistic.

通常来讲，巴比伦神话没有地狱判官的神话的那种形而上学的性质，更加唯物世俗一些。

transcribe [træns'kraib] *v.* 抄写，转录

When you ***transcribe*** your notes, please send a copy to Mr. Smith and keep the original for our files.

在转录记录时，请送给史密斯先生一份，原件你保存好给我们存档用。

比较记忆：transcript（成绩单），transcription（抄本）

transfigure [træns'figə] *v.* 美化；使改观. transform

trans (across) + figure → 改观

transfix [træns'fiks] *v.* 戳穿；使麻木. impale

trans (through) + fix (piece) → 戳穿

transformer [træns'fɔːmə] *n.* 变压器

transfuse [trænsˈfjuːz] *v.* 输（血）；灌输. influx

trans (across) + fuse (pour) → 输血

transgress [trænsˈgres] *v.* 越界；违背. encroach

trans (across) + gress (step) → 越界，冒犯

transition [trænˈsiʒən] *n.* 过渡时期；转变. transformation

transitional [trænˈsiʒənəl] *a.* 过渡的；过渡时期的

Current data suggest that although *transitional* states between fear and aggression exist, fear and aggression are as distinct physiologically as they are psychologically.

目前的信息表明,尽管恐惧同侵犯行为间存在中间过渡性状态,但二者在生理上和心理上都是截然不同的。

transitory [ˈtrænsitəri] *a.* 短暂的. transient

Conscious that all things pass, the psalmist relates the *transitory* happiness and fame.

意识到一切都会成为过去,唱赞美诗的人叙述着短暂的欢乐和名誉。

translucent [trænzˈljuːsnt] *a.* 半透明的

We could not recognize the people in the next room because of the *translucent* curtains which separated us.

隔着中间一道半透明的帘子我们认不出隔壁房中的人。

比较记忆：transparent（透明的）

transmogrify [trænzˈmɔgrifai] *v.* 变得古怪；使完全变形

transpire [trænsˈpaiə] *v.* 泄露；散发（蒸汽）. blab

When Wu writes the sentence "it had just *transpired* that he had left gaming debts behind him," her meaning is not that the debts had just been incurred but that the shocking news had just leaked out.

当吴写下这句话："刚刚发现他身后留下一屁股的赌债"时,她不是指赌债是刚有的,而是指这一惊人的消息刚泄露出来。

transport [træns'pɔːt] *v.* 传输；(使)狂喜. enrapture

Margo was a creature of extremes，at one moment in *transports* of joy over a vivid sunset，at another moment in transports of grief over a dying bird.

马戈是个十分极端的人，一会为生动的日落而欣喜，一会儿又转而为垂死的鸟儿而悲哀。

Unit Thirty-Seven

trapezium [trə'piːzjəm] *n.* 梯形；不规则四边形

参考：triangle（四边形），hexagon（六边形）

trappings ['træpiŋz] *n.* 服饰；马饰

He loved the ***trappings*** of success, the limousine
stock options, the company jet.

他喜爱这种象征成功的外部标志：豪华轿车、股票的特权、公
专用喷气客机。

trash [træʃ] *n.* 废物，垃极. refuse

After cleaning up the attic, we dumped a heap of ***trash***
into the litterbin.

清扫完阁楼后，我们往废物箱倾倒了一堆垃圾。

比较记忆：thrash（摔打）

trauma ['trɔːmə] *n.* 精神创伤，外伤

traumatic [trɔː'mætik] *a.* 损伤性的

In his nightmares, he kept on recalling the ***traumatic***
experience of being wounded in battle.

恶梦中，他总记起战争中负伤的痛苦经历。

travail ['træveil] *n.* 艰苦劳动；剧痛. toil

How long do you think a man can endure such ***travail***
and degradation without rebelling?

你认为一个人能忍耐多久这种艰苦劳动和贬黜而不反抗？

travelogue ['trævəlɔg] *n.* 旅行见闻讲座；旅行记录片

travel + logue (discourse) → 游记

traverse ['trævə(ː)s] *v.* 横过；横贯. transverse

When you ***traverse*** this tract of shrubs, be careful of the bull.

当你横穿这片灌木丛时，小心点儿牛。

travesty ['trævisti] *v.* 歪曲；拙劣地模仿. ↔ paradigm

The ridiculous decision-the jury has arrived at is a ***travesty*** of justice.

陪审团作出的这一荒唐的决定是对公正的曲解。

参考同类词：burlesque（嘲弄），mimicry（摹拟），parody（拙劣地模仿），caricature（笨拙地模仿）

[trɔ:l] *n.* 拖网；　　*v.* 用拖网捕鱼；搜罗

erous ['tretʃərəs] *a.* 背叛的；危险的. perfidious；perilous

Treacherous currents make swimming in this part of the river dangerous.

危险的水流使在河的这段游泳很危险。

treacle ['tri:kl] *n.* 糖蜜；糖浆

Treacle is more highly refined than molasses.

糖蜜比糖浆加工得更加精细了。

treadmill ['tredmil] *n.* 踏车；乏味的工作

参考：stodge（乏味的作品）

treason ['tri:zn] *n.* 叛国罪

In time of war, ***treason*** is a crime punishable by death.

战争时期,叛国罪以死刑论处。

treatise ['tri:tiz] *n.* 论文. dissertation

He wrote a ***treatise*** on the development of the Gregorian chant.

他就格雷戈里赞美诗的创作过程写了篇论文。

比较记忆：treaty（条约）

treble ['trebl] *a.* 最高音部的

The boy sang in ***treble*** tone.

男孩用高音在唱。

trek [trek] *v.* 长途跋涉. tramp

342